IRIS SMITH

Strategic Management Skills

Strategic Management Skills

Daniel J. Power
University of Maryland

Martin J. Gannon
University of Maryland

Michael A. McGinnis
Shippensburg University

David M. Schweiger
University of Houston

 ADDISON-WESLEY PUBLISHING COMPANY

Reading, Massachusetts ● Menlo Park, California
Don Mills, Ontario ● Wokingham, England ● Amsterdam
Sydney ● Singapore ● Tokyo ● Madrid ● Bogotá
Santiago ● San Juan

ISBN: 0-201-13978-2
CDEFGHIJ-AL-89876

Preface

Strategic Management Skills provides students and professors with a unique approach to the business policy or strategic management course that is both meaningful and easy to understand. This is the first book that helps business students acquire and master strategic management skills in a systematic, sequential fashion. Students and professors using this book are immediately engaged in an **active** learning process leading both to a high degree of skill development and satisfaction. In addition, this book emphasizes practical skills that students can use not only in the course, but also in their first jobs and subsequent jobs as managers and planners.

We strongly recommend that professors use our book and the accompanying videotape early in the course. Chapters 1 through 9 provide an effective orientation to strategic management and business policy. Also, these chapters introduce the major concepts and methods that students need in order to complete case analyses. We recommend using this book in combination with other instructional materials, a computer game, or a basic textbook in business policy/strategic management. We have used a number of different combinations in our teaching. In addition, our book can be used in a two- or three-day management training session; then it is not necessary to assign any other book.

Strategic Management Skills is distinctive in at least five ways. **First**, this book describes in detail a complete set of skills that a manager needs to master in order to be an effective strategic planner. **Second**, the skills are presented systematically and sequentially. Concepts are clearly defined and examples are provided. **Third**, students will view videotaped presentations by MBA students that are linked to the text. In this manner students are shown role models they can critique and emulate. **Fourth**, students are encouraged to complete action exercises, analyze cases and create an **active** learning environment. **Fifth**, this book includes several distinctive pedagogical devices, e.g., action exercises, a student report, detailed appendixes and checklists, and a videotape, that are designed to enhance student learning. In short, this book creates a learning system for the strategic management course.

The book itself is divided into three major parts. Part one includes nine chapters describing strategic management skills. The first chapter is a general introduction to strategic management; the remaining eight chapters focus on specific strategic management skills. Each of these eight chapters concludes with:

- tips to remember
- action exercises
- suggested readings.

Part two contains the written cases that student teams have analyzed on the videotape. It also includes a written report on the Anheuser-Busch case completed by one of the MBA teams. There are three example cases and four videotaped presentations; two teams analyze the Anheuser-Busch case so that your students can see how two excellent strategic analyses of the same situation can differ. We strongly recommend that students read at least the first four chapters of Part 1 before reading and analysing any cases and watching a videotaped presentation. Since the entire videotape can be viewed in approximately two hours, one or more class sessions can be devoted to viewing the videotape. We recommend three separate sessions, one for each case, although we have found that one viewing of all three cases is also feasible.

Part three contains two current cases - Apple Computer and Federal Express. Students should use these case situations to practice skills they have learned in this book. There is also a glossary of terms so that all students understand the basic concepts and words associated with business policy/strategic management.

There are many individuals we would like to thank for helping us with this book. First and foremost we want to express our appreciation to Rudolph P. Lamone, Dean of the College of Business and Management at the University of Maryland at College Park. He was an early and ardent supporter of the concept of an MBA Case Competition. During the regular school year every graduating MBA student at Maryland is involved in this competition. As in the case of many new endeavors, this one was plagued with many problems and trouble spots. Dean Lamone's help and encouragement made possible our own Maryland MBA Case Competition and our participation in the Rutgers University at Camden/Harrah's 1984 and 1985 Invitational MBA Case Competitions. We are proud of the Maryland MBA students who won the first-place award in 1984 and the second-place award in 1985 in this competition. Dean Lamone and Professor Edwin Locke also arranged Daniel Power's schedule so that he would not have teaching responsibilities during the Fall 1985 semester. Those four months of "free" time were used to produce this innovative book using an Apple Macintosh, Microsoft Word and an Apple LaserWriter printer.

We would also like to thank Ming Jer Chen, a doctoral candidate at Maryland who helped with our glossary; Lisa Forry, an MBA student at Shippensburg University who helped us with the appendixes in Chapter 5; Mary Cabrera, Carol Power, Karen Craig and Karen Litwyn, who typed parts of the manuscript for us; Barbara Armstrong and Elizabeth Ashton, who reviewed and edited the manuscript; Earl W. Douglas, who helped with production; and our colleagues at the University of Maryland, the University of Houston, and Shippensburg University, especially Steven J. Carroll, Frank T. Paine (deceased), Curtis Grimm, and Kenneth Smith.

We also want to thank the case writers and the MBA student presenters. Theresa M. Brady and Robert S. Berlin deserve special thanks for all of their extra efforts under severe time pressure. Finally, we want to thank everyone at Addison-Wesley Publishing Company, including Steven Dane, Jim Heitker and Shirley Rieger. Addison-Wesley people provided the advice and resources that made this book possible.

As a final note, we definitely think that there are many advantages associated with the use of a skills-based approach in strategic management and business policy courses, and we have highlighted only some of them. You will probably identify additional advantages as you use the book. We want your comments and feedback about how to use and improve our book. The "bottom-line" is that we want students to be able to genuinely say that they have taken a strategic management course that was *interesting* and *stimulating*, and that it *helped prepare them for successful careers* in the business world.

We hope you enjoy reading **Strategic Management Skills**.

College Park, Maryland   D.J.P.
College Park, Maryland   M.J.G.
Shippensburg, Pennsylvania   M.A.M.
Houston, Texas   D.M.S.

Table of Contents

Strategic Management Skills

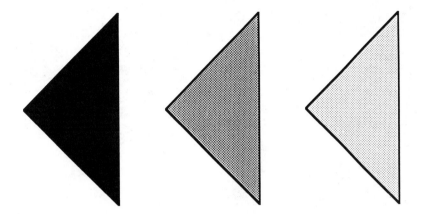

PART 1

Skills

Chapter 1

Mastering Strategic Management Skills

Lewis Carroll wrote in his book *Alice in Wonderland*: "If you don't know where you are going, any road will take you there." This provocative passage captures the essence of why strategic management skills are so important. They can help you think about, discuss, and act to create a road map and a future for an organization. Mastering them is a key to your career success. And if you apply them effectively, the chances of organizational success should increase. These skills include:

- **Cognitive, intuitive, and judgmental skills**
- **Interpersonal and team skills**
- **Communication and presentation skills.**

Research and our experience indicate that many people can acquire and master strategic management skills. By improving your **cognitive, intuitive,** and **judg-mental** skills, you will be more effective at integrating quantitative and qualitative business information into meaningful patterns and conclusions. Hence your ability to make effective decisions when faced with uncertainty and ambiguity should be enhanced. In addition, improved **interpersonal** and **leadership** skills will help you become a better team member and leader. Finally, improved **communication** and **presentation** skills -- crucial for writing reports and making oral presentations -- can help you convince others to adopt your plans and ideas. This book is designed to help you develop and master these skills.

You will read about skills used by effective general managers, planners, con-sultants, and other key personnel in organizations. Reading about these skills will not, however, magically transform you into a strategic thinker, an intuitive strategist, a team leader, or a good communicator. You must practice the skills identified and discussed in this book if you seriously want to master them. You, your fellow students, and your instructor will want to discuss each skill, analyze your current level of proficiency, practice these skills through action exercises and case analyses, view videotapes of outstanding team presentations, and plan specific additional actions that will result in skill mastery.

Probably this book has been assigned as part of a strategic management or business policy course or a management training program. You may have heard that strategic management is important only for executives or that the material is conceptual and abstract. Studying strategic management **is different** from such business courses as finance or marketing, for now you are required to use all of the knowledge you have learned in more specialized areas. You will acquire new knowledge as well as specific, concrete skills. Additionally, you are expected to be an active learner in a strategic management course.

You will be involved in team case studies or industry analyses, and you will need to work hard to analyze case situations and practice new skills. It will also be important that you plan and manage learning activities and assignments. You should try to think and to act like a top-level manager or a high-priced strategic management consultant. Finally, you will need to demonstrate that you have mastered the skills of a professional manager.

In the next two sections, we briefly discuss the general area of strategic management, including the strategic management and planning process, and define some key terms. We then identify who uses - and hence who needs to master - strategic management skills, with a focus particularly on the role of general managers in organizations. Then, because many of the specific strategic management skills discussed in subsequent chapters are directly related to more basic skills, we briefly review these basic skills. In the final section, we describe the plan of this book.

WHAT IS STRATEGIC MANAGEMENT?

Strategic management is an ongoing process of analysis, planning, and action that attempts to keep a firm aligned with its environment while capitalizing on organizational strengths and environmental opportunities and minimizing or avoiding organizational weaknesses and external threats. **Strategic management** is also a future-oriented, proactive management system. Managers who use strategic management skills are seeking a competitive advantage for their firms and long-run business success.

According to Kenneth Andrews, a professor at the Harvard Business School, **a corporate strategy** is the pattern of company purposes and goals, and the major policies and actions for achieving them. Together they define the business or businesses the company is to be involved with and the kind of company it is to be (see Suggested Reading 1.1). A written statement of strategy should communicate both a company's mission or missions and its primary goals. The written strategy should also include the company's major direction or thrust in products, markets, research, and production methods. A supporting strategic plan should indicate the major actions, resource allocations, and other changes that will occur during the planning horizon -- usually five years.

Strategy content. Much of the research and discussion related to strategic management emphasizes the content of strategies. So you should be familiar with and consider generic strategies. Michael Porter, a Harvard Business School professor, has identified three well-known generic strategies that may lead to competitive success (see Suggested Reading 2.1). His first strategy is pursuit of **overall cost leadership** for the **entire** market. Firms such as Dupont and Emerson Electric are well-known for such a strategy. Various actions such as increasing production efficiencies, underpricing competitors, and cutting costs are directly related to the successful pursuit of this strategy. Porter's second strategy is **differentiation** of products so that the customers see them as unique or very distinctive. General Motors takes this tack in the automotive industry. Distinctive brands, a heavy investment in product innovation, and memorable marketing campaigns are linked directly to this general strategy. The third strategy involves **focusing** on only a narrow segment of a larger market, emphasizing either overall cost leadership or differentiation to achieve the goals that top managers set for the organization.

According to Porter, the major and supporting strategic plans would first identify a company's generic strategy and then describe specifics, that is, how the company plans to pursue this strategy. A number of other authors have also developed lists of generic strategies. Chapter 4, Developing a Strategic Business Plan, discusses the content of corporate and business unit strategies in more detail and explains portfolio reorganization, multinational expansion, and diversification strategies.

Strategy content is discussed with various audiences. Edward Wrapp, a professor at the University of Chicago, identifies four strata or levels of corporate strategy (see Suggested Reading 1.2):

Stratum I -- corporate strategy for the annual report. Usually this version is sterilized by top management and edited by the public relations staff. For the shareholders, it conveys a sense of direction and an assurance that management knows where it is taking the company.

Stratum II -- corporate strategy for the board of directors, financial analysts, and middle managers. This statement provides a somewhat more comprehensive and revealing view of corporate strategy than Stratum I. Segments of the company and growth opportunities are often discussed in more detail. Major problems or obstacles are usually camouflaged.

Stratum III -- corporate strategy for top management. In an organization of any size or complexity, several members of top management usually participate in discussions considering moves and countermoves, the strength of the competition, the competence of operating management, and sometimes the survival of the current top management team.

Stratum IV -- the CEO's private corporate strategy. "If the CEO is a strategic thinker, he is seldom inhibited by anyone -- not by his top managers, not by his directors, not by his professional planners, and not by his outside advisors. He may be mulling a range of moves that he discloses to almost no one."

Strategic management skills are useful at all four strategy levels. Your written strategy and planning documents will probably be focused at a Stratum II and III audience, middle and top management. Strategic management skills are used to develop industry analyses, strategic business analyses, and strategic business plans for this audience.

Strategic management process. At its best, the strategic management process includes participation by many individuals in an organization, open two-way communications among individuals, systems for the effective use and integration of quantitative and qualitative information, norms for openness to innovative ideas and for the acceptance of reasonable risk-taking when making decisions, and finally, experienced managers who can make subjective decisions using incomplete, conflicting, and extraneous information.

The actual strategic management process is most often described as a rational and analytical one involving the following steps (see Fig. 1.1):

1. **Environmental scanning.** This step examines and forecasts competitor actions, industry forces and industry and company-specific threats and opportunities.
2. **Company analysis.** In this step, managers analyze and assess company activities to identify current performance, corporate cultures, strengths, weaknesses, and managerial values; and to examine current mission, goals and strategic thrusts.
3. **Strategic goal-setting.** Strategic goal-setting generates and sets a mission and long-run goals.
4. **Generating an overall strategy and major strategic actions.** This step uses information from the three previous steps to generate a new strategy that fits the organization's environment and its strengths.
5. **Strategy evaluation and choice.** This step involves a reconciliation of the previous steps with market opportunities, corporate capabilities, the values of general managers, and legal requirements and social responsibilities.
6. **Strategy implementation.** This is the step where strategies are translated into organizational actions. Actually implementing a strategy involves providing leadership, communicating with managers, adjusting the strategy, and making many tactical plans and day-to-day decisions.
7. **Strategy control.** This step monitors strategies and strategic planning to improve both future performance and the planning process.

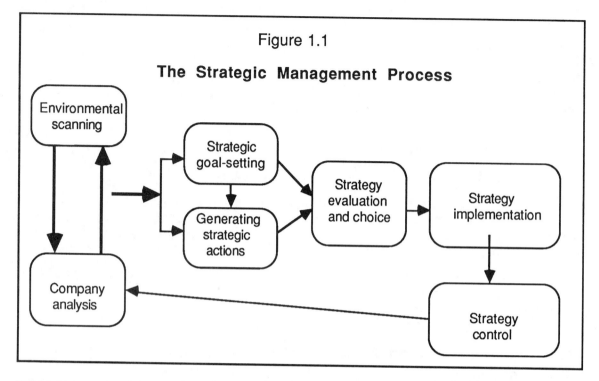

Figure 1.1

The Strategic Management Process

WHAT FACTORS IMPACT STRATEGIC MANAGEMENT?

In every situation, factors exist that constrain the design of the strategic management process and the plans that are developed. Managers and planners need to recognize these factors and take them into account when they design and use a strategic management process. Some of the factors can be altered by managers, while others are more permanent. At a minimum, the following five factors need to be considered:

- Organizational size
- Environmental turbulence and dependence
- Attitudes toward operational risk
- Power relationships
- Organizational structure.

Organizational size. Generally as the size of the organization increases the strategic management process becomes more complex and formal. A small firm with 20 employees usually has no formal strategic management process. The president makes plans, but sometimes keeps them in his or her mind. A better approach for a small company is to create a simple strategic business plan. In some large diversified corporations, planning forms exist, a formal planning process occurs once a year, and a major planning document is prepared. Such a formal approach may actually inhibit rather than promote strategic management. It is important not to become so bogged down with paperwork that the essence of strategic management - proactive future-oriented thinking - is lost.

Environmental turbulence and dependence. Companies in turbulent envi-ronments need managers with a strategic management orientation, but the actual process must be flexible and innovative to fit the environment. Firms that are heavily dependent on a major customer also need to innovate when using the strategic management process.

Managers may have to develop a plan to reduce that dependence. Other real or perceived dependencies may also limit the strategic management process and strategic plans.

Attitudes toward operational risk. Managerial attitudes affect the boldness of strategic plans. Operational risk refers to the possibility that new strategies and plans will fail. This type of risk is difficult to assess. Generally, the better your analysis, the greater your openness to alternate points of view, the greater your success in past similar situations, and the lower your fear of making a wrong decision, the better your assessment of operational risk during the strategic management process. Excessive concerns about operational risk encourage the development of a rigid, bureaucratic planning process.

Power relationships. Those who have power and authority in the organization must be actively involved in the strategic management process. Planning is not just a rational, analytical process; bargaining and trade-offs are also important.

Organizational structure. The structure of an organization partially determines power relationships. It also embodies the current way of doing business, the so-called status quo. The strategic management process must fit the structure of the organization.

The design of the strategic management process is important and managers need to critically take into account the above factors.

WHO NEEDS STRATEGIC MANAGEMENT SKILLS?

Probably you are currently using planning skills to examine various career options and the strengths and weaknesses of different companies that may offer you employment. Strategic management and planning skills also are routinely used by managers and planning staffs of large corporations, owners of small businesses, consultants, and managers in a wide variety of organizations ranging from prisons to hospitals.

In single-business companies, the president is often the only general manager and the primary strategist. In larger organizations, there are many levels of general managers with strategic management responsibilities. General managers are those responsible for the performance of an entire organization or a significant part of an organization, which is often called a strategic business unit (SBU). Each SBU has its own market niche and products. For example, General Electric has 45 SBUs. Thus, at GE, strategic planning occurs at the top corporate level as well as at each of these 45 SBUs

General managers direct the activities of others in the organization and control the acquisition and use of resources to provide the product or service offered by the company. Also, general managers are normally responsible to many internal and external constituencies and stakeholders, including stockholders, creditors, customers, and many other groups such as citizens' or advocacy groups. As Frank Lucier, former chairman of the Black and Decker Company, has noted, he was not his own boss, and no CEO that he knows is his own boss because of these constituencies or stakeholders. Reconciling the conflicting demands of stakeholders is a major part of the general manager's job.

Several authors have developed profiles of the general manager's job. These profiles tend to include the following responsibilities:

- Establishing challenging and attainable long-term objectives for the organization
- Developing plans to achieve stated goals
- Leading the organization by setting an example for others
- Resolving conflicts and making trade-offs.
- Reconciling conflicting demands of stakeholders.
- Monitoring and assessing the performance of the organization.

General managers are not confined to private, profit-making organizations. Such positions exist in all organizations, including governmental and educational organizations. Further, they are not the only ones who must possess strategic management skills. Line or operating managers should possess a long-run or strategic management perspective and strategic management skills. So, too, should staff managers responsible for planning. In fact, **all business students and managers aspiring to become general managers need to develop and refine strategic management skills.**

Strategic management skills are especially helpful in a rapidly changing and unpredictable world. Today the reality of our world is one of uncertainty. In many industries, the product life cycle has decreased significantly in the past 40 years. The life cycles of electric appliances took about 30 years to mature before World War II; the market for newer appliances such as microwave ovens has taken about 10 years. Similarly, the half-life of an electrical engineer -- the time from graduation to when he or she becomes technically obsolete -- was about 15 years in 1940 and is now about 4 years. A *Fortune* author has coined the term "high-speed management" to signify the importance of the change (see Suggested Reading 1.2).

The need for managers to predict and manage the changes in their industries or markets has never been greater. They need to possess the skills to deal effectively with situations that cannot be fully anticipated. Reasoning, analysis, and planning skills are important; proficiency in using them can help to provide some stability, predictability, and order for individuals and entire organizations.

The major benefits of mastering and using strategic management skills include the following:

- Managers become more future oriented.
- Managers can use systematic analyses and plans to inform and persuade colleagues, subordinates, and the board of directors.
- Managers can better anticipate what resources are needed, what decisions must be made, and what actions must be taken.
- Managers can use plans to evaluate future performance and accomplishments.

In summary, general managers clearly must develop strategic management skills, but so must students pursuing managerial careers in many types of organizations, owners of small businesses, the planning staffs of large organizations, and upwardly-mobile individuals who aspire to be line managers.

WHAT ARE THE BASIC SKILLS?

Effective general managers and planners have mastered many skills, the most important of which include the following:

- Analyzing and interpreting data and situations
- Diagnosing problems to uncover their causes
- Predicting and forecasting
- Planning and goal setting
- Communicating
- Implementing plans and monitoring them.

Managers are constantly bombarded with a variety of data about business situations that they must analyze, interpret, and assess. They must use basic cognitive, intuitive and judgmental skills. **Analyzing** means separating the situation into parts and examining the parts to better understand what is occurring. **Interpreting** means explaining and providing your own view of the situation. **Assessing** means estimating the value or worth of elements of the situation. In applying these basic skills, you will be sorting data and identifying consistent and plausible interpretations. These data are often important, so the analysis must be as rigorous and complete as possible, and the interpretation must be systematic and cautious. Assessments and interpretations of the data indicate importance, plausibility, and worth or value. Plausible explanations of the data should be discarded only when there is a sufficient amount of evidence to clearly rule them out. The key problem facing managers is that data in business situations are often incomplete, conflicting, and extraneous. So you must exercise care and identify missing, erroneous, or extraneous data. You need to develop skills to aid you in:

- Coping with partial information
- Recognizing and assessing contradictory data
- Identifying unreliable data
- Making realistic assumptions
- Developing complicated reasoning chains supported by assumptions and evidence
- Using your intuition to reach defensible assessments and interpretations.

Futhermore, because general managers and planners are business generalists, they must diagnose problems affecting not only individuals but the entire organization. **Diagnosing** is the process of determining the cause and nature of problems. Usually you will need to draw inferences and make judgments to reach a diagnosis. **Inferring** means reaching conclusions based upon what is known and assumed. **Judging,** a skill that peo - ple use often, is the process of forming opinions and estimates relevant to a situation or problem. As a skilled management diagnostician, you will need an understanding of the entire organization, the relationships among units within the organization, and the rela - tionships of the organization with its environments. You need to be especially skilled at the following:

- Using incomplete and conflicting information
- Separating symptoms and causes from problems
- Collecting relevant diagnostic information.

But general managers must do much more than analyze, interpret, and diagnose. An important strategic management skill is forecasting and predicting the future. This skill involves determining what one believes is likely to happen in the future. Sometimes models of the past or present are useful aids in forecasting. In other situations, the models introduce false confidence and exaggerate errors and discontinuities about anticipated events occurring over time. The predictors or variables used by managers to help them anticipate the future can change rapidly as events unfold, thus requiring managers to adjust their plans. General managers need an adequate understanding of causes and consequences to help them anticipate events and adjust planned actions over time. Hence managers must be skilled at:

- Considering and assessing multiple possible futures
- Making use of diverse types of data from many sources
- Considering contingencies and uncontrollable factors
- Assessing the likelihood of events.

Naturally, two basic skills that managers must possess are planning and goal-setting. **Planning** is the process of designing a consistent integrated program of actions that when carried out will accomplish specific goals. **Goal-setting** is the process of identifying desired accomplishments and targets. General managers and planners should be especially skilled at long-run planning and goal-setting for the business enterprise. They should be able to construct plans that achieve long-run goals without consuming excessive resources or violating constraints. If long-run goals of the business are in conflict, then planners must be able to establish priorities. Skilled strategic managers are flexible and opportunistic in situations that are not fully known or that change with time. They can work with predictions and develop plans that are responsive to the uncertainty and contingencies associated with them. These managers are also skilled at coping with the following key problems:

- Assessing the likely consequences for alternative actions
- Sorting out irrelevant issues, and focusing only on the most relevant
- Resolving goal conflicts
- Preparing for possible contingencies
- Coordinating the actions and actors in the plan.

General managers and planners must also work and communicate with a wide array of individuals at all levels of the firm. In order to be effective, general managers and planners must possess well-developed communication, interpersonal and team skills. Ef - fective communication includes **both** the ability to influence and inform others **and** the openness to be influenced and informed by others. Effective strategic managers, then, have communications-receiving skills such as listening openly to new ideas, and effective communication-sending skills such as speaking persuasively.

Finally, general managers must be skilled at implementing and monitoring plans. Once a plan has been communicated to those who will execute it, general managers and planners must not only carry out their assigned tasks and assist those people who need help, but must also interpret signals and feedback from others who are executing the plan. Effectively implementing and monitoring a plan that has been skillfully crafted can greatly increase the likelihood of success.

WHAT IS THE PLAN OF THIS BOOK?

This book is divided into three major parts. In this first part, the specific strategic manage - ment skills are described and discussed in detail. Chapter 2 develops your skills for analyzing an industry; Chapter 3 helps you hone the skills necessary for conducting a strategic business analysis for a company; Chapter 4 explains the skills needed to develop a strategic business plan; Chapter 5 provides assistance in finding strategic management information; Chapters 6 and 7 explain such team skills as developing and participating in strategic management teams; Chapter 8 examines the skills required for a team to write a competent formal business report; and Chapter 9 highlights the skills needed to make a high-quality formal business speech.

Each of these chapters begins with a list of the skills discussed; each of the skills is then explained in a separate section of the chapter. Each chapter includes "tips to remember," some short exercises for mastering the skills, and suggested readings.

This first part of the book is intended to help you prepare four different types of strategic management documents:

- a strategic industry analysis (Chapter 2)
- a strategic business analysis (Chapter 3)
- a strategic business plan (Chapter 4)
- a strategic business analysis and plan.

In most situations, you will prepare either an industry analysis or a report combining a business analysis and a plan. You will use the skills discussed in Chapters 2, 3, and 4 to develop these reports.

The second part of the book contains three strategic management cases -- American Safety Razor, Inc., Anheuser-Busch Cos., Inc., and Levi Strauss, Inc. -- and a written student analysis and strategic plan for Anheuser-Busch. First read each case, then view the appropriate videotaped presentation by an outstanding MBA student team. We have found that these role-modeling videotapes are enormously helpful; you should learn quickly what is required in a strategic business analysis and strategic business plan. Also, the tapes should help you improve your oral presentation •kills.

Finally, Part 3 contains two additional strategic management cases so that you can practice strategic management skills. The cases are Apple Computer, Inc. - Fall 1985, and Federal Express, Inc. - 1985. It also includes a glossary and short biographical sketches of the student presenters.

TIPS TO REMEMBER

1.1   Skill mastery results from understanding and practice, not from reading about skills.

1.2   Try to think like a general manager or strategic management consultant when you analyze strategic management cases.

1.3   Strategic management is a systematic process. Keep the entire process in mind as you read about specific skills.

1.4   Specific strategic management skills use more basic cognitive, interpersonal and communication skills. Master both the basic skills and the specific strategic management skills.

SUGGESTED READINGS

1.1   Andrews, K.R., *The Concept of Corporate Strategy* (rev. ed.). Homewood, Ill.: Richard D. Irwin, Inc., 1980.

   This book helped define the field of strategic management. Andrews clearly and succinctly established the Harvard Business School perspective.

1.2   Andrews, K.R., Corporate Strategy as a Vital Function of the Board. *Harvard Business Review*, November/December 1981, pp. 174-184.

   Andrews discusses the function of the board of directors in strategy formulation. He includes materials on the strata of strategic management excerpted from a letter he received from Edward Wrapp, University of Chicago.

1.3   Fraker, S., High-speed Management for the High-tech Age. *Fortune*, March 5, 1984, pp. 62-68.

   This article describes the shortening of the product life cycles in many industries and the management problems that have resulted from such changes.

1.4   Kotter, J.P., *The General Managers*. New York: The Free Press, 1982.

   Kotter summarizes a research study on the jobs of 15 general managers. The book is well-written and helps clarify the scope and diversity of general management jobs.

1.5   Quinn, J. B., *Strategies for Change: Logical Incrementalism*. Homewood, Ill.: Richard D. Irwin, 1980.

   Quinn criticizes formal planning and offers an alternate approach - Logical Incrementalism. He tries to document his position with a number of company examples.

Chapter 2

Analyzing an Industry

MAJOR SKILLS

- DEFINING AN INDUSTRY
- REVIEWING AN INDUSTRY'S HISTORY
- ANALYZING INDUSTRY FORCES
- ASSESSING INDUSTRY COMPETITIVE STRUCTURE
- EVALUATING INDUSTRY MARKETING PRACTICES
- IDENTIFYING INDUSTRY-WIDE THREATS AND OPPORTUNITIES
- EVALUATING INDUSTRY INVESTMENT REQUIREMENTS
- RECOMMENDING STRATEGIC CHANGES

Analyzing an industry is an important skill related to the environmental scanning step in the strategic management process. Environmental scanning includes ongoing management activities such as reading newspapers. But periodically managers need to develop a formal comprehensive analysis - a strategic industry analysis. This analysis includes an overview of strategic forces affecting a target industry, an analysis of strategies of various companies in the industry, and forecasts and recommendations.

A formal strategic industry analysis is useful in many strategic management and planning situations. First, such an analysis helps managers understand their company's current strategic position. Specifically, the industry analysis should define the scope and direction of competitor actions so that company strategic moves are focused and targeted.

Second, an industry analysis should pinpoint and analyze the general threats and opportunities facing all companies in an industry. This knowledge can provide an advantage to managers who respond appropriately, making them better able to capitalize on the available opportunities while minimizing or avoiding the threats facing firms in the industry.

Third, a formal industry analysis aids managers in deciding whether to enter or leave a particular industry. For instance, several years ago, both General Electric and RCA independently decided to liquidate their respective computer mainframe divisions. Analyses completed by these two companies probably indicated that the costs associated with continued competition in this industry would be very high and the returns would be unacceptable.

Finally, preparing an industry analysis aids managers in understanding the strategies and behavior of specific competitors. For example, the motel industry has evolved into three tiers of companies linked to upscale, mid-range, and budget customer segments. Recognizing and identifying these three customer segments helps you see why several motel companies are now developing multiple chains positioned in different tiers under the same parent corporation.

The remainder of this chapter explains the specific skills used in preparing a formal strategic industry analysis. When you have mastered these skills, you should be able to develop a complete and meaningful strategic industry analysis.

DEFINING AN INDUSTRY

An industry is a group of companies or organizations providing similar products and/or services to an identifiable set of customers or clients. You must define an industry before you apply other skills. The definition of an industry sets boundaries and provides a frame of reference for other analyses. You should choose one or more of the following approaches when you define the target industry for your strategic industry analysis.

First, you could use the Standard Industrial Classification (SIC) system. In the United States, each industry is given a SIC code. This code classifies products and services. For example, the SIC code for home refrigerators is 3632, while the SIC code for home laundry (washing) machines is 3633. Thus a firm that manufactures both home refrigerators and home laundry machines would compete in two industries identified by SIC codes 3632 and 3633. A specific firm, such as General Electric, might be identified with several hundred product categories.

The SIC code can also help you find information about specific industries. Chapter 5, Finding Strategic Management Information, discusses information sources in detail.

A second way of defining an industry is by enumerating all of the companies that participate in that industry. For example, in preparing a strategic industry analysis of the fast food industry, our students found that it was necessary to enumerate those firms that are burger-oriented (i.e., McDonald's, Wendy's, Burger King, and some regional burger chains like Roy Rogers). In this way, they excluded from their analysis firms specializing in pizza, chicken, seafood, or Mexican food. Any attempt to analyze a complex industry such as fast food, may require segmentation into strategic groups. Enumeration of the competitors in those groups will then be necessary. So a comprehensive analysis of the entire fast-food industry might include individual analyses of burger-oriented, pizza-oriented, chicken-oriented, seafood-oriented, and Mexican-oriented chains.

A third approach is to use specific criteria to aid in classifying companies as participants in an industry. For example, to define the Baltimore--Washington, D.C. retail furniture industry, the following criteria could be used to identify participants in the industry:

• Within 25 miles of Baltimore or Washington, D.C.
• Two or more locations
• At least 100,000 square feet of showroom space
• More than $1,000,000 in annual retail sales
• More than 15 employees in furniture retailing
• Listings in the Baltimore and Washington telephone book

This third approach is often useful for analyzing regional markets or new, evolving industries.

REVIEWING AN INDUSTRY'S HISTORY

Once you have defined the target industry, the next step is to review and identify those issues that historically have been strategically important to the industry. Do not detail every historical event; rather try to develop a historical overview and a list of strategically important events, trends, and competitor actions. Making a list of challenges and issues also helps develop a historical perspective for subsequent analyses. Not every issue and challenge facing an industry is new; many of them have a long history.

Your review of an industry's history should answer the following questions:

√ How was the industry created? What was occurring at that time?
√ How has the industry changed and developed?
√ What challenges and issues has the industry faced over the years?
√ How has the industry responded to these challenges and issues?

Your assessment of the industry's history should include a time span sufficient to develop an overall historical perspective. Thus, a strategic industry analysis that focused on only the past five years might overlook long-term forces affecting the industry. For example, an analysis of the petroleum industry that focused on 1980-1985 would probably conclude that the industry is stagnant and unattractive. However, a **brief** historical review of that industry's past 50 years would suggest that the fortunes of this industry ebb and flow over time and that recent history should be viewed from that perspective. On the other hand, the personal computer industry is less than 10 years old, so its historical review will cover less than a decade.

ANALYZING INDUSTRY FORCES

Six major external forces seem to influence strategies and the profit potential of an industry:

- Technological changes
- Resource availability
- Socioeconomic trends
- Government actions
- Customer needs and actions
- General business developments.

In examining each of these forces, consider both the current status and likely future directions of the forces and assess the importance of each for the target industry.

Technological changes. The first step in analyzing the current and future impact of technological changes on an industry is to identify what is occurring. You should specify the current level of technology (simple versus highly technical), the availability of technologies,and the rate of technological change. For example, changes in information-processing technology, such as computerized grocery checkouts, have dramatically altered the technological assessment of the grocery retailing industry. The level of technology is sophisticated, and new technologies are widely available and rapidly changing. Technology has become a major force in that industry.

The second step is to examine technological threats to the industry. For instance, changes in telecommunications technology pose a direct threat to the express mail delivery industry, including the U.S. Postal Service and Federal Express, organizations that move correspondence, financial data, and other types of printed information.

The final step in analyzing technological changes is to assess strategic implications. You should ask: How will technological changes alter company strategies? In some instances, your research will clearly indicate how strategies will be altered. However, in many situations, you will have to deduce or infer them. For example, a student team in early 1985 concluded that electronic imaging technology would substitute for the silver haloid photographic technology and make the film industry based on that technology virtually obsolete by 1990. Subsequent articles in the business press have discussed the threat of electronic imaging to traditional consumer photographic products.

Resource availability. All competitors in an industry are dependent on the same general pool of resources. The availability and control of critical resources can influence levels of output and company profitability. The first step in analyzing this external force is to evaluate what resources are critically needed for companies in the industry. These resources could include raw materials, energy sources, managerial skills, technical personnel, and transport and logistics capabilities. The relative importance of these resources varies from one industry to another. In the accounting industry, for example, raw material availability and energy considerations are of little importance, but managerial capabilities and technical personnel are currently critical resources.

The second step is to determine the availability of critical resources. Your analysis should address the following questions:

√ What are the critical resources?
√ How available are critical resources?
√ What are the trends in the availability of these resources?
√ What impact will resource availability have on the industry in the near
   and long term?

Also try to assess the impact of strategic changes initiated by firms that provide capital goods and raw materials to the target industry. Supplier issues that should be con-sidered include these:

√ Is the number of suppliers changing?
√ How are suppliers performing financially?
√ Is it possible suppliers will integrate forward into the target industry?

Socioeconomic trends. Your analysis of socioeconomic trends should consider the broader changes occurring in society that may affect the target industry: demographic changes, changes in consumer behavior patterns, consumer lifestyle changes, and changes in consumer values. For example, the housing industry may be influenced by changing attitudes toward marriage and family, changes in savings behavior, shifting housing preferences, increased levels of education, and an aging population. Ask the following questions:

√ What major socioeconomic changes are occurring?
√ What socioeconomic changes may have an impact on the target
   industry?
√ What is the potential impact?

Government actions. Local, state, and federal governments and associated agencies can have both positive and negative impacts on industries. At the federal level, trade laws, environmental protection laws and equal employment opportunity laws influence many industries. You should evaluate the impact of pending legislation, regulations, and current laws on the target industry. Your assessment is important because it establishes rules and constraints on acceptable company strategies. Also, your analysis may suggest opportunities for joint actions with other companies through trade associations to influence laws and regulations. Examples of issues that should be considered in the assessment include the following:

- Antitrust problems
- Changing interpretations of laws and regulations
- Social and consumer legislation
- Other legislative trends.

Customer needs and actions. Customer behavior can be influenced but not con-trolled, so managers need to be especially sensitive to this important external force. In some cases, customers are large and powerful and can have a major influence on company actions. For example, General Motors is a powerful customer for automobile parts manu-facturers. Usually, powerful customers will try to create strong ties to their suppliers. In consumer goods industries, the customer and marketing practices become a key to company success. Therefore you should attempt to develop for the industry a customer profile that answers the following questions:

√ What are the major customer groups?
√ How many customers are in each group? How much of the industry's output is sold to each group? What are the trends?
√ Are there changes in customer buying practices?
√ Can customers substitute products from other industries?
√ Can customers integrate into the target industry?
√ Are changes occurring in markets served by your customers?

General business developments. Large companies may consider entering the target industry as part of a diversification move. An embryonic industry that can provide a substitute product may have attracted venture capital. Companies producing comple-mentary products may have difficulty attracting capital, thus retarding sales of the target industry's products. Changes in the financial services industry or public accounting indus-try can affect many other industries. As the preceding examples suggest, scanning the general business environment is important. External business developments may influence the target industry. Therefore you will want to assess what changes are occurring and how they may influence the target industry, especially in terms of the following questions:

√ Are there potential entrants to the target industry?
√ What is happening in industries that do or could produce substitute products?
√ What is happening in industries that produce complementary products?

Finally, consider the combined influence of all industry forces. In some instances the net effect of these forces may constrain the industry. In other instances the net effect may nurture the industry. Seldom will all of the industry forces work together. However, your analysis should enable you to identify the impact of forces and assess the net effect.

ASSESSING INDUSTRY COMPETITIVE STRUCTURE

There are three steps in assessing industry competitive structure: categorizing the structure, evaluating successful and unsuccessful firms, and developing strategic group maps.

Categorizing industry structure.   Your first step is to categorize the target indus - try's structure. Is the industry oligopolistic? Why do you think so? Economists discuss the competitive structure of an industry by using the following categories: perfect competition, monopolistic competition, oligopoly, and monopoly. Perfect competition, as you probably recall, refers to an industry with many small firms, none of which can influence or set prices. Monopolistic competition involves a few large and medium-sized competitors, and many small competitors. The larger competitors are severely restrained in their ability to set prices. Oligopoly involves four or five large competitors that control most of the output of the industry. Such firms can implicitly collude to set prices. Follow-the-leader pricing and similar practices are common in such an industry. Monopoly means that a single company dominates and controls prices in an industry.

Evaluating firms.   The next step is to evaluate successful and unsuccessful firms in the target industry. Identifying successful and unsuccessful firms within an industry helps you recognize that there may be more than one strategy that works. For example, in the domestic airline industry, American Airlines has been successful as an "aggressive market leader," while U.S. Air has been successful by appealing to a specific segment or "niche" in the market - less dense, short-haul markets in the Northeast. Regardless of the number of successful strategies that exist in an industry, try to develop some generalizations con - cerning successful and unsuccessful firms.

Developing strategic group maps.   The third step is to develop strategic group maps. This technique is useful for formalizing relationships among industry competitors. A strategic group map divides competitors in an industry into meaningful groups based on at least two strategic variables. Developing strategic group maps involves creativity and trial and error. The following steps can help you develop useful groupings:

1. Identify relevant dimensions of competitive strategy for your industry.
2. Pick two important, independent dimensions.
3. Position companies in terms of those two dimensions.
4. Evaluate and interpret the resulting strategic group map.
5. Repeat the above steps until you are satisfied that you have meaningful strategic group maps.

Figure 2.1 identifies a list of competitive strategy dimensions that seem relevant to many target industries. This list is provided as a basis for analyzing competitive strategies in an industry. Seldom will all dimensions be relevant to a specific industry.

Strategic group maps can help you visualize relationships among industry par - ticipants. In the example shown in Fig. 2.2, the domestic airlines have been categorized by the type of market served (national or regional) and their cost position.

Interpreting a strategic group map is not always easy and it certainly requires that you use your intuition and judgment. For example, in Fig. 2.2 you can see that there are five groups of companies. As noted in the figure, group-B companies are following similar strategies. Also, the arrow in the figure indicates that group-B companies are expanding into additional markets. You may develop many maps during your preliminary analysis, only to discover that just a few provide meaningful insights appropriate to your final analysis. The number of strategic group maps that you develop for a specific industry will usually vary from two to six.

Figure 2.1

Possible Dimensions for Strategic Group Maps

Dimension	Explanation
1. Specialization	Narrow or broad range of products
2. Product quality	Level of quality, consistency of quality
3. Technological leadership	Technological leader or follower?
4. Vertical integration	Extent of backward integration into sources of supply or forward integration in customer markets
5. Cost position	High cost vs. Low cost
6. Service	Intangibles such as credit, customer assistance, post-sales support
7. Pricing policy	High price vs. low price, aggressive pricing vs. reactive pricing

Adapted from Michael E. Porter, <u>Competitive Strategy: Techniques for Analyzing Industries and Competitors</u> (New York: The Free Press, 1980).

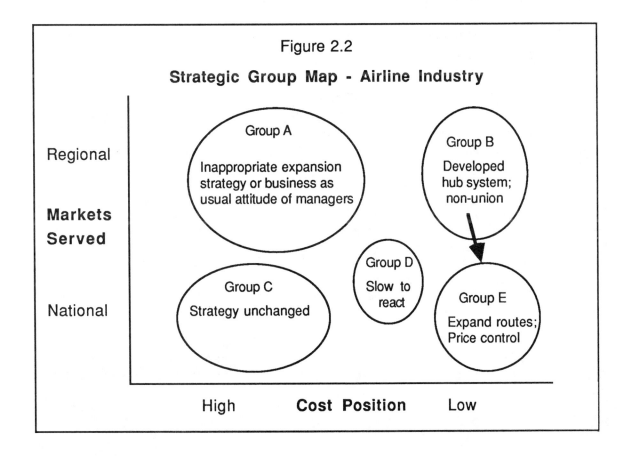

Figure 2.2

Strategic Group Map - Airline Industry

EVALUATING INDUSTRY MARKETING PRACTICES

You need to critically assess industry practices regarding **the marketing mix,** which is defined as follows:

- *Product* (the array of tangible and intangible attributes capable of satisfying customer needs)
- *Price* (including discounts for prompt payment, quantity orders, preseason orders, and long-term commitments)
- *Promotion* (advertising, personal selling, sales promotion, public relations, and publicity)
- *Place* (channels of distribution, inventory policies, customer services policies, and number of distribution points).

Both industry-wide patterns and variations among industry participants should be evaluated. In addition, an evaluation of industry marketing practices should identify relevant trade associations, which are frequently a major component of the industry's marketing program. The following discussion examines the industry marketing mix.

Product. The product is usually superficially homogeneous within an industry. While it may be difficult to differentiate meaningfully the products in some industries (such as cement, grain, gravel, or coal), a closer examination of many industries reveals a level of product differentiation that enables each firm to insulate itself from much of the direct competition one would expect to find in an industry. For example, McDonald's and Wendy's are not really direct competitors. McDonald's targets its products for the family segment, whereas Wendy's focuses its products on the adult segment.

Price. The evaluation of pricing activities within an industry seeks to address such ques - tions as these:

√ Are pricing practices consistent or do they vary from firm to firm?
√ Are pricing patterns stable over time or do they vary with the business cycle?

Promotion. The evaluation of industry promotion practices provides a great deal of insight into the behavior of the industry. For example, the Coca Cola Company dominated the soft-drink industry for many years, a situation that changed dramatically after Pepsi began a concerted drive to unseat Coke by means of (a) aggressive comparative advertising stressing that Pepsi was preferred over Coke by most consumers, and (b) the heavy use of promotional pricing practices to make Pepsi more attractive than Coke.

Place. Further subtle but important differences between competing products are often revealed through the evaluation of industry distribution (place) practices. While the soft drink bottlers use similar channels (syrup production --> bottler --> all possible retail points), an assessment of the television manufacturing industry would reveal several different strategies. Some firms in this industry emphasize exclusive, or limited, distribution (Curtis Mathis), while other firms use intensive, or mass, distribution (General Electric).

In general, the **marketing mix evaluation** helps you develop an overall pers - pective on a particular industry's traditions and practices. An understanding of the simil - arities and differences among the industry participants will help you develop an intuitive feel for that industry.

Finally, identification of industry trade associations is useful for two reasons. First, the number and types of trade associations give you a feel for the nature of that industry. For example, a list of 30 trade associations will suggest an industry of much diversity, whereas a short list of trade associations may suggest either an industry that has a clear identity or an industry that possibly is somewhat stagnant.

IDENTIFYING INDUSTRY-WIDE THREATS AND OPPORTUNITIES

A **threat** is an external problem or potential problem for most or all companies in an industry. An **opportunity** is a benefit or potential benefit most companies in an industry may realize. This chapter focuses on threats and opportunities from an industry-wide standpoint. The next chapter discusses threats and opportunities from the perspective of an individual company.

When evaluating threats to an industry, attempt to identify **the source** of the threat and **any harm** that may occur. Your evaluation should include your suggestions concerning how firms in the industry can avoid or minimize the impact of each threat. When evaluating opportunities for an industry, identify **the source** of the opportunity and **the benefits** that may occur. Your evaluation should include your suggestions for capitalizing on each opportunity. The assessment of industry threats and opportunities should also include an evaluation of the significance of each threat and opportunity. Figure 2.3 presents a threats-and-opportunities profile for the personal computer industry.

A list of specific industry threats or opportunities may evolve from the overall impressions you have developed. You need to evaluate these impressions. They represent your subconcious mind integrating the information you have gathered. You also need to systematically brainstorm a list of threats and opportunities. In some cases, reviewing the

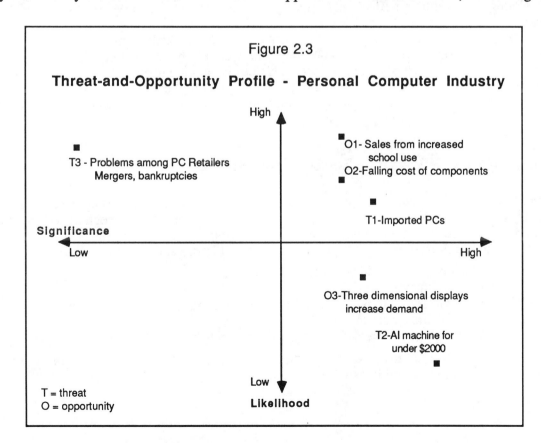

Figure 2.3

Threat-and-Opportunity Profile - Personal Computer Industry

major industry forces will help you identify threats and opportunities. If your strategic industry analysis is a group project, then the group creativity and decision techniques discussed in Chapter 6 may help your team identify threats and opportunities.

EVALUATING INDUSTRY INVESTMENT REQUIREMENTS

Each industry has differing investment requirements. In some situations these requirements will have strategic importance. Your evaluation of industry investment requirements must answer three key questions:

√   How much capital investment is needed by current competitors?
√   How much working capital is needed?
√   How much capital is needed to enter the industry?

While precise numbers cannot always be developed for the investment requirements of an industry, a qualitative investment evaluation is needed to answer such questions as:

√   Is this industry capital intensive?
√   Does the level of capital intensity or the rate of technological change result in any unusual capital needs?
√   Does the cyclical nature of this industry suggest that investment requirements will fluctuate either seasonally or cyclically?
√   Are capital requirements changing?

Investment evaluation can be difficult. First, although many students feel that they will be able to "look up" or "find" the answer, there is seldom a single precise quantitative number that answers the critical question: Should a firm invest heavily in this industry? Completing this evaluation effectively usually involves synthesizing a perspective based on research.

Second, investment requirements in many industries are changing rapidly. For example, the investment mix between buildings and technology has changed dramatically in many industries. Previously, investment needs could be categorized as those involving primarily building, bricks, mortar, and equipment. Now a higher proportion of investment needs are in less tangible areas, such as research and development, computer software development, and promotional programs.

RECOMMENDING STRATEGIC CHANGES

Forecasting industry changes and making strategic recommendations are major parts of an industry analysis. Picture yourself as a consultant who is preparing a speech or writing an article for an audience that includes industry executives. What can you say that would be interesting and provocative? Some questions you should pose and answer include:

√   What changes should firms consider?
√   What are the investment needs?
√   How can firms capitalize on opportunities and minimize or avoid threats?
√   How significant are the threats?
√   What significant events or changes are likely to occur in the next 10 years?

Don't be afraid to provoke disagreements; try to make forecasts and recommend-ations that are distinctive and logical.

TIPS TO REMEMBER

2.1 Think 5 to 10 years ahead as you proceed in your analysis. Your recommendations should anticipate the future.

2.2 Focus first on the major competitors.

2.3 Use multiple sources of information. Depending on a limited number of sources can mislead you.

2.4 Try to verify your intuitive conclusions.

2.5 Determine key forces that affect performance in the industry. These forces will differ from industry to industry.

2.6 Consider both sales and profit potential of the industry.

ACTION EXERCISES

2.1 Using the most recent *Forbes* Annual Survey of American Industry, identify those American industries that are responding most effectively to foreign competition. Identify those industries that are responding least effectively to foreign competition. *Forbes* includes many feature articles on company and industry strategy. Each January the second issue is an Annual Report on American Industry. This Annual Report is probably the best single source of information on American industry.

2.2 Prepare a strategic industry analysis for one of the following industries:

Real Estate	Petroleum Products
Domestic Airlines	Trucking
Fast Foods	Hospitals
Motels	Forest Products
Construction Equipment	Corrugated Boxes
Life Insurance	Microcomputers
Public Accounting	Meat Packing
Supermarkets	Banking
Home Construction	Soft Drinks

SUGGESTED READINGS

2.1   Porter, M. E., *Competitive Strategy: Techniques for Analyzing Industries and Competitors*. New York: The Free Press, 1980.
   This book provides a comprehensive methodology for analyzing industries and individual firms. It is very readable, makes liberal use of relevant illustrations and examples, and is well indexed.

2.2   Porter, M. E., *Cases in Competitive Strategy*. New York: The Free Press, 1983.
   This book has many well-written industry and competitor analyses. Most of the analyses were prepared in the mid-1970's, but they can serve as useful examples and sources of ideas.

Chapter 3

Conducting a Strategic Business Analysis

MAJOR SKILLS

- ASSESSING A COMPANY'S CURRENT POSITION
- ASSESSING A COMPANY'S INTERNAL CAPABILITIES
- ANALYZING THE EXTERNAL ENVIRONMENT
- EVALUATING STRATEGIC FIT

Now that we have discussed strategic industry analysis, let's turn our attention to the strategic evaluation of one organization. Once we understand the industry or industries in which a company is competing, we need to evaluate thoroughly its strategic position by conducting a formal strategic business analysis. This analysis critically evaluates a company's current position, internal strengths and weaknesses, and external threats and opportunities.

A strategic business analysis is useful in several different strategic management situations. First, this analysis helps you develop a thorough understanding of a company and what its managers are trying to accomplish. Without the insights provided by a strategic business analysis, effective strategic planning is not likely to happen. Second, a strategic business analysis aids in evaluating competitors. Competitive strategies should exploit competitors' weaknesses and avoid their strengths. Finally, completing a strategic business analysis of a merger or acquisition prospect aids in the assessment of the fit of that company with the prospective buyer.

While the skills for conducting a strategic business analysis may seem simple and straightforward, you should remember two important points:

- Each analysis differs.
- Your cognitive, intuitive, and judgmental skills are important.

The remainder of this chapter describes the skills needed for preparing a strategic business analysis. When used together, these skills will enable you to do the following:

- Prepare a meaningful analysis that considers both the internal and external environments of a company.
- Evaluate the appropriateness of a company's mission, goals and strategic thrust.

ASSESSING A COMPANY'S CURRENT POSITION

This assessment involves developing an overall perspective on a company's current stakeholders, culture, performance, current mission and strategic thrust, and strategic business units (SBUs). A strategic business analysis begins with this step because you need to know a company's current position before you can decide where a company should be going and how managers can make any needed changes. In analyzing some companies, you may find it necessary to subdivide them into component divisions, subsidiaries, or SBUs. These companies are usually involved with a diversified array of products or businesses. In other situations you will need only to assess the company as a whole. When it is necessary to analyze the firm in terms of divisions, subsidiaries, or SBUs, you should also integrate your findings into a more global assessment.

Assessing the current position of the firm involves many interrelated skills. Among the most important are these:

- Identifying the stakeholders or constituencies of the firm
- Evaluating the corporate culture(s)
- Profiling company performance
- Assessing the current mission and strategic thrust
- Identifying strategic business units.

Identifying stakeholders. Stakeholders are those organized groups that have a vested interest in a specific company. These groups may be external (society, the local community, stockholders, customers, suppliers, creditors) or internal (top managers, other managers, staff, hourly employees). The purpose of identifying stakeholders is to determine the relative influence that they have on managerial decisions. Stakeholder influence can constrain general managers and limit strategic choices. Knowing the "players" is an important step in determining what strategic actions are feasible.

Two approaches are useful in identifying stakeholders. You can begin by examining a company's publications. Questions to ask as you review company publications include the following:

√ Which stakeholder groups does management seem to recognize as important?
√ How well do company policies and strategies reflect these stated concerns?
√ Which stakeholders have an impact on decisions?

Some companies will formally identify their employees as important stakeholders but have high rates of employee turnover at all levels. This anomaly suggests that employees may not really be valued stakeholders. Similarly, a company may profess concern for environmental issues, but constantly engage in litigation with various local, state, and federal agencies over environmental pollution. In such companies environmental groups are weak stakeholders.

The second approach for assessing stakeholder priorities is to evaluate what is written in public sources about a company and its strategies. Questions to keep in mind include the following:

√ Is the company sensitive to its customers?
√ Is the company sensitive to the long-term needs of its suppliers, or is it in constant conflict with them?
√ Does the company experience a great deal of conflict with the communities in which it does business or is there only minimal conflict?
√ Do the company's financial policies result in conflict with its lenders?
√ Are shareholders receptive to overtures from take-over threats?

When you are identifying stakeholders, remember that some are more influential than others. You will not have time to consider all possible stakeholders so it is especially important to focus on the most important ones.   After you have identified a number of stakeholders, try to list and rank them in terms of their importance to the company.   Also, you should try to specify the impact they have on managerial decisions.

Evaluating the corporate culture(s).   Corporate culture is an important internal characteristic of a company.   The culture can influence managerial behavior and constrain management decisions and actions.   If you understand the corporate culture, you can better assess what is occurring and judge what mission, goals, and strategies managers can effectively implement.   Corporate culture includes the assumptions, values, traditions, and behaviors that prescribe the actions of individuals within a company.   Terrence Deal and Allen Kennedy (see Suggested Reading 3.1) have developed a typology that will help you understand a company's culture.   They use the following two dimensions to define culture:

- Degree of risk (low or high) that an organization and its members are willing to tolerate
- Rapidity of feedback (slow or fast) from the external environment that an organization and its members experience when they pursue a particular course of action.

As shown in Fig. 3.1, Deal and Kennedy developed four general types of organization cultures: Tough-guy, Macho; Work Hard/Play Hard; Bet your Company; and Process.   Descriptions of each type are provided in Fig. 3.2.   Deal and Kennedy also indicate that large divisions or departments within a company may have quite different cultures.   For example, the sales department may have a "Work Hard/Play Hard" culture whereas the production department may have a "Process" culture.

These four types of cultures represent a good point of departure for evaluating the culture of a company.   Use Fig. 3.1 as a starting point for developing your own description of a company's culture.   Invent a name for the culture that fits your assessment.   Examples of corporate cultures that have been identified in student analyses include "Work Hard but Bet your Company," "Innovation and Concern for the Employee," "Drift without Aim," and "Persistence in the Face of Adversity."

Figure 3.1

Summary of Corporate Culture Types

Level of Stakes

		High	Low
Speed of Feedback	Quick	Tough-Guy, Macho	Work Hard/ Play Hard
	Slow	Bet your Company	Process

Developed from Terrence A. Deal and Allen A. Kennedy, *Corporate Cultures: The Rites of Corporate Life*, Reading, MA: Addison-Wesley, 1982, chap. 6.

Figure 3.2

Descriptions of Four Corporate Culture Types

<u>Culture</u>	<u>Characteristics</u>	<u>Business Environment</u>
Tough-Guy, Macho	High stakes, quick feedback, individualism, high pressure, speed over endurance, emotional, self-centered, short-term emphasis,impulsive, win-lose, score points off other people, superstitious, high risk	Unstable, competitive, changing markets
Work Hard/ Play Hard	Low stakes, quick feedback, team orientation, energetic, short-term emphasis, friendly competition, quantity over quality,individual decisions not crucial, persistent, low risk.	Customer oriented, mass market
Bet Your Company	High stakes, slow feedback, hierarchical decision making, very deliberative, steady pressure, interdependence, team oriented, future oriented, many meetings, lower energy, quality over quantity, high risk	Capital intensive, changing technologies or customer needs
Process	Low stakes, slow feedback, bureaucratic, hierarchical, means over ends, technical perfection, regimented, cautious, perpetuation, slow moving	Noncompetitive, low growth

Developed from Terrence E. Deal and Allen A. Kennedy, *Corporate Cultures: The Rites of Corporate Life*, Reading, MA: Addison-Wesley, 1982, chapter 6.

Evaluating the corporate culture is a useful step in a strategic business analysis, because it helps you accomplish the following:

- Understand how strategies develop in the company
- Evaluate which strategies may be appropriate for the company
- Assess whether current strategies are appropriate
- Assess the environment/culture fit
- Identify changes that are needed in the company's culture.

Profiling company performance. This skill involves both an examination of facts about company performance and an assessment of what they mean. This analysis helps you determine how well a company is performing and if the company has the financial capability needed for strategic changes. Calculating and examining financial ratios such as profitability, liquidity, leverage, and activity is an important first step in developing a profile. You will need to make three types of comparisons to develop a reasonable profile. First, examine what has occurred during the past 5 or 10 years and develop **historical** comparisons. This will help you identify trends. Second, compare the company with its **competitors**. Since strategic behavior focuses on competitive moves, you need to determine how the company is currently performing relative to competitors. Finally, apply standards to financial ratios and other organizational characteristics, and make **normative** comparisons between these standards and company performance. Normative comparisons help put your analysis in perspective. A company may be doing better than competitors, but in terms of normative standards the performance levels may be unacceptable.

Basically, a company profile summarizes your perceptions of how the company is performing and why. The following questions should help you develop a profile:

√ Is the company financially successful? What are the trends?
√ How does the company's performance compare with that of competitors?
√ Has performance improved during the past five years?
√ Why has the company been successful or unsuccessful?

It is important to keep in mind that financial performance data reflect the successes and failures of previous strategic actions. The data are historical. Do not assume that the trends you observe will automatically continue in the future. Future performance will be a function of past, current and future strategic actions.

Assessing the current mission and strategic thrust. The mission statement defines a company's purpose. In some cases, the mission statement is published in such outlets as the annual report and/or it can be deduced easily from interviews with company officers or other sources. In other situations there will be no direct statement about the intended mission of a company; in that case you will need to spend a considerable amount of time trying to infer the mission from company actions and policies. In some situations actions and policies will differ from the written mission statement. Policies are written guidelines, procedures, and rules that influence managerial decisions and actions. You will find that policies and actions most accurately reflect a company's true mission. While some companies have well-developed mission statements, many do not.

In determining and analyzing the mission of a company, it is helpful to keep in mind the following questions:

√ What does the company do?
√ Who are the customers? What do they buy?
√ What can the company do?
√ What should the company be doing in five years?

In addition, a firm usually follows a specific strategic thrust. A strategic thrust is a broad statement of strategic actions pursued by a company. You should identify specific strategic actions a company is, and has been, pursuing. It is important that you use facts to support your conclusions and that you avoid generalities that cannot be supported. It may be useful to develop a hierarchy of strategic actions and relate this hierarchy to the mission statement. Chapter 4 discusses the mission statement and strategic thrust in more detail.

Identifying strategic business units. As we have already noted, sometimes it is necessary to divide a company into strategic business units (SBUs) to make a meaningful strategic analysis. Your task is to divide a company into relatively homogeneous units. The following criteria developed by William Rothschild (see Suggested Reading 3.6) should help you identify strategic business units.

- An SBU **must** serve an external, rather than an internal, market; that is, it must have a set of external customers and not merely serve as an internal supplier or opportunistic external supplier;
- An SBU should have a clear set of external competitors which it is trying to equal or surpass;
- An SBU **must** have control over its own destiny. (This means managers must be able to decide what products to offer, how and when to go to market, and where to obtain its supplies, components, or even products. This does not mean that the SBU cannot use pooled resources such as a common manufacturing plant, or a combined sales force, or corporate research and development (R&D). The key is choice.);
- An SBU should be able to measure its performance in terms of profit and loss; that is, it should be a true profit center.

While no organizational unit is a pure SBU, all SBUs must meet the first and third criteria - external market and control over their own destiny. When a company has multiple SBUs, you should conduct your analysis on two levels, for the whole company and for individual SBUs. Whether to assess the whole company or the individual SBUs first will depend on the particular company. Generally, if the company seems to be relatively cohesive, assess the whole company first and then assess the individual SBUs. Conversely, if the SBUs are relatively autonomous, assess the individual SBUs first and then develop an overall assessment of the company.

ASSESSING A COMPANY'S INTERNAL CAPABILITIES

Assessing internal capabilities involves identifying and evaluating the strengths and weaknesses of a company. Identification of strengths and weaknesses is crucial, because a company must develop strategies that capitalize on its strengths and minimize or avoid its weaknesses. Weaknesses that cannot be minimized or avoided must be corrected, or another strategy must be developed.

Strengths are characteristics of an organization that make it uniquely adapted to carrying out its tasks, or characteristics of the company that its competitors don't have and that provide a competitive advantage. **Weaknesses** are characteristics of an organization that inhibit its ability to carry out its tasks, or characteristics that the company doesn't have that competitors do, and which create a competitive disadvantage.

In identifying strengths and weaknesses, keep two questions in mind:

√   What are the key organization capabilities required for success?
√   How do the key success requirements match up with the company's major strengths and weaknesses?

Your initial listing of strengths and weaknesses may result in a large number of both. Identify the critical (or most relevant) strengths and weaknesses. Analyzing each according to its **significance** can help you reduce a bewildering number of strengths and weaknesses. For example, in evaluating a list of strengths and weaknesses for Gerber Products Company, a group of students developed the following list:

<u>Strengths</u>	<u>Weaknesses</u>
1. Well-established reputation	1. Inability to develop a successful geriatric food line
2. Identifiable brand name	
3. Diversification in other markets	2. Promotion problems for some product lines
4. 60-70% market share	3. The Gerber name is associated primarily with baby foods
5. Integrated management information system	
6. Good R & D department	

Be sure to develop reasons why you are classifying characteristics as strengths or weaknesses. You can use the Strengths and Weaknesses Checklist in Appendix 3.1 as a starting point for your assessment, adding items as you proceed.

ANALYZING THE EXTERNAL ENVIRONMENT

You must also assess the external environment in which a company operates. This assessment involves two steps:

- Forecasting the external environment
- Assessing threats and opportunities.

Forecasting the external environment. This step focuses on environmental changes a company may encounter in the near and long term. Your forecasts of the external environment will establish key assumptions you will use to develop conclusions about threats and opportunities. Some forecasting methods include mechanical extra - polations of past trends, barometric techniques, opinion polling, and econometric models.

Mechanical extrapolations include the use of statistical techniques, such as a moving average, to evaluate past data for the purpose of projecting relationships into the future. These techniques can be very useful if the past statistical relationships continue to hold. Barometric techniques also use a statistical analysis of past relationships to predict the future. However, barometric techniques examine the relationships between causal or coincidental events to predict future events. Outlets such as *Business Week* regularly publish such data. An example of such forecasting applied to the sales of major appliances is a manager who uses the level of building permits as a barometer to gauge the demand for appliances several months in the future. Barometric forecasting techniques can be useful if past statistical relationships remain stable.

Opinion polling involves surveying knowledgeable individuals (such as executives, industry analysts, sales representatives, or purchasing agents) to develop a consensus regarding future activity. Many magazines and consulting services provide forecasts based on opinion polling. Econometric models are large-scale computer models used to predict future economic activity. These models depend on relationships among the model variables and the analyst's assumptions about the future.

Generally, forecasting is most accurate when a combination of the above techniques is used. The insights developed from various sources are then evaluated and forecasts are developed.

Because of the uncertainty of the environment during the 1970s and 1980s, the process of forecasting has become relatively more qualitative and less quantitative. The emphasis should be on identifying directions and types of change using scenarios rather than on trying to make single-assumption quantitative forecasts. In many situations you will want to identify multiple directions of change rather than predict a single, specific direction of change.

Assessing threats and opportunities. In this step of your environmental analysis you must identify environmental threats and opportunities and then evaluate the timing, likelihood, and significance of these threats and opportunities.

The assessment should include both current and potential threats and opportunities in the external environment. As you recall, an industry-wide threat is a problem or potential problem for all companies in an industry. Similarly, an industry-wide opportunity is a benefit or potential benefit that most or all companies in an industry may realize. However, a **company-specific threat** can be defined as a problem or potential problem that may result from the interaction between specific company weaknesses and present or future negative environmental variables and industry-wide threats (see Fig. 3.3). Threats can keep a company from achieving goals or from competing effectively. Similarly, a **company-specific opportunity** is a benefit or potential benefit that may result from the interaction between specific company strengths and present or future positive environ-mental variables and industry-wide opportunities.

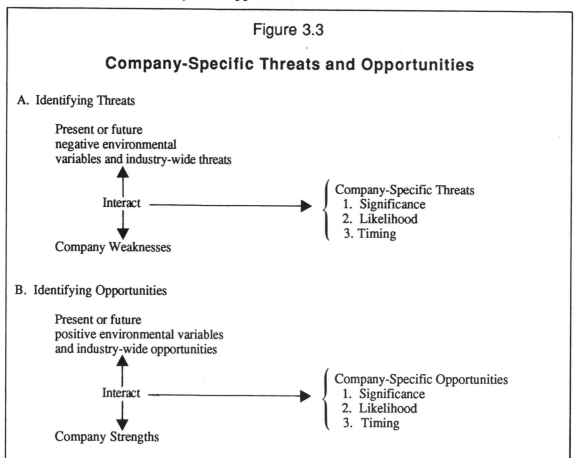

Figure 3.3

Company-Specific Threats and Opportunities

A. Identifying Threats

Present or future
negative environmental
variables and industry-wide threats

Interact ────────────▶ { Company-Specific Threats
  1. Significance
  2. Likelihood
  3. Timing

Company Weaknesses

B. Identifying Opportunities

Present or future
positive environmental variables
and industry-wide opportunities

Interact ────────────▶ { Company-Specific Opportunities
  1. Significance
  2. Likelihood
  3. Timing

Company Strengths

In identifying threats and opportunities in the organization's environment, keep three questions in mind:

√ Which threats are critical and how can they be avoided or turned into opportunities?
√ Which opportunities are critical and must be exploited?
√ Which threats and opportunities are short term and which are long term?

Your assessment of threats and opportunities will evolve in much the same way as did your asssessment of strengths and weaknesses. Analyzing each threat and opportunity according to its **time frame** (near term or long term), **significance**, and **likelihood** of occurrence can help you to focus on the most important threats and opportunities. For example, a group of students developed the following list of important opportunities and threats for Gerber Products Company:

<u>Opportunities</u>	<u>Threats</u>
1. Increase in sales due to an increasing number of births per year	1. Reduced baby-food consumption
2. Increase in number of baby products	2. Price regulation/price wars
3. Increase in market share	3. Failures of new product introductions
4. Expansion of foreign markets	

Once you have developed a list of critical threats and opportunities, assess their significance. This assessment is important because many of your assumptions about future strategies will be based on conclusions you reach. Some questions that will help you assess the significance of threats and opportunities are these:

√ How much could be gained or lost? When?
√ Is the current or future survival of the organization threatened?
√ When will these threats and opportunities begin to affect the organization?
√ How much time is available to act?

Finally, you can use the Environmental Variables Checklist in Appendix 3.2 as a starting point for your assessment, adding items as you proceed in your analysis.

EVALUATING STRATEGIC FIT

Once you have assessed the current position of the firm and its internal capabilities and analyzed the external environment, you should have an excellent overview of the company. Based on data and your judgment and intuition, you will have developed insights that enable you to evaluate a company's strategic position.

Your evaluation of strategic fit indicates how well a company's mission, strategic thrust and culture fit its internal capabilities and its external environment. Many strategies fail because management did not adequately evaluate strategic fit. Figure 3.4 provides a list of questions that should help you evaluate strategic fit.

Figure 3.4

A Checklist for Evaluating Strategic Fit

1. Are the current mission, objectives, and strategic thrust consistent with the interests of stakeholders?

2. How well are the interests of the various stakeholders met?

3. Is the current mission and strategic thrust consistent with the corporate culture?

4. Is it possible to change the corporate culture so it is consistent with the strategy?

5. Is the strategy maximizing company performance?

6. Is the strategy consistent with the financial resources available?

7. Will continued support be available from society, the local community, and public-action groups?

8. Is the organizational structure consistent with the strategy?

9. Is the strategy consistent with the company's strategic business units (if any)? Are the strategic business units appropriate for the strategy of the firm?

10. Is the strategy appropriate, given the company's strengths and weaknesses?

11. Is the strategy responsive to environmental threats and opportunities?

12. What risk of bankruptcy exists if the strategy fails?

13. What costs will be incurred if the strategy is abandoned?

14. Have possible competitive reactions to the current strategy been anticipated?

After you have asked the questions in Fig. 3.4, you should be prepared to reach specific conclusions concerning the following:

- Where the strategy is strong
- Where the strategy is weak
- How the strategy will help the firm to achieve its objectives.

Recommending changes involves identifying and justifying actions that will enable the company to survive and achieve its objectives. You may recommend general or specific changes. However, your recommendations should be consistent with the perspectives you developed at various stages of the strategic business analysis. Chapter 4, Developing a Strategic Business Plan, discusses skills that can help you develop an entire plan and consistent set of recommendations.

TIPS TO REMEMBER

3.1   Avoid broad generalities and search instead for inconsistencies and conflicts.

3.2   Assume that competitors will react to strategic changes. Don't underestimate your competition.

3.3   Remember that strengths, weaknesses, threats, and opportunities change over time.

3.4   Keep in mind that strategies are difficult to revise or terminate.

3.5   Assess the significance of the strengths and weaknesses.

3.6   Assess the timing, likelihood, and significance of threats and opportunities

3.7   Evaluate strategic fit.

ACTION EXERCISES

3.1   You have learned to use many analytical tools in other courses. Spend a half hour trying to list additional techniques and tools that can aid you in the following activities:

a) Assessing a firm's internal capabilities
b) Analyzing a firm's external environment.

3.2   Select two firms from the same industry. Choose either one firm that is performing well and another that is performing poorly, or two firms that are performing well but are following different strategies. For these two firms prepare a comparative strategic business analysis that answers the following questions:

a) What are the similarities between the two firms?
b) What are the differences between the two firms?
c) What conclusions regarding strategies for the industry have you reached?

3.3   Select a firm and conduct a strategic business analysis for 1975 and another analysis for 1985. Answer the following questions:

a) How has the profile of this company changed?
b) How have its internal capabilities changed?
c) How has its external environment changed?
d) How has its mission and strategic thrust changed?
e) How well have its managers dealt with changes in the environment?

SUGGESTED READINGS

3.1   Deal, T. E., and Kennedy, A., *Corporate Cultures: The Rites of Corporate Life*. Reading, MA: Addison-Wesley, 1982.
      This book provides a very readable and informative introduction to the concept of corporate culture.

3.2   Gross, C. W., and Peterson, R. T., *Business Forecasting* (2d ed.). Boston: Houghton Mifflin Company, 1983.
      This is a simple introduction to forecasting. Quantitative techniques such as time-series analysis, regression, and modeling are emphasized.

3.3   Levinson, H., *Organizational Diagnosis*. Cambridge, MA: Harvard University Press, 1972.
      Levinson provides a comprehensive framework for identifying and diagnosing organizational problems. His ideas and examples can help you master strategic business analysis. See especially Chapter 7, Current Organizational Functioning.

3.4   Naisbett, J., *Megatrends: Ten New Directions Transforming Our Lives*. New York: Warner Books, 1984.
      This book discusses a wide range of issues shaping our society. Naisbett's trends provide a background for analyzing a firm's external environment.

3. 5   Porter, M.E., *Competitive Advantage*. New York: The Free Press, 1985.
      Porter develops a framework for analyzing company activities to identify competitive advantage. He also discusses the construction of industry scenarios.

3.6   Rothschild, W. How to Ensure the Continued Growth of Strategic Planning, *Journal of Business Strategy*, Summer 1980, pp. 11-18.
      Strategic planning from the perspective of the General Electric Company is discussed. Rothschild presents criteria for identifying SBUs.

APPENDIX 3.1

Strengths and Weaknesses Checklist

1. Marketing

Y N   Product Quality
Y N   Number of Product Lines
Y N   Product Differentiation
Y N   Market Share
Y N   Pricing Policies
Y N   Distribution Channels
Y N   Promotional Programs
Y N   Customer Service
Y N   Marketing Research
Y N   Advertising
Y N   Sales Force

2. Research and Development

Y N   Product R&D Capabilities
Y N   Process R&D Capabilities
Y N   Pilot Plant Capabilities

3. Management Information System

Y N   Speed and Responsiveness
Y N   Quality of Current Information
Y N   Expandability
Y N   User Oriented System

4. Management Team

Y N   Skills
Y N   Value Congruence
Y N   Team Spirit
Y N   Experience
Y N   Coordination of Effort

5. Operations

Y N   Control of Raw Materials
Y N   Production Capacity
Y N   Production Cost Structure
Y N   Facilities and Equipment
Y N   Inventory Control
Y N   Quality Control
Y N   Energy Efficiency

6. Finance

Y N   Financial Leverage
Y N   Operating Leverage
Y N   Balance Sheet Ratios
Y N   Stockholder Relations
Y N   Tax Situation

7. Human Resources

Y N   Employee Capabilities
Y N   Personnel Systems
Y N   Employee Turnover
Y N   Employee Morale
Y N   Employee Development

APPENDIX 3.2

Environmental Variables Checklist

1. Societal Changes

Y N   Changing Customer Preferences --- Impacting Product Demand or Design
Y N   Population Trends --- Impacting Distribution, Product Demand or Design

2. Governmental Changes

Y N   New Legislation --- Impacting Product Costs
Y N   New Enforcement Priorities --- Impacting Investments, Products, Demand

3. Economic Changes

Y N   Interest Rates --- Impacting Expansion, Debt Costs
Y N   Exchange Rates --- Impacting Domestic and Overseas Demand, Profits
Y N   Real Personal Income Changes --- Impacting Demand

4. Competitive Changes

Y N   Adoption of New Technologies --- Impacting Cost Position, Product Quality
Y N   New Competitors --- Impacting Prices, Market Share, Contribution Margin
Y N   Price Changes --- Impacting Market Share, Contribution Margin
Y N   New Products --- Impacting Demand, Advertising Expenditures

5. Supplier Changes

Y N   Changes in Input Costs --- Impacting Prices, Demand, Contribution Margin
Y N   Supply Changes --- Impacting Production Processes, Investment Requirements
Y N   Changes in Number of Suppliers --- Impacting Costs, Availability

6. Market Changes

Y N   New Uses of Products --- Impacting Demand, Capacity Utilization
Y N   New Markets --- Impacting Distribution Channels, Demand, Capacity Utilization
Y N   Product Obsolescence --- Impacting Prices, Demand, Capacity Utilization

Chapter 4

Developing a Strategic Business Plan

MAJOR SKILLS

- DEVELOPING KEY PLANNING ASSUMPTIONS
- CLARIFYING BUSINESS AND PLANNING TERMS
- PREPARING A MISSION STATEMENT
- SETTING PERFORMANCE GOALS AND TARGETS
- CHOOSING A STRATEGIC THRUST
- PLANNING STRATEGIC ACTIONS
- ALLOCATING RESOURCES
- DEVELOPING CONTINGENCY PLANS
- CREATING AN APPROPRIATE ORGANIZATION DESIGN
- PREPARING PRO FORMA FINANCIAL STATEMENTS
- ASSESSING THE STRATEGIC BUSINESS PLAN

Planning is a key strategic management skill. Most managers make plans. Many managers at different levels in the organization claim to exploit opportunities and develop plans as needed. General managers, at the very least, have a notion of long-term goals and future actions for their firm. Systematic long-range planning is, however, somewhat contro-versial. Some managers view such planning as bureaucratic and unnecessary. Such a view often results in a self-fulfilling prophecy whereby planning does become bureaucratic.

As you have probably gathered by now, this book strongly advocates the use of systematic, strategic business planning. The skills discussed in the previous two chapters provide the analytical foundation for strategic business planning. This chapter describes the skills needed to develop a strategic business plan.

A written strategic business plan is an action-oriented document that describes the mission, strategic thrusts, and major actions for an entire firm, a division, or a strategic business unit (SBU). Such a plan usually includes the following sequence of topics:

- Mission, objectives, and performance targets
- Strategic thrust
- Strategic actions related to products and markets
- Resource allocations
- Major implementation steps
- Pro forma financial statements.

For a small firm or a large single-product firm, only one strategic business plan is needed. However, for large multi-product companies, an overall strategic business plan and separate SBU strategic plans are usually prepared. The skills discussed in this chapter are applicable to planning in both types of firms. Much of the analysis and information used in strategic business planning is derived from industry analyses and strategic business analyses. Chapter 5, Finding Strategic Business Information, can aid you in finding any additional information. As noted in Chapter 1, the planning process is usually a group process and the skills discussed in Chapter 6, Developing a Strategic Management Team, and Chapter 7, Participating in Strategic Management Team Activities, can also aid you in managing a business planning process.

The major content sections and subsections of a formal strategic business plan are generally prespecified and incorporated into a table of contents, which is usually based on tradition or perceptions of what is needed for an effective strategic planning and control process. The skills discussed in this chapter are related to preparing action-oriented strategic business plans, but the skills should also equip you with ideas and materials that can be shaped and crafted into a variety of planning documents. In addition, these skills are related and must be used in concert to build a plan. For example, assumptions are stated and used in subsequent planning activities, then revised if necessary. Goals are stated, tested, and refined. At this point, strategic actions are proposed and consequences and resource allocations are examined. The actions then need to be modified. As you read about and practice planning skills and develop the elements of a strategic business plan, note the dynamic interplay that emerges among skills.

DEVELOPING KEY PLANNING ASSUMPTIONS

Strategic business plans are developed on the basis of facts, forecasts, analyses, and assumptions. An **assumption** is a condition, relationship, or state of affairs that is regarded as true without actual knowledge that it is or without direct supporting facts. As a planner, you must explicitly develop key assumptions. Knowing your assumptions helps you adjust your plans when circumstances change.

Your key assumptions may be based on indirect evidence, forecasts, business common sense, or an educated guess. Developing assumptions can be difficult, but you should critically review environmental information and forecasts rather than rely solely on educated guesses. Assumption-making and testing are important first steps in the strategic planning process, particularly since developing your key assumptions may help you come to grips with your preconceptions and biases. The following questions indicate categories of assumptions that should be explored in strategic business planning:

√ How will major competitors react to strategic changes?
√ What are forecasted levels of customer demand and/or market acceptance?
√ What is the ability of suppliers to meet resource needs?
√ What technological changes are anticipated?
√ What strengths will be exploited in the plan?

Prepare a list of your key planning assumptions. This list should include only significant and meaningful assumptions. Try to strike a balance between a long list with many possibly trivial assumptions and a brief list that neglects important assumptions. If you find that the success of your strategic business plan depends on a long list of implausible or questionable assumptions, then either revise your plan or review your assumption analysis.

CLARIFYING BUSINESS AND PLANNING TERMS

Defining terms and concepts used during the planning process and in the written plan is necessary. Planners and readers need a common language so they can act in concert and communicate effectively. In many cases the context in which a term is used clarifies it for listeners and readers, but that is not always true. This book provides you with a general planning language. Terms such as strategy, plan, strength, and weakness are defined and discussed.

A brief illustrative review of strategic actions planned for a large "multi-modal" transportation company demonstrates the need for specifically defining and clarifying novel business terms. The plan calls for the use of "non-vessel operating common carriers (NVOCCs)," aggressive use of the "spot market," and the use of "rates that vary from the conference rates." Many people would find such terms incomprehensible. The planners were specialists and these terms were satisfactory when they spoke with other specialists. However, the terms could be confusing to bankers and other external stakeholders. A written plan would indicate that the term "multi-modal" means a transportation company with some combination of trucks, rail, pipelines, air, and water transport modes. An "NVOCC" is a for-hire ocean carrier that does not own any ships. The "spot market" is a mechanism for setting freight rates. Rates are quoted for a limited amount of time or for a limited number of shipments. Such terms are not, however, usually discussed in planning meetings. Nevertheless, in those meetings you should not hesitate to ask for clarification of ambiguous or vague terms.

Planners make a major mistake when they casually assume that everyone in their organization uses the same vocabulary for technical, marketing, production, or strategic management terms. Spending some time defining key terms will clarify your thinking and improve your ability to communicate with others.

PREPARING A MISSION STATEMENT

In Chapter 3, we noted that a firm's mission statement is a broad statement of its direction and purpose. A written mission statement is a major element of a written strategic business plan, so it should be a clear and concise statement. The mission statement answers two questions: What business do we want to be in? What are the major long-term objectives?

In the fall of 1977, the mission of the American Safety Razor Company (ASR) was poorly defined (see Part 2). Reading the case one notes that:

> ASR is primarily a personal razor and blade manufacturer and secondarily a manufacturer of industrial and surgical blades and that it has some non-razor businesses. The long-run goals are continued and improved profitability and sales growth.

Managers at ASR are not really customer or product-oriented and the long-term goals are vague and general. A more specific statement of ASR's mission would be:

> ASR is in business to provide high-quality blades and shaving products for individuals, hospitals, and industrial customers. We strive to provide our customers with both value and service. In the long term, we will have the dominant market share in all of the market segments we serve. We are striving for a 5% return on sales, and we want to double our sales in five years primarily through improved market penetration.

Most mission statements can be refined and improved. At a minimum, the statement should be a meaningful and useful guide for stakeholders. In his classic 1960 article "Marketing Myopia," Theodore Leavitt pointed out the danger of defining a company mission too broadly or too narrowly (see Suggested Reading 4.4).   For example, managers of railroads in many cases failed to recognize that their company's mission was really to provide all types of transportation.   Conversely, today some managers perceive that the mission of their company is to provide high-technology products.   In many instances this is an overly broad mission.   These same managers then proceed to make inappropriate mergers and acquisitions to try to fulfill this poorly defined mission.

The following questions should be asked as you think about and develop a comprehensive mission statement:

√   What customers are we trying to serve? Why?
√   What products or services can we effectively provide?
√   Why are we running this business?
√   What do we really want to accomplish in the next 5-10 years?
√   Are our objectives clearly defined?

As you apply other skills, you may find it necessary to revise the mission statement. A clear, meaningful mission statement can guide or structure the rest of the planning process, communicate your strategic vision for the company to others, and provide broad criteria for evaluating proposed performance targets and strategic actions.

SETTING PERFORMANCE GOALS AND TARGETS

Establishing a mission and broad performance objectives is important, but more specific business objectives and performance targets also must be set. Managers need to consider setting specific short- and intermediate-term goals and targets concerning revenues, profits, capital investments, promotional support, production capacities, and any other strategic variables that can be influenced by managerial actions. These more specific goals and targets can help managers:

• Evaluate the progress of the strategic plan
• Identify problem areas
• .Focus corrective action.

Actually setting performance objectives and targets is an iterative process. The mission statement, assumptions, and your strategic analysis of the business can guide you in the selection of key performance areas and help you develop a realistic first approximation of the goals or targets. As you analyze the feasibility of strategic actions, evaluate the costs of those actions, and prepare pro forma projections, you will likely identify problems resulting from the initial goals and targets. A process of reconciliation must then occur. That process may involve changing assumptions, targets, and/or actions.

For instance, the initial performance goals and targets for American Safety Razor might be as follows:

Planning Horizon

Performance areas	1978	1979	1980	1981	1982
Gross Sales	40M	45M	48M	51M	55M
Profit	1.5M	1.7M	2M	2.2M	2.6M
Sales force	60	75	80	80	80

You would probably want to include additional performance areas such as net return on assets and the rate of managerial turnover. And you may find that another format works better for your own planning situation. Many organizations use preprinted forms to standardize the setting of performance objectives and targets for SBUs. As you set goals and targets, ask the following questions:

√ Are the targets realistic?
√ Will you be able to determine whether the target is met?
√ Do managers clearly understand the performance areas?
√ Are the performance areas of strategic importance?

CHOOSING A STRATEGIC THRUST

A **strategic thrust** is a broad statement of strategic actions that will occur during the planning horizon -- usually a five-year period. Often, the mission statement and performance goals and targets will indicate if the strategic intent is sales, product and market growth, retrenchment, stability, or a combination of these goals. The strategic thrust indicates actions that will be taken to accomplish the mission and performance goals and targets. Basically, managers determine how they intend to compete with other firms when they choose a strategic thrust.

A number of corporate-level generic strategic thrusts should be considered in developing a strategic thrust. A **diversification strategic thrust** involves acquiring related or unrelated businesses, and in some cases developing major new product lines. Exxon's diversification thrust in the late 1970s involved establishing an entrepreneurial new venture unit that purchased and managed small high-technology firms and developed new products. A **multinational expansion thrust** may involve joint ventures with partners in other countries, wholly-owned subsidiaries, or expanded distribution channels. A **portfolio reorganization thrust** involves actions to change the SBUs of the corporation. A major change in the mission of a diversified company often involves a portfolio reorganization thrust. For example, United Technologies' mission change to a high-technology company necessitated divesting some low-technology companies and acquiring new businesses in semi-conductors and other high-technology areas.

As noted in Chapter 1, generic business-level strategies have been widely discussed in strategic management. Let's briefly review Michael Porter's generic strategies or strategic thrusts:

• Overall cost leadership
• Broad market differentiation of products and services
• Focused cost leadership
• Focused differentiation of products and services.

Each of these business-level or SBU strategies is associated with general strategic actions. For example, a group of managers pursuing an overall cost leadership strategic thrust must emphasize general actions such as plant modernization to achieve economies of scale, product redesign to develop a product that is less expensive to manufacture, and changes in distribution channels to increase product sales.

Another way of looking at the strategic thrust is in terms of the company's posture toward competitors. Some managers want an aggressive, confrontational posture and strategic thrust. Others want to avoid direct challenges to market leaders. Strategic thrusts also include internal company changes, such as staff reductions or quality control. Finally, strategic thrusts may differ in terms of product innovation and market introduction. According to Raymond Miles and Charles Snow, some managers want their company to take a **prospector** approach, actively searching for new products and markets and aggressively seizing opportunities. Other managers favor an **analyzer** approach, a wait-and-see attitude toward innovation and change that requires proven demand before new markets are developed. Finally, some managers emphasize a **defender** approach, aggressively defending current businesses rather than introducing new products or entering new markets (see Suggested Reading 4.5).

The following strategic variables should be considered as you create a strategic thrust: markets, products, R&D expenditure, capital expenditure, marketing resources, and product engineering. A possible statement of a strategic thrust for ASR could read like this:

> During the next five years, we will pursue a focused low-cost leadership strategy. We will concentrate on markets in which we currently have a strong position. We will cut production costs by reducing down-time and waste. Our sales and marketing efforts will be expanded 50% per year and will be targeted toward narrow market segments. Market development will be focused on hospital and industrial markets. Product innovation will be a low priority; efficient product engineering will be a high priority.

You should generate and consider a number of alternative strategic thrusts. The questions listed below should help you choose a strategic thrust:

√ Does the strategic thrust fit with the mission and performance targets?
√ Are the changes in strategic variables consistent?
√ Is the strategic thrust realistic given past experience?
√ Is the strategic thrust focused and meaningful?
√ Does the strategic thrust clearly indicate how the company intends to compete during the planning horizon?

You should be able to describe your strategic thrust briefly and succinctly. If your description is long and involved, you probably have not clarified the strategic thrust adequately in your mind. Until the strategic thrust is clear to you, you will not be able to plan for strategic actions.

PLANNING STRATEGIC ACTIONS

Planning actions associated with the strategic thrust requires a framework for organizing your thinking. A number of possible frameworks can be used, including a functional approach, a product approach, and a business-unit grouping approach. Functional and product approaches are useful in developing strategic business plans for single business units and functionally organized companies. When using a functional approach, consider strategic actions for each business function: marketing, production, finance, engineering. When using a product approach, consider actions for each major product or product line. A business-unit grouping approach works well in diversified companies. When using a business-unit grouping approach, first examine actions to change business groupings, then consider actions for each SBU or group of SBUs.

All of these approaches involve choosing target markets and products, product development plans, capital expenditure plans, and marketing plans. For all major actions, you should consider timing and sequencing. **When** major actions are expected to occur is an important issue. If actions are interdependent, the **sequencing** of those actions is also important.

Choosing target markets and products is very important. The choice of target markets and the identification of products should be the end result of your previous research on industries, competitors, and market needs, as well as on your firm's strengths, weaknesses, threats, and opportunities.

The following questions should help you create and choose strategic actions:

√   What actions have worked in the past?
√   What are competitors doing?
√   What types of actions have we done well in the past?
√   What actions will have the greatest impact?

ALLOCATING RESOURCES

All of the strategic actions you choose to include in the strategic business plan will use valuable company resources.   Therefore it is important to ask the following critical question: What resources are available and how will we use them? Companies do not have unlimited resources, so it is important to decide how to use available resources efficiently and effectively. Most resource-allocation decisions focus only on budgets and spending, but you should also consider the availability of people, facilities, and raw materials.
Questions to keep in mind include the following:

√   What resources are needed to accomplish major actions?
√   Are resources adequate for all major actions?
√   What resources should we hold in reserve?
√   Can we make trade-offs between alternate resource demands?

In allocating resources, it is sometimes helpful to keep in mind that there is seldom one "right" answer to the issues with which you are dealing.   If your analysis was well done, and if you have a good grasp of the mission and strategic thrust, then some of the conflicts between resource demands will be best resolved through the use of your intuition.

DEVELOPING CONTINGENCY PLANS

Contingencies are low-probability events anticipated by the planner.   Contingency plan - ning is a "What if" skill important in business planning. The purpose is not to identify and develop a plan for every possible contingency. That would be impossible and a terrible waste of your time! Rather, the purpose is to get you to think about major contingencies and possible responses. Few business changes actually unfold according to the plan. However, managers who have given thought to contingencies and their possible reponses are more likely to meet major goals and targets successfully.   The following questions can help you develop contingency plans:

√   What is the worst case scenario of events?
√   What is the best case scenario of events?
√   What event would cause the greatest disruption of our plans?
√   How will we adjust our plans if costs are greater than projected or
     if revenues per unit are less than expected?
√   How will we adjust our plans if key people leave the organization?
√   What are the expected moves of our competitors? How should we
     respond or preempt these moves?

CREATING AN APPROPRIATE ORGANIZATION DESIGN

General managers and planners also need to develop and use organization design skills. The overall design of an organization must fit the strategic thrust and major action strategies. Therefore major design changes should be reviewed in a strategic plan.

During the strategic planning process, managers should briefly review the organ-ization's design and evaluate its fit with the proposed mission and strategic actions. A list of design problems and issues should be prepared. General solutions to these problems need to be considered and the best ones should be adopted. The discussion that follows touches only on major design questions; it is not intended to provide extensive knowledge about organization design.

In analyzing the fit of a proposed strategic plan with the organization's current design, you should critically assess the current organization hierarchy, authority relationships, information and communication systems, and reward systems. The next few paragraphs discuss each of these areas and suggest some assessment questions.

Current organization hierarchy. An organization hierarchy refers to how people and tasks are grouped. An organization may be structured in functional units such as accounting and marketing, with only one type of specialist working in each of these units. Or an organization can be structured in product units. In this instance, specialists of all types are grouped together within one unit. An examination of the organizational hierarchy provides valuable information about how planned tasks and actions are divided among organizational units. In some cases, most of the burden of implementing strategic changes will fall on only a few units. Also, major changes in strategic thrust may require changing from a functional to a product structure. The following questions should be asked:

√ Do the current units in the structure facilitate accomplishment of the proposed mission and strategic thrust?
√ Are relationships and task responsibilities of organizational units well-defined and effective?

Authority relationships. The organization design basically determines who the key decision-makers are in an organization. Decision-making authority is usually delegated to ensure that all of the tactical and day-to-day decisions will be made expeditiously. Those who will hold key decision-making roles should be in general agreement with any proposed changes in mission and strategic thrust. Asking the following questions can aid in your assessment:

√ Do key decision-makers support the proposed strategic change? If some do not, why not?
√ Do key decision-makers have adequate authority to complete planned tasks?

Information and communication systems. To execute strategic changes effectively, managers must inform, guide, and encourage organization members. Also, some managers need to coordinate tasks and share important information. Finally, top managers must monitor the progress of strategic changes and communicate adjustments. The current information and communication systems must be capable of handling this load. Some current business strategies rely heavily on improved information and communication systems to gain competitive advantages. To determine the adequacy of present systems, you will need to assess both computerized and non-computerized systems. At a minimum, the following three questions should be asked:

√ Will people quickly and accurately receive information needed to implement and monitor the proposed strategic changes?
√ Will information about key results be gathered and transmitted quickly to general managers?
√ Are current systems capable of meeting any special tasks proposed in general marketing or production plans?

Reward systems. Most of us realize that who gets rewarded and for what influences the success of proposed strategic changes. We also recognize that changing reward systems is difficult and problematic. People are sensitive about changes in pay, benefits, promotion policies, and other rewards. For example, many of the U.S. Auto and Steel companies are encountering resistance to strategic changes in their reward systems.

The basic planning guideline is to develop reward systems tied directly to performance of assigned tasks. Managers, in particular, need to be adequately rewarded for successfully implementing strategic changes. Managers also need to be encouraged to identify the major problems of a plan before irreparable harm is done. A strategic business plan is not the document in which to propose detailed changes in reward systems. But major changes such as adopting performance-based pay, bonuses, or profit-sharing, can be discussed and proposed in the plan. Because of the sensitivity surrounding changes in reward systems, carefully consider the following questions before recommending changes:

√ Will current reward systems encourage managers to implement the proposed strategic changes?
√ Is cost cutting a major part of the strategic change? If so, can rewards be altered without major disruptions in the organization?
√ Can more non-monetary rewards be linked to job performance?

Considering these four organization design components may help you identify problem areas in the firm's structure. Listing these problems and assessing the importance of each is a good way to begin the creative part of organization design. Usually there are no simple solutions to these problems. Sometimes a solution can be found that solves multiple design problems. The following possible design changes are reasonably common today. They do not solve all problems, but they may improve the fit for organizations making strategic changes in uncertain, rapidly changing business environments.

Design-change possibilities. Some companies create more organizational slack, for example, by hiring additional workers or extending delivery dates of products to eliminate problems. Other companies emphasize the use of flexible resources. For example, sometimes "firefighting" teams are created to deal with special tasks, or some units (especially research and development departments) are isolated from other parts of the organization.

In addition, some companies are purchasing more sophisticated computerized information systems. In some cases, this is a very effective solution to some design problems; in other cases, the machines sit unused and the problems persist. Computer hardware and software can improve the collection, storage, retrieval, and analysis of information, but a well-designed analysis and plan for the new system must be developed. Many of the skills you are practicing in this book can help you evaluate such proposals.

Finally, some organizations strengthen lateral relationships among individuals and groups to facilitate information sharing and task coordination. Jay Galbraith, a well-known management consultant, defines lateral relationships as joint decision processes that cut across lines of authority (see Suggested Reading 4.3). Examples of lateral relationships include temporary interdepartmental task forces, management teams with shared decision authority, and the use of a program or project manager to integrate activities.

Preparing organization charts. A final task that is often part of designing an organization is preparing a proposed or revised organization chart. These charts can communicate major changes in the organization hierarchy and in authority relationships. The following are characteristics of a well-prepared organization chart:

- An accurate, descriptive title
- Readable names of position incumbents and position titles
- Clearly specified reporting relationships
- Well-organized and easy to follow
- A key for symbols used on the chart.

Creating organization designs is part of the strategic management task. But, as we have noted, a full-scale design is not usually included in formal, written strategic business plans. Redesigning an organization incurs major costs, so design changes need to be carefully considered when resources are allocated.

PREPARING PRO FORMA FINANCIAL STATEMENTS

Financial analysis and projections are very important in strategic planning. In many ways, developing financial projections forces you to become concrete and to deal with business reality. You must quantify financial outflows and inflows to arrive at projected financial statements for the proposed strategic plan. Spreadsheet computer programs such as Lotus 1-2-3 or Multiplan make it much easier to develop financial projections. You can develop projections that are either revenue or profit driven. Also, the various pro forma statements can be linked together to speed up "what if" analyses in which assumptions and numbers are changed.

Pro forma financial statements are useful for developing detailed financial plans, evaluating the progress of the strategic plan, pinpointing problem areas, and taking corrective action. The pro forma financial statements are also valuable when used as aids in the implementation of the strategic plan.

Key questions to keep in mind when developing pro forma financial statements include these three:

√ What assumptions underlie these financial statements?
√ How sensitive are these financial statements to changes in assumptions?
√ Can we justify the numbers of the pro forma financial statements?

For outside stakeholders, the pro forma financial statements will be a critical part of their evaluation of the strategic plan. For this reason, the statements must present a convincing case, be consistent with other elements of the strategic business plan, and present a realistic picture of the financial consequences of strategic actions.

ASSESSING THE STRATEGIC BUSINESS PLAN

You have reached the point where you need to make an evaluation of the overall plan. Your plan should minimize the harm from threats and weaknesses while capitalizing on strengths and opportunities. It is critical that the recommended plan be as **specific** as possible. The plan should be based on your strategic business analysis. Potential strategic actions should have been tested to determine if they fit the environment and the organization's strengths and weaknesses. A proposed strategic business plan must pass three primary tests.

Workability test. This test determines if what is proposed can really be accomplished and whether it is likely that the intended results will be realized. It is important to ask:

√ Are critical resources such as money, expertise, and facilities adequate?
√ Will key managers support the proposal?
√ Can objectives and targets be met in the specified time period?
√ Are there major implementation barriers?

Economic feasibility test. This test focuses on returns and costs in both the short and long term. A long-term strategic plan that bankrupts a company in the short term is not economically feasible. Neither is a plan that neglects long term-investment for transitory short-term gains. Pro forma financial analyses should help you answer some of the following questions:

√ Does the plan project acceptable returns on investment?
√ Can funds for required investment be obtained at an affordable rate?
√ Will the firm be solvent in the short run even if it operates at worst-case loss levels?
√ Can the firm respond to competitor retaliation and incur the losses that may result? Are financial reserves adequate?

Acceptability test. This test forces you to examine the attitudes that major stakeholders will have toward the proposed strategic business plan. Acceptability means that major stakeholders will be either neutral or favorable toward the proposal. In some cases, the negative attitudes of only a few stakeholders will make the proposal unacceptable. The following questions should help you apply the acceptability test:

√ Do projected benefits seem to outweigh associated social and psychological costs?
√ What stakeholders will be harmed by potential changes? Can compensation be provided to them?
√ Are incentives for supporting the proposal known to those affected by proposed changes?
√ Will stakeholders accept the risk associated with the proposed actions?

Applying these three tests may suggest some revisions to a proposed strategic business plan. Such a plan will never be perfect. You will be predicting the response of competitors. You will make compromises. And you will make some timing mistakes because the future can only be anticipated, not known. You and other managers will need to resolve many problems once you begin implementing the plan. The plan, however, will serve as a benchmark and a guide as you attempt to steer an organization toward long-term goals.

TIPS TO REMEMBER

4.1   Look ahead at least five years -- be proactive.

4.2   Use facts, forecasts, and analyses as a basis for your strategic business plan.

4.3   Reconcile and adjust elements of the plan.

4.4   Creativity is important in developing the plan.

4.5   Apply planning skills systematically and rigorously.

4.6   Anticipate what can go wrong, and develop plans for major contingencies.

4.7   Prepare financial projections. Learn to use spread-sheet computer programs such as Lotus 1-2-3 and Multiplan.

4.8   Apply the workability, economic feasibility, and acceptability tests to the proposed strategic business plan.

ACTION EXERCISES

4.1   Watch the videotape of American Safety Razor. Assume that you are John Baker, president of ASR and one of the new owners. Take notes on the proposed plan, then apply the workability, economic feasibility, and acceptability tests to the plan. Does the plan pass those tests? What changes would you recommend to improve that strategic business plan?

4.2   Prepare a list of alternative strategic thrusts that you think the management of ASR should consider. Try to assess the benefits, costs, and risks associated with each.

4.3   Write a proposed mission statement for a new business venture. What would you include in the statement? How can you tell if the proposed mission is meaningful and realistic? How long is your mission statement? Ask someone to quiz you about your proposed mission statement. What questions are they likely to ask?

4.4   Think about a major decision you made recently. List all of the assumptions that you made. Which assumptions now appear to have been correct?

4.5   Prepare a strategic business plan for a strategic management case such as Apple Computer or Federal Express. Apply the skills in this Chapter. Prepare a detailed outline. Read Chapter 8, Writing Strategic Management Reports, and write the plan.

SUGGESTED READINGS

4.1   Abell, D. F., *Defining the Business: The Starting Point of Strategic Planning*. Englewood Cliffs, NJ: Prentice-Hall, 1980.
        Abell's book provides a detailed model and examples relevant to defining a company's business or mission. His book is a detailed discussion of this important topic.

4.2   Curtis, D. A., *Strategic Planning for Smaller Businesses*. Lexington, MA: Lexington Books, 1983.
        Although this book describes strategic planning for smaller business, the topics and techniques discussed should be useful to anyone involved in the strategic planning process. This approach is simple and practical.

4.3   Galbraith, J.R., *Organization Design*. Reading, MA: Addison-Wesley Publishing Co., 1977.
        Galbraith's book is a good starting point if you are unfamiliar with the concepts and principles of organization design. He includes good case examples and his information processing orientation integrates the concepts and his practical design suggestions.

4.4   Leavitt, T., Marketing Myopia, *Harvard Business Review*, 38:4, July/August 1960, pp. 45-56.
        Marketing Myopia is a classic article in the strategic management literature. Leavitt identified the dangers of defining a company's business either too narrowly or too broadly.

4.5   Miles, R., and Snow, C., *Organizational Strategy, Structure, and Process*. New York: McGraw-Hill, 1978.
        This book develops an original typology of generic strategies. It explains the prospector, defender, and analyzer strategies discussed in this chapter.

4.6   Osgood, W. R., *Planning and Financing Your Business: A Complete Working Guide*. New York: Inc./CBI Publications, 1983.
        This is a guide for budding entrepreneurs. It is workbook oriented, but worksheets are explained. Each section of a business plan format for functionally organized companies is discussed in detail.

4.7   Salter, M. S., and Weinhold, W. A., *Diversification through Acquisition Strategies for Creating Economic Value*. New York: The Free Press, 1979.
        This book can benefit managers who are contemplating diversification as part of the strategic business plan. It raises the important planning issues and contains practical suggestions for planning and executing a diversification program.

4.8   Steiner, G. A., *Strategic Planning: What Every Manager Must Know*. New York: The Free Press, 1979.
        This book is a reasonably comprehensive discussion of formal strategic planning. Chapter 4 presents a framework for a corporate planning manual.

Chapter 5

Finding Strategic Management Information

MAJOR SKILLS

- ASSESSING INFORMATION NEEDS
- IDENTIFYING AND USING INFORMATION SOURCES
- DEVELOPING A SEARCH PLAN
- ORGANIZING AND MANAGING INFORMATION

Strategic management activities often require large amounts of information. Also, preparing meaningful industry and company analyses and strategic business plans requires detailed and accurate information. Strategic management cases provide a basic information source for practicing analytical and planning skills. But in actual business situations, information must be gathered, organized, and evaluated. You need to master a number of skills to find meaningful strategic management information.

This chapter discusses those major skills and lists many important sources of business information. Spend some time reviewing the business information sources in the appendixes so that you can intelligently apply planning and analysis skills in actual strategic management situations.

ASSESSING INFORMATION NEEDS

Information gathering should be a planned, systematic activity. The first step is to assess what information is needed. Managers work in information-rich environments. Newspapers, news magazines, meetings, reports, and colleagues provide a steady stream of potentially relevant information. This information provides a background for analysis and planning, but additional information is frequently needed. In many cases extensive research, computations, or interviews are employed to find key pieces of information.

The discussions of strategic management skills in Chapters 2, 3, and 4 describe many types of strategic management information: demand forecasts, competitor information, industry ratios and similar measures. Information search needs vary depending upon the purpose of the search. *Ad hoc* special-purpose searches differ from searches that are part of an on-going strategic management process. In an *ad hoc* search you may need to gather large amounts of new information or a specific piece of information. Searching that occurs as part of an on-going strategic management process adds to an existing base of information. In both cases the starting point is determining the general purpose of the search, which can be ascertained by answering the following questions:

√   Are you preparing an industry analysis?
√   Are you preparing a strategic business analysis?
√   Is the analysis for a strategic business unit (SBU)?
√   Have some analyses been completed?
√   Are you preparing a strategic business plan?

Once you have determined the general purpose of the search, prepare an initial list of information needs. Then prioritize this list. Gathering information is costly. In most cases, resources are not available to collect all of the information that is initially desired. You should assess what resources are available for conducting a search. You also need to consider the time available, the cost to gather a specific type of information, the availability of the information, and the validity of the information that will be gathered. A number of information sources are discussed in the next section. Each source differs in terms of time required, cost, availability, and validity. In some cases, for example, interviews are not appropriate for student projects because they are time-consuming and the data gathered may have little general validity.

IDENTIFYING AND USING INFORMATION SOURCES

Three primary sources of strategic management information are libraries, interviews, and company data. Trade associations are also useful sources of information for some tasks. Computerized data bases, when available and cost-effective, are valuable early in the search process. Sophisticated bibliographic or company data bases can be useful but are not a prerequisite for an excellent industry or strategic business analysis.

Libraries. Generally, libraries and reference librarians are useful sources of company and industry information. Library card catalogues and indexes help you find sources of information relevant to your needs. Some of the references in the appendixes can serve as a starting point when you visit a university or company library.

Start identifying sources by consulting bibliographic references such as the *Business Periodicals Index* and the *Predicasts F&S Index*. Once references have been identified and consulted, some questions usually remain. At this point, reference librarians can provide invaluable assistance. They can suggest additional references that you have not considered or help you to use your current sources more effectively. In many situations, reference librarians will confirm that your search strategy was appropriate and that you have obtained all of the information that is available from library sources.

Learning to use the Standard Industrial Classification (SIC) system is a particularly valuable library search skill. As mentioned in Chapter 2, the U.S. government and many private companies classify information through SIC codes. The SIC systematically divides economic activities into broad divisions (manufacturing, mining, retail trade, etc.). Each division is further broken down into major industry groups (two-digit SIC code), then into industry sub-groups (three-digit SIC code), and finally into industries (four-digit SIC code). A detailed description of the SIC, including industry definitions, is contained in the 1972 edition of the *Standard Industrial Classification Manual*, published by the U. S. Office of Management and Budget.

To get the most information out of a library information source, take a few minutes to read the introduction before you begin using it. The introduction usually explains (a) how to use the source, and (b) what information it contains. People often waste considerable time and effort by failing first to become familiar with a source.

Each of the references in the appendixes for this chapter provides the title of the source, the publisher, Library of Congress call numbers (LCC), a brief description of the source, and in some instances a brief example of the types of information provided by the source.

Interviews. Many analysts find that personal or telephone interviews with executives, trade association personnel, or research experts can help them fill in missing information, evaluate the accuracy of library information, develop additional perspectives, or confirm their own perspectives regarding industries and companies.

Telephone interviews, unlike personal interviews, allow you to speak with either individuals outside a geographic area or those who do not have time to spare for personal interviews. Whether using telephone or in-person interviews, there are several guidelines to consider before proceeding:

1. Become familiar with as much library information as is possible before conducting interviews. This will help you determine what information is needed and thus which questions to ask. It also demonstrates to interviewees that you are knowledgeable about the industry and company.

2. Identify the names and titles of those people whom you would like to interview. This will save time and help you avoid run-arounds. (Names and titles can be found in some of the sources cited in the appendixes at the end of this chapter.) Further, ask friends, professors, and contacts if they would be willing to refer you to people they know.

3. When setting up interviews, explain who you are and what you are doing. Do not misrepresent yourself.

4. If no one in a company can be identified beforehand, ask to speak with someone in public relations or personnel. They might be able to provide you with names of people to talk to and with company and industry data and statistics.

5. When arranging an interview, choose a time convenient for your interviewee. Also realize, especially in the case of a busy executive, that interview time will be limited. Clarify exactly how much time you will need and how much time the interviewee has available. Most executives are willing to allocate between 30 and 45 minutes for student interviews.

6. If more than one interviewer will be present at a personal interview or if you want to tape record the conversation to ensure complete notes, clear these requests with the interviewee first. **Never** begin an interview with unexpected requests.

7. When preparing for an interview, develop a few **key** questions to ask. Specific questions ensure that you get desired information. Remember, time will be short so a few questions will have to suffice. Several minutes before the end of the scheduled time, ask the interviewee, "Is there anything else that we have not discussed that I should know?" This question may give you additional insights.

8. During the interview, spend most of your time listening. (See the discussion on effective listening in Chapter 7). Also take detailed notes that can be used later.

9. At the end of the interview, thank the interviewee and ask if he or she has any questions or requests. You should also write a thank-you note.

10. After the interview, review your notes and summarize them as soon as possible. This will reduce the amount of information lost due to gaps in memory.

Company data sources. Many companies maintain files and records that facilitate finding strategic management information. Also, companies often have computerized information systems that contain personnel, production, and financial data. Some company information is quite widely distributed to the public and press. For example, annual reports, 10K reports to the Securities and Exchange Commission (SEC), and company newsletters and press releases often contain valuable strategic management information. Students can often receive packets of company information by writing to the public relations manager.

Trade associations. Trade associations are voluntary groups formed by companies or professionals to promote joint interests. These associations often conduct research studies and maintain libraries. Staff members at an association often develop broad expertise about industry problems or problems of the professional group. An association can be an important information source for both company and industry studies. Association executives may agree to interviews, furnish you with written information, and provide useful leads such as companies and executives who might be willing to be interviewed. Two directories that can provide you with the names of relevant trade associations are found in many university and public libraries:

- *Encyclopedia of Associations*
- *National Trade and Professional Associations of the United States.*

Computerized data bases. Data bases have become an increasingly useful source of industry and company information during the last 10 years. Many university libraries have access to a wide range of data bases, often at modest cost. Because the availability and cost of using data bases vary widely from library to library, you should check with your own university reference librarian concerning available data bases. In addition, many companies subscribe to various data base services. If you are employed, you may be able to access company data bases through the research department.

Data bases can be used to compile a bibliography or a set of facts pertinent to a specific topic. Usually a reference librarian serves as an intermediary in conducting the search. The librarian helps you identify key words to use in the search and then types that information into the computer terminal.   A competent reference librarian can improve the quality of the search and reduce the cost.   Before you talk with the reference librarian who conducts computerized searches, take the following steps: First, write down the purpose of your search.   Second, identify some sources that may have the needed information. Finally, list key words that can be used for searching the data base.

Computerized data bases can save you time, increase the breadth and comprehensiveness of your search, and ensure that your references are up-to-date.   The cost of a search depends on three factors: (a) the data bases used, (b) the number of citations retrieved, and (c) the amount of connect-time to the computer.   Charges average about $.50 per connect minute to the computer and $.10 per citation retrieved and printed.

DEVELOPING A SEARCH PLAN

Searching for strategic management information should be a planned activity.   Two basic search strategies are usually used.   The first is called **breadth first** search.   Its goal is to explore many sources and topics and then search for detailed information.   The second search strategy is called **depth first** search.   Its goal is to research in detail a few key areas first and then broaden the search to other areas as that becomes necessary.   A breadth first search is usually best when you know very little about an industry, company, or topic. A broad survey of topics helps you determine what is really important. If you are more familiar with a topic, a depth first search can often reduce the costs of a search.   We have prepared two general search strategies that many of our students have found effective in their company and industry analyses. The steps included in these search strategies enable you to conduct a systematic search that minimizes the number of pitfalls and dead ends you may encounter.   Try to focus on broad strategic issues during your search. Minor points, historical information and other facts can be interesting, but you may let these materials divert you from your actual search goals.

Strategy 1. Strategic Industry Analysis Search

Step 1. Identify the SIC code for the industry.

Step 2. Gather basic economic, financial, and statistical data.
   a)   Sales, including the percentage growth rate
   b)   Trend predictions for the industry
   c)   Comparative industry analyses
   d)   Market statistics
   e)   Industry overviews

Step 3. Assess financial ratios.

Step 4. Assess general business indicators.
   a)   Trade (import/export) data
   b)   Population demographics
   c)   Employment statistics
   d)   Key business events

Step 5. Gather product data.
   a)   Product consumption per capita
   b)   Annual production rate

Strategy 2. Strategic Business Analysis Search

Step 1. Gather background material on the company and subsidiaries.

Step 2. Identify the appropriate SIC codes.

Step 3. Gather general information about the company.
   a) Headquarters address
   b) Corporate officers
   c) Description of businesses and operations

Step 4. Gather basic economic, financial, and statistical information.
   a) Income statements and balance sheets
   b) Stock report data
   c) Financial ratios

Step 5. Examine forecasts of sales.

Step 6. Gather comparative industry data.

Step 7. Tailor the search strategy for specific requirements.

ORGANIZING AND MANAGING INFORMATION

As you conduct your research, keep careful notes on each source. Record what you found and how the information relates to your information-gathering task. These notes will often save you many hours of work as you reach the end of the project and need to retrieve specific pieces of information. Using index cards can help you organize and sort information. Also, preparing citation cards with a complete reference for each source used can save much effort. If a number of team members are gathering information, you must coordinate information gathering tasks and information recording. In some cases you will want to make copies of articles or materials so that other team members can read them.

Sorting and organizing large amounts of information is often a difficult task. The search strategies discussed above suggest topic areas that you can use for sorting information. Also, the skills discussed in Chapters 2, 3, and 4 can provide an organizing framework for your materials. Managing this information base means more than ensuring that pieces of information are not lost or distorted. You also need to ensure that the information is available when it is needed for subsequent analyses and for writing reports and preparing presentations. At the beginning of your search, you should develop a procedure for organizing and managing the information you gather. Then you should try to follow that procedure.

The information you find should help you develop insights, conclusions, and perspectives relevant to an industry or company. Your insights and conclusions will be based on both facts and reasoning. Because you are relying on information - some of it misleading, incorrect, or incomplete - you must make judgments about the importance and validity of the data you gather. Make these judgments both as you collect the information and when it is analyzed. During a search, biases toward specific conclusions can limit or distort the search. You can minimize this possibility by following your search strategy and recording discrepant or contradictory information. Your search will be productive and useful if you are diligent and keep an open mind about how each piece of information fits with other information.

TIPS TO REMEMBER

5.1   List and prioritize information needs.

5.2   Consult reference librarians.

5.3   Develop search plans. They can save considerable time, energy, and aggravation.

5.4   Seek interviews with people who may have useful information. A surprising number of people will be cooperative and helpful.

5.5. Take time to sit back and reflect on what you have found in your research, then organize your information.

5.6. Start early. If you delay your search until the last minute, you will be less successful.

5.7. Be resourceful and creative. You may be surprised that so much relevant information is available.

ACTION EXERCISES

5.1. Visit your university library to identify the locations of the sources listed in this chapter. Are any of the sources unavailable?

5.2. Identify the data bases available to you in your university library, where you work, or from other sources.

5.3. Role play an interview. Practice asking questions and taking notes.

APPENDIX 5.1

Financial, Historical, and Statistical Sources

5.1.1   *Almanac of Business and Industrial Financial Ratios.* Troy, L. (Ed.), Englewood Cliffs, NJ: Prentice-Hall, published annually. LCC # HF5681.R25 T68

This almanac profiles corporate performance for many industries. You can use the data to compare company to industry data on profit, sales, net worth, and other financial and operating information.

5.1.2   *The Dow Jones-Irwin Business and Investment Almanac.* Homewood, IL: Dow Jones-Irwin, published annually. LCC # HF5003.d68a

Dow Jones provides comparative industry statistical information in this almanac. The almanac also includes "Business in Review," industry surveys, a summary of top-growth companies, and other important information.

5.1.3   *Dun and Bradstreet Million Dollar Directory.* Parsippany, N.J.: Dun and Bradstreet, published annually in 3 volumes. LCC # HC102.D8

Almost 100,000 companies are listed in this directory. Information includes addresses, officers, number of employees, annual sales, subsidiaries, and SIC codes. The three directories are divided by company size. Listings are arranged alphabetically with indexes by geographical areas and SIC codes.

5.1.4   *Fortune.* Los Angeles, CA: Time, Inc., published bi-weekly. LCC # HF5001.F745

Fortune publishes a number of special monthly issues that contain directories of company information concerning sales, assets, net income as a percent of sales and stockholder's equity, earnings per share, and total return to investors. For example, the May issue includes the directory of the 500 largest Industrial Corporations, and the June issue has a directory of the second largest 500 Industrial Corporations.

5.1.5   *Moody's Bank and Finance Manual.* New York: Moody's Investors Service; published annually. LCC # HG4961.M65

Moody's covers banks, insurance companies, investment firms, and real estate companies in this manual. It includes information on companies, officers, capital stock, earnings, etc..

5.1.6   *Moody's Industrial Manual.* New York: Moody's Investors
         Service; published annually.
         LCC # HG4961.M67

         In this manual, Moody's provides financial data on companies
         listed on the New York and American Stock Exchanges. Securities
         are rated and prominent companies are featured in a special
         section called "Corporate Visibility-Plus."

5.1.7   *Predicast's Basebook.* Cleveland, OH: Predicast's Inc.; published
         annually.
         LCC # HA214.B3

         The data in the Predicast's Basebook are measures of market size.
         The time series reflect the cyclical sensitivity of the various
         products and industries. The series are arranged according to a
         modified version of the SIC. You can find information using an
         alphabetical guide and SIC codes or you can use the table of
         contents. Approximately 28,000 time series are included.

5.1.8   *Predicast's Forecasts.* Cleveland, OH: Predicast's, Inc.; published
         annually.
         LCC # HA214.P6

         Arranged by SIC code, this source publishes forecasts of the
         U.S. economy, products, and services. Each forecast indicates
         source, short- and long-range projections, and implied annual
         growth rates.

5.1.9   *Securities and Exchange Commision (SEC) Corporate Filings.*
         Washington D.C.: Securities and Exchange Commission; published
         annually.

         Numerous reports are filed by companies with the SEC; these reports
         provide a variety of information about companies. The 10K report
         is a common source. It provides information concerning financial
         analysis, names, background data, compensation of directors,
         strategic changes, and background information on a company and
         its markets. Many libraries keep copies of the 10K reports on
         micro-fiche.

5.1.10   *Standard and Poor's Industry Survey.* New York: Standard
         and Poor's Corp.; published annually.
         LCC # HC106.6 .574

         This source provides economic, financial, and statistical data on
         69 major U.S. industries. Articles examine prospects and investment
         outlook. Trends and problems are placed in an historical context.

5.1.11   *Standard and Poor's Register of Corporations, Directors and
         Executives.* New York: Standard and Poor's Corp.; published
         annually.
         LCC # HG4501.S7664

         This register includes names of corporate officers, corporation
         background data, business locations, stock data, and income
         and balance sheet data.

5.1.12   *Standard Industrial Classification Manual.* Washington, D.C.: Office
of Management and Budget, U.S. Government Printing Office, 1972.
LCC # HF1042.A55

This manual explains the SIC system and indexes SIC codes.

5.1.13   *Statistical Abstract of the United States: 1985.* (106th edition)
Washington D. C.: U.S. Bureau of the Census, published annually.
LCC # HA 202.U5

This is a compilation of statistics on the social, political, and
economic make-up of the United States. Each table provides
notes that refer to additional statistical materials.

5.1.14   *U.S. Industrial Outlook.* Washington, D.C.: U.S. Department of
Commerce, Bureau of Industrial Economics, Government Printing
Office; published annually.
LCC # HC106.6.A23

This is the major channel through which the Department of
Commerce makes its data and analytical resources readily
available. The 5-10 page industry analyses cover industries at the
3- and 4-digit levels of the Standard Industrial Classification (SIC)
system. Forecasts are given in "real" terms, i.e., in 1972 dollars,
and as a percent change in constant dollar values.

5.1.15   *Value Line Investment Survey.* New York: Value Line, Inc.;
published weekly, each company covered twice yearly.
LCC # HG4501.V26

This investment survey examines industries and specific companies.
Ninety industries are covered and ratings and reports are provided
for specific companies. Financial information is included.

5.1.16   *Ward's Directory of 55,000 Largest U.S. Corporations.* Petaluma, CA:
Baldwin Ward Publications; published annually.
LCC # HG440557.W37

This directory covers 55,000 corporations in 21 manufacturing and
37 non-manufacturing SIC industry categories. Materials cover
both private and public companies. Private company data includes
address, CEO, sales, and number of employees. Public company
data also includes 25 indices such as profits, assets, number of
employees, cash flow, and current ratio.

5.1.17   *Yearbook of Industrial Statistics.* New York: United Nations;
published annually.
LCC # HC59.U512

This U.N. publication compiles world industrial statistics in two
volumes. Volume One, Part One contains basic data for each
country or area, and Part Two contains indicators that show
global and regional industrial trends. Volume Two has detailed
information about world production of industrial commodities
for a 10-year period.

APPENDIX 5.2

Journal and Newspaper Indexes

5.2.1   ABI/Inform

This computerized data base provides bibliographic information plus abstracts of articles for 400 English-language business journals from August 1971 to present.

5.2.2   *Business Information Sources*. (L.M. Daniells). Berkeley, CA: University of California Press.
LCC # HF5030.D3

Describes the basic kinds of business reference sources, such as bibliographies, indexes and abstracts, directories, statistical and financial sources and data on current and business trends.

5.2.3   *Business Periodicals Index*. New York: H.W. Wilson Co.; published monthly with an annual volume.

This is a cumulative index to business periodicals. The main body of the index has subject entries arranged alphabetically.

5.2.4   *Encyclopedia of Associations*. Detroit, MI: Gale Research Co.
LCC # HS17.G32

First published in 1956, it contains detailed information concerning non-profit American membership organizations of national scope. Detailed information includes the location, size, objectives, and many other essential aspects of more than 18,100 trade associations, professional societies, labor unions, and other types of voluntary groups.

5.2.5   *Encyclopedia of Business Information Sources*. (P. Wasserman, ed.). Detroit, MI: Gale Research Co.
LCC # HF5353.E9 1976

This encyclopedia contains detailed lists of primary subjects of interest to managerial personnel, with a record of source books, periodicals, organizations, directories, handbooks, bibliographies, and other sources of information.

5.2.6   *National Trade and Professional Associations of the United States*. Washington, D.C.: Columbia Books; published annually.
LCC # HD24225.D532

This directory lists names, addresses, telephone numbers, officers and budgets of 6,000 national trade associations, labor unions, and professional and scientific or technical societies.

5.2.7   *Predicasts F&S Index.* Cleveland, OH: Predicast's, Inc.; published monthly with an annual volume.

This index covers company and industry information from more than 750 financial publications, newspapers, and trade magazines. Topics also include mergers, new products, and technological developments.

5.2.8   *Reader's Guide to Periodical Literature.* New York: H.W. Wilson Co.; published monthly and an annual volume.
LCC # AI3.R48

This reader's guide is a cumulative author and subject guide to periodicals of general interest published in the United States.

5.2.9   *Wall Street Journal Index.* New York: Dow Jones; published monthly.

An index of *Wall Street Journal* articles organized by company name or general news topics.

Chapter 6

Developing Strategic Management Teams

MAJOR SKILLS

- UNDERSTANDING TEAMS
- STRUCTURING TEAMS
- ORGANIZING TEAM MEETINGS
- MAKING TEAM DECISIONS
- CONTROLLING TEAMS

Teams commonly complete industry and company analyses and develop strategic business plans. Hence the success of each student -- and the success of any executive who is assigned to a team project -- is partially and sometimes totally dependent upon the performance of the team. Thus even individuals possessing the analytical and intuitive skills described in the previous chapters of this book may well experience failure purely because of the composition of their team.

Student teams are put together to accomplish several purposes:

- Analyze an industry
- Analyze the strategic position of a specific firm
- Develop business plans
- Write a team report for any of the above
- Make a team oral presentation for any of the above.

Instructors tend to use different approaches with student teams. Some give only one assignment to a team. Many other instructors ask each team to complete several assignments. Teams are usually charged with responsibility for all aspects of problem solving and decision-making and are relatively permanent for the duration of a semester or quarter. It is likely that membership in these teams is determined by a random selection or self-selection process, but some instructors do attempt to assign individuals from different areas of academic concentration (e.g., marketing, finance, general management) to each team.

Student teams simulate several aspects of strategic management teams in industry. Individuals with different information and viewpoints are brought together to arrive at solutions and recommendations for strategic problems. These teams provide you with opportunities to work with and learn from others and to understand the importance of honoring differences and blending them into a meaningful report. The processes by which these viewpoints are assimilated are influential in determining the quality of a team's solutions and recommendations.

Further, you are graded primarily on "team" rather than individual products. Hence the use of teams helps you understand the problems involved in generating "team" solutions. Since the primary grading focus in the classroom is high-quality solutions rather than "politically" feasible ones, team members will most likely be committed to accepting high-quality solutions. In this sense, student teams provide only a partial simulation of the "political side" of many real organizations.

Teams also serve a developmental function. Rather than focusing on preparing you for top management positions in a particular company, they provide you with some of the skills necessary to function effectively in management teams.

In the remainder of this chapter, we will describe the major skills required for developing effective strategic management teams.

UNDERSTANDING TEAMS

The first skill that you need for developing effective strategic management teams is understanding them. In this section, we focus on the following issues:

- The nature and importance of strategic management teams
- Types of strategic management teams
- The composition of teams
- The effective team.

Nature and importance. Many strategic decisions are made by teams of top executives who have the responsibility for shaping and influencing the long- and short-term directions of their firms. These decisions are quite diverse. For example, a board of directors may decide to merge a firm with another firm, or a chief executive officer (CEO) and his or her key division managers may spend a week at a planning retreat, developing a strategic business plan. Such teams are very important in that the quality of the decisions made by them can exert a profound effect on the profitability and survivability of their firms.

Teams of top managers are formed for three reasons. First, they provide the CEO with an opportunity to bring together key executives who possess diverse information and viewpoints needed to solve complex problems and make decisions. This diversity is necessary since, except in the case of a small firm, the CEO rarely has sufficient information and knowledge to complete these activities alone. The more complex the problems or decisions, the more likely that other executives and individuals will be brought into the decision process. For example, in deciding whether to acquire another firm, a CEO will certainly need the involvement of financial, legal, and planning executives, as well as investment bankers. Similarly, when a CEO is considering a major expansion of product lines, it is expected that marketing, financial, and operations executives will be involved in the decision process. Whatever the issue, it is evident to most CEOs that the input and involvement of multiple executives is often needed for the effective solution of problems.

Second, top management teams can facilitate the executives' acceptance of and commitment to decisions. Executives who have been directly involved in the actual decision processes are likely to have had some degree of influence over decisions and thus "partial ownership" of them. Ownership enhances commitment in that individuals have responsibility for seeing that decisions are carried out successfully. In an organizational context the involvement of key executives also ensures that the views and values of constituents who may be affected by a team's decisions are fully represented in the decision-making process.

Finally, top management teams may provide an opportunity to develop emerging executives who have been identified as long-term successors to the top managers. This involvement exposes these individuals to the nature of top management problems prior to succession and provides them with needed experience in dealing with such problems. It also exposes them to the cadre of top managers in a firm and helps them establish the internal organizational networks necessary to succeed as they move up the firm's hierarchy.

Types of teams. There are several types of strategic management teams. Some of them, such as boards of directors, exist on a permanent basis to deal with ongoing strategic problems. Others, such as task forces or advisory groups, are constructed on a temporary basis to handle specific issues. When their tasks have been completed, they are usually disbanded or assigned to another task. In many cases it is common to find subgroups within larger teams. For example, within the board of directors of a firm, a compensation committee composed of some external board members has the responsibility for suggesting types and levels of compensation for top executives to the overall board.

Teams may also have different roles in the overall strategic management problem-solving and decision-making process. Teams may be responsible for dealing with all aspects of the process, including the choice and implementation of alternatives. Or they may be responsible only for one phase of the decision-making process: analyzing a problem, developing alternative strategies, choosing an alternative, or implementing a strategy. The number of possible roles for strategic management teams is numerous.

Composition of teams. From our previous discussion, it is apparent that the composition of teams tends to vary enormously. Who participates should be, and often is, determined by the nature and type of team. Deciding whom to include should be influenced by such criteria as who possesses needed information or essential viewpoints, who represents critical constituencies, and who has developmental needs. Any or all of these criteria may be essential in making this choice. For example, in constructing a board of directors, we may want to include bankers, CEOs from other firms, business school professors, and executives from our own firm who represent key constituencies. In creating a task force to analyze the sudden moves of a key competitor, we may include individuals from planning and marketing and others in the firm who may be knowledgeable about competitors.

The effective team. There are two important criteria for determining the effectiveness of strategic management teams. The first and most obvious is that a team's products meet or exceed some standard of quality.

The second criterion is that the team experiences are reasonably pleasant for members and that they either maintain or enhance the ability of team members to work together on future projects. In some team situations, such as temporary task forces, there is no need for team members to work on future projects. Although the second criterion may not apply directly in this case, it is likely that team members will have to interact with each other in the organization at future times. From the perspective of student teams, the members have to "live" with one another for the duration of a semester or quarter and complete several course projects. A semester can be a very long period of time when you are a member of an unproductive or unpleasant team.

Now that the criteria for effective teams have been established, the next important issue is how to achieve them. Effective teams are a function of many factors. It is beyond the scope of this chapter to list them all. The essential factors, presented in Fig. 6.1, are the quality of the individual members and member task performance; the structure, organization, and control of teams; and the interaction among team members. The most desirable situation is one in which individuals on a team possess all the necessary information and knowledge for a project and can work in a structured, organized and cooperative manner to achieve high-quality products. Unfortunately, we are not always afforded all of these luxuries. Many times in organizations all of the knowledgeable people cannot be identified easily or are not available. In classroom situations, students may have no control over team membership if instructors make the assignments. Also it is not always clear how best to structure or organize strategic management teams. Finally, individuals are not always cooperative; and they may define high-quality products in different ways.

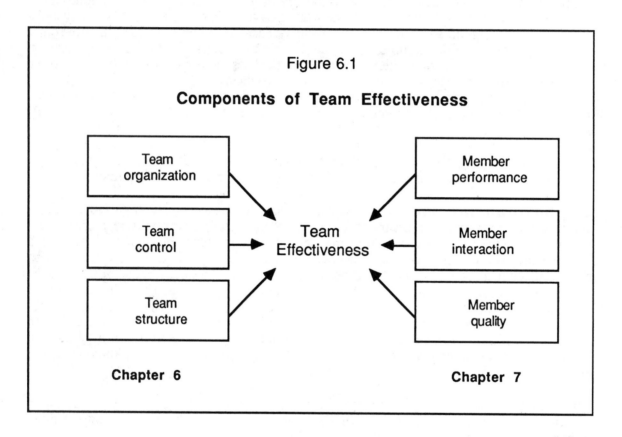

Figure 6.1

Components of Team Effectiveness

STRUCTURING TEAMS

Many teams that break down and become ineffective attribute their failure to "personality differences" among members. Although personalities contribute their fair share of problems, such attributions are frequently nothing more than convenient rationalizations for the failure to structure a team properly. The manner in which teams are structured sets the stage for how team members interact with one another and how they work toward the successful completion of projects. Structuring primarily focuses on determining how a team will function, what its goals and products will be, and what each team member will be responsible for accomplishing.

Developing team leadership. For most strategic management teams, leaders are assigned by those who create the team. The CEO often leads or assigns leaders for particular teams. The classroom experience is somewhat unique in that instructors rarely assign team leaders. Leadership is often left to emerge on its own. If the issue of leadership is not addressed early in the team process, your team may either never choose leaders or experience "bloody battles" among some members for the leadership position. In either case, the results could be disastrous.

There are two ways to deal with the leadership issue. First, someone on a team should ask if anyone wants to be the leader. If more than one member does, let each one state his or her reasons for wanting to be team leader and present qualifications to the group. Through discussion, a team should choose the most acceptable leader.

Second, teams can share leadership. Sharing can be done in two ways. One method that works well is for teams, through discussion, to assign different members responsibility for leading projects or particular aspects of them. This procedure gives those members who want to be leaders a peaceful way of attaining this objective. Another approach is not to choose a leader, but to govern teams through mutual understanding and consent.

Whatever approach to leadership is chosen, it is **essential** that your team works in a structured, organized, and purposeful way with a focus on completing projects. Further, your team should be cohesive. Although it is difficult to define precisely the term cohesive, it is basically a team environment that fosters cooperative behaviors among team members and allows them to work together as a **single unit** in the pursuit of common goals and products. Cohesion is very important to teams. When team members work at cross purposes with one another, they are often unable to achieve the needed goals and products.

To create cohesive teams, especially student teams, it is important that team members not initially alienate themselves from one another. The individuals involved in new teams typically do not know one another and have no basis for being uncooperative or noncohesive. In ongoing groups, previous history or knowledge may play a major role in determining the degree of cohesiveness of a group over time.

Maintaining cohesion in a team over time is always challenging. As team members work together and agree or disagree on issues, cohesiveness may be challenged. Many teams become less cohesive because they do not fully understand what a team should do, how it should be done, and who should do it. Sometimes cliques form and divide the group into factions. In student teams, cliques often develop because some team members seek high grades whereas others do not, or some members are friends from other classes. However, if teams are properly structured and organized at their inception, and if acceptable team-member interaction is specified for all participants, cohesion will be enhanced.

If cliques do form in teams, every effort should be made to confront them at an early stage and try to understand why they are operating. Cliques are often the outcome of a breakdown in structure, organization, or interaction.

Developing team expectations. It is essential early in the team process for **all members** to understand what is expected of the team by those who created it. Since there are numerous types of strategic management teams, expectations will vary by team type. Some teams (e.g., task forces) will be expected to develop solutions to a single problem, whereas others (e.g., the board of directors) will be expected to consider and evaluate strategic issues on an ongoing basis. Student teams are expected to complete a number of high-quality projects. These may include analyzing and evaluating cases or researching issues in the library, with either written or oral reports as the final products.

When possible, team leaders should clarify the group's goals and products. Teams can function effectively only if they know what products must be generated and how they will be evaluated. Many teams fail precisely because the members do not fully understand what the required products are. Once external expectations are clarified, all members should be made aware of them.

As discussed earlier in this chapter, a key component of team effectiveness is the assignment of individuals with proper knowledge, information, and skills to teams. Although this may be possible with strategic management teams, you may not have control over member assignment. Therefore you often have to work with the talent assigned.

Utilizing team talents. To assess knowledge and skills and develop a cohesive team, members should in a round-robin fashion summarize background knowledge and skills pertinent to the course. Members should take notes on each individual as the discussion progresses. After all members have presented their backgrounds, each member should entertain questions to clarify levels of knowledge and skill. This approach provides a useful assessment and helps team members become acquainted with each other.

Assess the skills, knowledge, and information that will enable the group to make the best use of available talent. This talent may include experience obtained from work, library research, reading, or courses. After completing this exercise, individuals usually find that there is more talent among group members than they had assumed when the teams were created. This assessment also identifies team members with similar knowledge and skills. This duplication of knowledge and skills provides teams with an opportunity for these members to work together and help one another when necessary.

Defining team tasks. Once it is clear what team products are expected and the knowledge, information, and skills available, team tasks should be defined. Each project for which teams are responsible should be broken down into its component parts. For example, in analyzing and presenting written cases, team members will usually be required to prepare an industry analysis, strategic business analysis, problem analysis, and recommended solutions. They will also need to draft, type, and proofread papers. Several tasks will be completed by individuals working alone (e.g., an industry analysis), whereas others (e.g., choosing solutions) will require team interaction and discussion.

Defining team tasks serves two purposes. First, it clarifies the short-run products that must be accomplished in the pursuit of major projects. Thus, it eliminates ambiguity about what team members are supposed to do. Second, it helps a team establish the frequency and necessity of team meetings.   When teams are disorganized and unclear about the tasks to be accomplished, they tend to meet more often than needed. These meetings are frequently spent trying to figure out what to do rather than doing it. Since time is scarce, team meetings should be used only when **team member interaction** is necessary. Such meetings might include planning sessions for scheduling projects and discussing each member's research. Minimizing meetings also helps to maintain the harmony of teams.

Assigning team tasks. At this point in a team's evolution, responsibility for completing tasks should be assigned to specific members. Teams can use several alternative approaches. First, members may be assigned or volunteer for tasks based on a knowledge and skills assessment. This approach obviously attempts to fit closely the knowledge and skills of individuals to the various tasks. A second approach takes a more developmental view. In this instance members may be assigned a different task for each project. This procedure provides each member with an opportunity to acquire and apply new skills and knowledge. A third approach requires that each member work on every project task independently. Later, the team meets to discuss all of the tasks and reconcile differences. This last approach applies specifically to analyses since teams need to arrive at one set of recommendations and one written paper or oral presentation. Although this appproach seems to be the least efficient use of time, it does provide the highest degree of development since each member is responsible for analyzing and understanding entire projects. Whatever approach is chosen, however, **all** team members should feel that tasks have been distributed equitably. Failure to do so could result in arguments.

Setting deadlines. Naturally, most team projects must be completed by specific dates. To accomplish this goal in an orderly fashion, the scheduling of tasks and team meetings should be planned at the beginning of projects. Although it is sometimes difficult to determine how long tasks will take to complete, deadlines are still necessary. Without them, coordination among individuals may be impossible and poorly conceptualized "rush jobs" may result. When there is uncertainty about how long the project will take, building slack time into plans and deadlines helps. Lack of planning tends to create squabbles among team members.

The planning process for most projects is not very complex. A simple time line chart, with each member's task responsibility and time frame defined, works well. Completion dates should be sequenced so that tasks that need to be finished before others can begin are clearly specified. Fig. 6.2 presents a basic project plan for the completion of a written case analysis. This plan itself, however, does not guarantee that tasks will be carried out. It is also necessary that all members accept their tasks and the time frames allocated for completing them.

Figure 6.2

Case Analysis Project Plan

OVERALL PROJECT PLAN

Month	SEP	OCT					NOV			
Week	19-26	27-03	04-10	11-17	18-24	25-31	01-07	08-14	15-21	22-03
Gather Information	xxxxx									
Analyze Data		xxxxx	xxxxx							
Lay out Scenarios				xxxxx	xxxxx					
Identify Strategic Alternatives						xxxxx	xxxxx			
Evaluate & Select a Strategic Alternative						xxxxx	xxxxx			
Propose Strategic Implementation Plan						xxxxx	xxxxx			
Write Up								xxxxx	xxxxx	
Edit										xxxxx

DATA ANALYSIS PLAN

Month	SEP	OCT					NOV				Responsibility
Week	19-26	27-03	04-10	11-17	18-24	25-31	01-07	08-14	15-21	22-03	
Business Definition Buyers Suppliers Report due 10/03		xxxxx									Bill
Potential Entry Substitution Report due 10/03		xxxxx									John
Competition Report due 10/03		xxxxx									Susan
Finance Report due 10/03		xxxxx									Joan
Management Operation Report due 10/03		xxxxx									James
GAP Analysis Meet on Oct 11 or 12 Team			xxxxx								Robert

ORGANIZING TEAM MEETINGS

In completing projects, you will need to meet with all team members to present and discuss issues and tasks. These meetings should be well organized, with members prepared to work and focus on these particular tasks. Since time is scarce, teams should not waste time by focusing on unimportant issues. If time is wasted, members may either leave the meeting or run out of energy before important issues are discussed. Such outcomes are certainly not desirable.

Establishing a meeting place. When and where to meet are always difficult decisions. Frequently, prior commitments force teams to make difficult decisions. However, some guidelines are helpful.

First, teams should meet as close as possible to the agreed dates presented in the project plan so that members with many commitments can plan for meetings. Second, within reasonable limits members should show some compassion for team members who have other time commitments and have difficulty participating in all meetings. You should try to accommodate one another's scheduling problems as much as possible and be prepared to make compromises. We all would like to meet when it is convenient for us, but this is not always feasible. Do not develop the attitude that "your other time commitments are your own problems, not mine." This approach will not solve scheduling problems and will serve to alienate team members. Third, try to find meeting locations that are convenient and accessible to all members. If members live near or on campus, find comfortable, central locations such as the library. If members live far from campus, rotate meetings among your homes, meet on campus, or choose neutral locations. Another approach would be to hold meetings before or after class, if schedules permit. The important point for all team members to remember is to be fair, compassionate, and flexible.

Developing team agendas. Written agendas facilitate the organization of the meeting giving members clear expectations of a meeting's purpose and the intended accomplishments.

Agendas may be structured in a variety of ways, but for the purpose of student teams they can remain rather simple. The first items to consider in agendas are tasks or issues that were not completed at the previous meeting. Before new issues are discussed, old ones should be resolved. Then reports that individual members are expected to give should be presented. Finally, new issues should be considered. Depending upon the reasons for the meeting, agendas may have few or many items.

Agendas should be written and, when possible, submitted to team members before meetings. Members should also be given the option to include other items for discussion. Written agendas ensure that all members possess the same information. Providing agendas in advance of meetings gives members sufficient time to think about and prepare for the issues to be discussed. Advanced preparation saves valuable meeting time and facilitates informed discussions.

Conducting team meetings. At the beginning of meetings, a brief review of progress made to date on each project is useful. Reference can be made to the plan discussed earlier. You might also mark off tasks as they are completed. This review helps maintain continuity on projects, provides team members with a sense of accomplishment, and serves as a basis of control to ensure that deadlines are being met. After the review, teams should discuss agenda items and work toward accomplishing them.

Further, team members responsible for presenting specific analyses or information should do so in writing. This approach facilitates the use of meeting time and keeps a project focused in several ways. First, it establishes an atmosphere of accountability. Since written reports are more easily scrutinized than verbal ones, it forces members to be more precise in their analyses. Second, it provides all team members with analyses and information that they can retain, rather than relying solely on the accuracy of notes taken while a member reports orally. These reports also allow members to concentrate on listening rather than on writing during meetings. Third, written reports can serve as preliminary drafts for overall project reports.

At the end of each meeting, a summary of what was accomplished and where it leaves the team with respect to plans should be given. It is also a good time to make any needed modifications of team plans. This summary helps ensure that all members have a common understanding of what was discussed and accomplished during the meeting. It also helps to prevent future disagreements, facilitates project continuity, and fosters a sense of accomplishment and control.

If possible, individual assignments due at the next meeting should be made. This procedure clarifies expectations, eliminates misunderstandings concerning individual responsibilities, and publicly commits members to complete their assignments.

MAKING TEAM DECISIONS

Strategic management teams are frequently responsible for defining and solving problems and making decisions. How teams approach these activities and work through them during meetings can influence the effectiveness of their solutions and decisions.

Developing team ideas. Effective strategic problem solving and decision making require careful problem definition, evaluation of causes, generation of alternatives, and evaluation of those alternatives. To accomplish these goals, a thorough canvassing and evaluating of ideas concerning problems, causes, assumptions and decision alternatives should be conducted. The greater the number of reasonable ideas considered, the greater the likelihood that high-quality solutions and decisions will result. One of the benefits of team problem solving and decision making is that there is a greater potential for generating innovative ideas.

Frequently, however, "potential" is not translated into actual ideas generated. Too often members of teams, in their haste to define causes or solutions, do not take sufficient time to generate a reasonable number of ideas before evaluating them. Many times teams never get beyond evaluating the first idea generated. As a result, many good ideas are either forgotten or suppressed.

It is essential that your team divide problem solving and decision making into two stages: idea generation and idea evaluation. The goal is to withhold evaluation until all reasonable ideas have been generated. This procedure also helps ensure that each group member has a chance to contribute. After idea generation is relatively complete, idea evaluation can begin.

Avoiding premature judgment. Another common problem for teams is their propensity to arrive at premature judgments. Effective strategic problem-solving and decision-making require that all ideas be examined and scrutinized before judgments and commitments are made.

Suspending judgment is difficult because teams tend to develop inertia toward developing solutions and arriving at decisions. This outcome occurs for several reasons. First, team members have only a limited amount of time in which to meet, and they must formulate solutions or decisions during this time frame. Second, team pressures toward conformity can suppress viewpoints that are not "on track" with the direction in which the team is headed. Rather than break the harmony of the team, members avoid rocking the boat. Third, to get out from under the time pressures of assignments, teams push toward solutions. Finally, stronger team members may push their ideas and solutions past weaker members without thorough evaluation, thereby reducing or eliminating useful ideas.

Three approaches can help a team's decision-making processes: brainstorming, the nominal group technique, and the devil's advocate approach. It is essential that you chose an approach that is appropriate for your situation and that all team members agree to use it.

Brainstorming. This approach is quite useful for **generating** ideas. It assumes that the greater the number of ideas generated, the greater the likelihood that "correct" or "better" ideas will be generated. The major objective of this approach is to push individual team members to free themselves from any inhibitions and criticisms and to generate as many ideas as possible. These ideas may focus on causes of problems, assumptions concerning them, or solutions and decisions. Brainstorming involves two separate steps: idea generation and idea evaluation.

Is it better to brainstorm together or individually? Research suggests that individual brainstorming generates more and better ideas because team interaction and possible criticism among members can inhibit individual generation of ideas.

The following steps are required for effective brainstorming:

1. Describe the problem or decision for which the team needs ideas and state the objective of identifying as many ideas as possible. (For example: Why did market share decline? or How to increase market share?)
2. Determine how team members are to be separated. Members may brainstorm in their offices, at home, or together at a meeting, provided that there is no criticism of ideas.
3. Provide time to brainstorm. Time needed depends on members' familiarity with the issue.
4. Encourage idea generation by asking members to do the following:
   • Withhold self-criticism of ideas
   • Be as creative as possible and do not worry if the ideas seem wild
   • Generate as many ideas as possible, quantity is what is wanted.
5. Hold an idea evaluation meeting, or at least separate the idea generation and idea evaluation phases of the meeting.

Although these steps seem simple, they are quite powerful in helping teams generate ideas. It is important, however, to reemphasize that idea generation and evaluation must be separated into two distinct phases.

Nominal group technique. This is a structured approach to strategic problem solving and decision making that clearly divides idea generation and idea evaluation into two stages. It is useful for eliciting ideas and information from team members. It also reduces interaction among team members.

The idea generation stage of this technique is very similar to **individual brainstorming** in that individuals work alone. The nominal group technique includes the following steps:

1. Present to team members, both orally and in writing, the issue for which ideas are needed.
2. Let team members list ideas on a yellow pad for about 10 minutes.

3. Have each member generate new ideas, using a variation of the individual brainstorming approach. Rather than brainstorming in isolation, individuals do so in the same location as other team members. A task-oriented work environment is created as team members observe each other working hard. However, cross-chatter and criticism of ideas are not allowed.

4. Record individual ideas on either a flipchart or blackboard by going around the team and asking for one idea from each member at a time (i.e., using a round robin procedure). Continue until all members' ideas have been recorded. This procedure ensures equal participation among team members, keeps the team involved in the process, and increases individual involvement.

5. Discuss, in order, each idea listed on the flipchart or blackboard. Discussion should focus initially on meaning and clarification of an idea.

6. After seeing the complete list of ideas, team members should individually brainstorm new ideas again. After viewing the entire list, members may have new ideas.

7. Shift focus to discussing agreement and disagreement about the importance and/or validity of each idea. Teams should be careful, however, not to "lose track" and discuss only one idea. This procedure will help team members familiarize themselves with the meaning, logic, and arguments for and against each idea.

8. Team members should then be asked to choose from the entire list a specific number of ideas (e.g., 7-10) that are most important and rank order them. Assign a score of one to the least important and so on. The most important item in the list should have the highest score.

9. Determine the team's preference by counting the ideas with the highest scores. Those ideas are considered the most important and valid ones.

Devil's advocate approach. This approach develops a solid argument for a reasonable recommendation, then subjects that recommendation to an in-depth, formal critique completed by a formally-appointed devil's advocate. The devil's advocate calls into question the data, facts, assumptions, ideas, and recommendations presented, and attempts to show why the recommendations should **not** be adopted. Through repeated criticism and revision, the approach leads to mutual acceptance of recommendations.

Proponents of this decision-making approach believe that good recommendations, ideas, and assumptions will survive even the most forceful and effective criticism and that this approach is more likely to yield sound judgments or recommendations.

The following are some guidelines and procedures to follow when using the devil's advocate approach:

1. Divide the team into two subgroups. Assign one subgroup the formal role of devil's advocate. The two subgroups should then meet separately.

2. Have the subgroups discuss the problem.

3a. The subgroup that is **not** the devil's advocate should develop a set of recommendations and build an argument for them, supported by all **key assumptions, facts, and data.** Individual brainstorming is useful for generating ideas.

3b. The devil's advocate subgroup should concurrently discuss the problem and any critical assumptions, data, etc., that they can identify as preparation for their critique.

4. The first subgroup should then present its written recommendations and assumptions to the devil's advocate subgroup. The devil's advocate subgroup subjects the recommendation to a formal critique prior to the next team meeting. The critique attempts to uncover what is wrong with the recommendations, assumptions, facts, and data and to expound the reasons why the recommendations should not be adopted.

5. At the next team meeting, the critique should be presented to the first subgroup orally and in writing. This subgroup then meets separately and revises its recommendations to satisfy the valid criticisms of the devil's advocate subgroup.

6. Steps 4 and 5 should be repeated until both subgroups accept the recommendations, assumptions, and data.

7. Record the final recommendations, assumptions, facts, and data.

CONTROLLING TEAMS

Although skills for structuring and organizing teams are essential for team effectiveness, they must be accompanied by control. Members responsible for key project activites must complete them by the required dates. For many strategic management projects, failure by one member to complete certain activites precludes other members from finishing their activities on time. It is often difficult, especially with student teams, to "force" individuals to meet deadlines. The best approach is to establish a team environment early in the process in which failure to meet plans and deadlines will not be tolerated. If you are serious about these plans and deadlines , efforts will be made to meet them.

Furthermore, all too often team members fail to communicate and provide one another with feedback. Team members should feel comfortable cri-tiquing each other's work. This approach can be quite constructive and establish expectations early in the process as to what is acceptable quality work. If you can make your reports and work available to other members prior to actual deadlines, they can provide feedback. If done constructively, feedback can help teams remain on course.

However, events frequently do not unfold as planned. A team member may become ill or fail to complete an activity on time. Regardless of the circumstances, teams must consider the possibility of these events and be flexible in dealing with them. Flexibility can be enhanced by building slack time into plans. Additionally, team members can be assigned secondary or back-up responsibilities. If one member fails to complete an activity on time or anticipates problems, the back-up person can help. It is important to remember that **all** members of the team are responsible for all the projects.

Occasionally a team will be assigned one or two members who are not driven to work hard and complete projects. This can be frustrating to motivated team members and makes it difficult for them to adhere to plans. It is hard to know early in the process whether a team member is marginal or unmotivated. Sometimes an individual does not complete an activity on time due to some extraordinary circumstances. It is usually not fair to conclude from this one event that the member is unmotivated. The most reasonable basis for assessment is to look for patterns. For example, does a member continually miss deadlines and team meetings? As the number of these events increases, so too does the likelihood that the member is marginal.

There are several courses of action that teams can take to handle marginal members. First, inform these members early in the process that they are failing to meet team expectations. Before concluding that they are marginal, first learn what the causes of the problems are. Find out if they are clear about what is expected of them, or if they are having trouble making deadlines or meetings. With some clarification of expectations, problems might disappear. Be careful however, that the explanations given are not just excuses. After a few confrontations, this issue should become clear.

Second, if it is apparent that certain members are marginal, put pressure on them to comply with team expectations. Inform them that the team will not carry them on projects and will inform the instructor of their failure to comply. When peer group evaluations are used the team may remind the marginal student of the consequences of his or her continued poor performance.

Finally, if it is apparent that marginal members cannot be made to carry out their responsibilities, bring this information to the attention of the instructor. If teams have made every **reasonable** attempt to deal with these members, this is a necessary final step. Most instructors do not want "free riders" and do want the teams to function equitably and effectively.

Some instructors make use of peer evaluations to assess individual contributions to total team effort. In such cases, members are usually requested to evaluate their relative contribution and that of other team members. When evaluating members (and in assessing marginal members) you must realize that contributions come in various forms. The best way to ensure that members' contributions are equitable is to allocate work fairly during the planning stages and to make sure that all members agree to and accept their assignments. Furthermore, make sure members understand that satisfactory completion of these assignments signals equitable contributions.

You must separate your personal feelings about others from your evaluations of them. If someone did a good job, he or she deserves a good evaluation. Too often, team members fail to distinguish between work contributions and feelings. When team members are either marginal or are failing to do a reasonable job, it is useful to document in writing what these individuals are doing or failing to do. If they miss meetings, record the date, time, and purpose of the meeting. If they turn in poor-quality work, make a copy of it and put it in a file. Having evidence available will make it easier to confront marginal members, to give accurate peer evaluations, and to discuss the performance of these members.

TIPS TO REMEMBER

6.1   Identify the team leader or leaders early in the team process.

6.2   Take time for all members to become acquainted.

6.3   Define team products and tasks as early as possible and ensure that members understand and accept them.

6.4   Assign members to tasks based on their knowledge, information, and skills.

6.5   Set plans and deadlines and see that members understand and accept them.

6.6   Choose meeting times and locations that are acceptable to all members.

6.7   Conduct meetings with written agendas, summarize accomplishments and review progress at the beginning and end of each meeting.

6.8   Have all members provide their analyses in writing, if possible.

6.9   Make the best use of team time by focusing on important tasks.

6.10   Avoid premature judgment and thoroughly assess ideas when solving problems and making decisions.

6.11   Adhere to plans and deadlines, but build in contingency plans in case of delays.

6.12   Do not let marginal team members have a free ride. Be objective in assessing individual member performance.

ACTION EXERCISES

6.1   This exercise is designed to be used at the first team meeting. It helps members become acquainted and provides a basis of discussion for deciding how to structure and organize teams. The steps are as follows:

a) Have members sit in a circle facing one another.

b) Get them to write their names on a sheet of paper with a marker and display the names so all members can see them.

c) Using the round-robin approach, members should introduce themselves and briefly describe their backgrounds (i.e., college major, work experience, etc.).

d) Using the individual brainstorming approach, have each member develop two lists. For the first list, members should think of an effective team on which they worked and describe all the things that the team did well. For the second list, they should think of an ineffective team on which they worked and describe all the things that went poorly. If members cannot think of effective or ineffective teams, have them list what they think would go well or poorly in such teams.

e) Using a round-robin approach, first list on a blackboard or flip chart all unique items associated with effective teams, then list those associated with ineffective teams.

f) Have members discuss each item and decide how to avoid the characteristics of ineffective teams and capitalize on those of effective teams (use the material contained in this chapter as a guide).

6.2   Following the assignment of projects by the instructor, develop plans based on Fig. 6.2. Use the following steps:

a) Break down the projects according to major tasks to be completed.

b) Determine the sequencing of the tasks.

c) Assign deadlines for each task.

d) Record this information on a sheet of paper, using the format presented in Fig. 6.2.

e) Break down each major task into subtasks, follow steps b-d.

f) Assign individual responsibilities for each task. Be sure that members are capable of carrying out and accepting their responsibilities.

g) Present each member with a written copy of plans.

SUGGESTED READINGS

6.1   Delbecq, A.L., Van de Ven, A.H., and Gustafson, D.H., *Group Techniques for Program Planning*. Glenview, IL: Scott, Foresman & Co, 1975.
       This is an excellent source for a complete step-by-step discussion of the brainstorming and nominal group technique approaches.

6.2   Huber, G.P., *Managerial Decision Making*. Glenview, IL: Scott, Foresman & Co., 1980.
       This book presents an overview of managerial decision making. Discussions of both individual and team decision making are provided.

6.3   Grove, A. S., How (and Why) to Run a Meeting. *Fortune*, July 11, 1983, pp. 132-135.
       This article, written by the president of Intel Corp., provides some guidelines for conducting effective meetings. The importance of the meeting as a controlled situation, rather than a free-for-all, is discussed.

6.4   Mason, R.O., and Mitroff, I.I., *Challenging Strategic Planning Assumptions*. New York: Wiley-Interscience, 1981.
       This book provides an excellent discussion of the use of dialetical inquiry in strategic problem solving and decision making. It focuses on both theoretical and practical issues concerning the use of this approach.

Chapter 7

Participating in Strategic Management Team Activities

MAJOR SKILLS

- ASSUMING INDIVIDUAL RESPONSIBILITY
- INTERACTING EFFECTIVELY IN TEAMS
- MANAGING TEAM PROBLEMS

As Chapter 6 indicates, it is important that you learn to structure, organize, and control teams. While these skills are necessary for success, they are not sufficient, for ultimately it is the willingness of each group member to participate in team activities that determines team effectiveness. This chapter is devoted to describing those skills that must be mastered by an individual who wants to participate effectively on a strategic management team.

Team members need to develop or refine three basic skills and several subskills. First, members must learn to assume individual responsibility for their assigned tasks. Second, they must interact effectively with other members. Finally, they must learn to manage team problems.

Team participation requires that members assume different roles at different times. Sometimes members need to be task-oriented and focused on completing individual assignments. At other times they need to be supportive, encouraging other team members to participate and helping those who are having difficulty completing assignments. In this chapter, we focus on skills that facilitate these two roles. Individuals should be more effective team members after acquiring and refining these skills.

ASSUMING INDIVIDUAL RESPONSIBILITY

The quality of team assignments is often as good as the contributions of its weakest member. This statement clearly highlights the importance of each team member assuming responsibility for and completing assignments. Failure to do so can adversely affect the ability of other members to complete their assignments and thus undermine the overall team effort. Individual responsibility to teams includes completing high-quality assignments, attending meetings regularly, and contributing positively to overall team products.

Often students complain that they cannot do what the team expects because of outside employment, heavy course loads, and other commitments. Although these are legitimate problems, students must realize when they enroll in a strategic management or business policy course that they assume the responsibility to contribute to their team.   When members fail in their responsibility, so does the team. In a classroom situation it is rare that teams can regroup effectively after such failure. Time frames are usually tight and it is difficult for instructors to remove or replace members during the semester.

In this section, we describe four specific subskills that are directly related to the major skill of assuming individual responsibility:

- Identifying time traps
- Avoiding time traps
- Adhering to team deadlines and meeting schedules
- Contributing quality work.

Identifying time traps. Time traps are unproductive activities and decisions. They serve to distract people from the important tasks at hand and may create conflicts among team members. The list of time traps is endless and varies among individuals, but it includes the following:

- Procrastination
- Indecision
- Inability to say no
- Overcommitment
- Lack of priorities
- Perfectionism
- Personal disorganization
- Lack of objectives
- Lack of deadlines
- Fatigue
- Socializing
- Lack of planning.

Avoiding traps. You can eliminate or minimize the impact of time traps through careful thought and planning. Let us examine some solutions for problems occurring because of time traps.

Procrastination and indecision are frequent traps for many people. To overcome them, you must first admit that they adversely affect your behavior and then attempt to understand why they occur. Typical reasons include these:

- Fear of failure
- Postponing or avoiding action
- Failure to set work priorities.

Fear of failure can be overcome by comparing the cost of failing to the cost of delaying. In many situations, the cost of delaying is much greater than the cost of failing. Postponing action can be overcome by tackling difficult activities or situations first. This procedure helps to get the worst problems out of the way quickly and provides you with a sense of accomplishment. In addition, setting priorities helps you focus on the most important items.

Further, learning to say "no" is a useful way to avoid overcommitment. Many people do not know how to say "no" and thus commit to so many activities that they do not have the time to do important ones properly. Overcommitment and its usual outcome, rushing, often result in low-quality work. Learn to avoid saying "yes" just to win approval and acceptance or to feel important. Take on those activities that are important and meaningful to you and that fit within your time constraints. It is perfectly acceptable to deny a request for your time. Do so, however, in a prompt and patient manner.

When faced with complex tasks, people tend to focus either on the easy parts of these tasks or on those that take only a few minutes. Sometimes tasks appear so overwhelming that we avoid them entirely. When possible, break tasks into simpler parts and then systematically prioritize these parts and work on them.

Some individuals suffer from perfectionism. This trap often prevents people from completing work on time and results in frustration. The key to avoiding this trap is to do the best job that you can the first time. Sometimes perfection is an excuse for procrastination. Always ask yourself whether the marginal improvements are worth the additional time spent.

Much time is also wasted on personal disorganization. Not knowing where material has been placed and having to spend hours looking for it is a time killer. Keeping neat and organized files goes a long way toward alleviating this problem.

Other time traps include a lack of objectives and deadlines. Setting objectives and deadlines helps you to define clearly what needs to be accomplished when. They ensure that effort and attention are directed at completing specific projects. It is useful for you to have daily as well as weekly objectives and deadlines. Objectives and deadlines motivate you to stay on target, and provide a sense of accomplishment when tasks are completed. Hence writing objectives and deadlines on paper and then crossing each out as it is finished is a useful approach.

There are many more time traps and solutions that are beyond the scope of this section. The key to solving the traps is to admit them, then work toward eliminating them. There are no magic solutions, just hard and thoughtful work.

Adhering to deadlines and meeting schedules. Team deadlines and scheduled meetings sometimes conflict with personal priorities. Many of us tend to believe that our lives and priorities are more important than deadlines and meetings. When personal priorities and team deadlines and meetings come into conflict, the key question becomes: Who should accommodate whom? This is difficult to answer because both personal and team priorities are legitimate. In deciding how to handle potential conflicts, the parties have one of two choices. First, each side can attempt to win at the expense of the other. This approach usually results in both sides losing and is not desirable in a "team" situation. Second, both sides can problem solve and seek out cooperative solutions. In this case both sides benefit. Individuals and teams must be willing to make some concessions to help one another. Frequently, team members will strive to cooperate with individuals who have legitimate problems in meeting deadlines and making meetings when these individuals are perceived as being responsible and genuinely interested in the team's success. When conflicts occur, teams should consider changing deadlines or assigning problem individuals to projects with longer deadlines. Meeting dates can be changed when they are continually inconvenient for a particular member. However, each individual should also consider adjusting personal priorities to be more consistent with team deadlines and meetings.

Regardless of the particular solution, it is unacceptable for members to fail consistently to complete projects and meet deadlines. If individuals and teams assume joint responsibility for deadlines, potential conflicts and problems concerning them should be minimized and creative solutions found.

Contributing quality work. A recurring problem with student teams is defining standards for quality work. This definition is often a subjective assessment that varies among team members. Before individuals can be held responsible for "quality" work, the team must set some standards of quality and clearly communicate those standards to each member. This procedure can be completed during early planning meetings. Quality issues to consider include the volume of work, the nature of its presentation, and the amount of original thought contained in it. Once these standards have been established and communicated, it is much easier to hold people responsible for them.

Individuals have responsibility for providing teams with quality work. Without high-quality work, the overall team effort suffers. However, individuals with varying abilities and levels of motivation comprise the team. The best way to ensure quality work is to match member's skills with appropriate assignments.

As we have noted, personal priorities reduce an individual's motivation to participate in groups and the level of effort allocated to produce high quality work. Sometimes individuals become overcommitted or fall into many of the time traps discussed earlier. The result is that they are forced to sacrifice quality by rushing through assignments in order to complete everything on time. Some members are just lazy and do not seek high grades. These individuals look for an easy way out and do not consider quality to be important.

When individuals fail to assume and fulfill team responsibilities, the costs are great for all involved. For the individual, it can mean personal embarrassment, although this is probably inconsequential for the lazy member. It might also mean the alienation and outrage of other team members. This outcome is certainly not pleasant. The costs may be most severe if peer evaluations are used by instructors. In this case, the result might be low or even failing grades for irresponsible members. Since students take the strategic management or policy course in the final semester or quarter, a failing grade could delay graduation.

For teams, the outcomes of individual failure are usually inferior products and lower grades for all members. Even if teams identify irresponsible members early in a semester or quarter, the costs in terms of emotion and energy expended can be quite high. Certainly the best approach is for all team members to contribute high-quality, timely work.

INTERACTING EFFECTIVELY IN TEAMS

As part of a team, members need to interact and communicate effectively with one another. Otherwise, the benefits derived from the team approach, such as the sharing of ideas, will be eliminated. Although effective interaction and communication seem easy to accomplish, that is not always true. Think about the number of times that you "listened" to individuals speak and did not remember what they said because you were thinking about something else. Also, how many times have you withheld or delayed sharing information with others because you did not trust them? These are just a few of the many situations in which interaction and communication are ineffective. In this section, we describe four skills for interacting more effectively in teams and communicating more openly with others:

- Dealing with personal insecurities
- Knowing when and how to speak and listen
- Admitting your mistakes
- Handling "ego" challenges.

Dealing with your insecurities. Before individuals can deal effectively with others, they need to understand what motivates them. Many people in our society are somewhat insecure. They worry excessively about such issues as whether their ideas are solid and acceptable, and they rely upon others' views of them rather than their own view to make such judgments. Although some insecurity is an inevitable and normal part of life, high levels of chronic insecurity can be psychologically detrimental both to individuals and to the team. Insecure individuals often try to protect or enhance their self-image. To accomplish this goal they may resist evaluation both of themselves and their ideas, try to prove to those around them that they are as good or better than others, and avoid interacting with others to minimize the probability of being evaluated.

The effects of such insecurity on teams are two-fold. First, some insecure members respond aggressively and try to protect themselves by taking overactive roles during team meetings. Such dysfunctional behavior includes dominating meetings; arguing excessively for positions, whether right or wrong; failing to listen to or attacking others' ideas; and preventing others from speaking. Second, some insecure members respond passively and try to protect themselves by withdrawing from team meetings. To prevent themselves from being evaluated, they do not contribute any ideas; as a result, their ideas are lost.

As these effects demonstrate, insecure members can be detrimental to team interactions and effectiveness. There is little that teams can do to handle insecure members other than tactfully and, if necessary, forcefully suppress aggressive members and support passive members. However, you are largely responsible for dealing with your own insecurities. Aggressive members should consider the worst that can happen to them if they do not dominate meetings. Perhaps more people would respect them or value their opinion if they were less aggressive. Dominating a meeting does not necessarily result in a greater degree of influence. Often aggressive behaviors make other individuals angry and intolerant. Eventually, aggressive members may be sanctioned or ignored by teams. Passive and insecure members must realize that there is little at risk in contributing. If teams are managed properly most members will welcome the contribution of other viewpoints. All members have something to contribute and should not be afraid to do so. If passive members withdraw, they will never have the benefits of testing their ideas and skills and making meaningful contributions.

It is quite common for individuals to be slightly insecure. How the insecurity is channeled, however, can be a significant determinant of team effectiveness. If you are insecure, consider the possible rewards of making a reasonable and supportive team contribution, then begin to participate.

Developing speaking and listening skills. To participate effectively, you must learn when and how to speak and listen. Think about your own experiences in group meetings. How many times were you rudely interrupted and, as a result, forgot what you wanted to say? How many times have you interrupted others with similar results? How did such experiences make you and others feel about the group meetings? What influence did they exert on the effectiveness of the group? These and similar questions should help you to understand why the skill of learning how and when to speak and listen is so important. Remember, communication and the exchange of ideas are enhanced within a team when knowledgeable members have an opportunity to present their ideas clearly and those listening are attentive and understand what is being said.

Although this guideline appears obvious, it is not always followed. People erect numerous barriers to effective communication every day. Individuals may approach a discussion with different frames of reference and interpret the issues quite differently. Some individuals engage in selective listening and block out information that disagrees with what they believe. Team members may discount the communication of individuals with low status or credibility, whether they are right or wrong. Individuals communicate with terms, jargon, and language with which other members are not familiar, or they assume too much background information on the part of their listeners. Finally, as discussed earlier, insecure and aggressive members may try to dominate meetings and refuse to give others ample time to participate. Whatever the barrier, the results are ineffective interaction and communication.

The following guidelines will help reduce communication barriers and aid team interaction:

- **Preparation**. To facilitate team use of time and enhance personal credibility, think before you speak. Prepare and evaluate ideas prior to speaking and then present them in an organized manner.
- **Follow-up**. When speaking during team meetings, stop at various points to ask if any members have questions or need clarification. Simply asking "Do you understand?" or "Is what I am saying clear to you?" can be quite helpful. As you are speaking, watch other members' facial expressions to see if they appear bewildered, then attempt to find out why. If you are listening to another person speak and are having trouble following the presentation, interject "Let me see if I understand what you are saying", and provide the speaker with a summary to which he or she can respond. But be careful not to interrupt the speaker at critical points in the discussion.
- **Choice of language**. Make sure that all members of a team are familiar with the terminology you are using when you speak. This procedure is most important when you are presenting research results or data no one else is familiar with. Make your presentation as clear and simple as possible.
- **Effective listening**. Only part of the responsibility for effective communication rests with the speaker. Frequently, communication does not occur because listeners do not use effective listening skills. Some practical guides for effective listening include:

    1. Give team members full attention. Do not **pretend** to be listening.
    2. Do not interrupt team members or finish their statements. Be patient and give them full courtesy before offering comments and questions.
    3. Listen not only to team members' words, but also to the context in which the words are being said, and thus to their implied meanings.
    4. Put team members at ease and encourage them by looking at them, smiling, and nodding. There is plenty of time for discussion after they have finished.
    5. Ask questions or ask team members to restate their ideas after their presentation if any issues remain unclear to you.
    6. Do not distract team members. Avoid working on other material or reading the newspaper while they are speaking, regardless of how uninterested you are.
    7. Fully consider and listen to ideas with which you disagree. Make sure you understand what is being said. Too often individuals fail to listen to a complete idea when they judge early in a presentation that it is wrong or simple. You do not always know where a speaker is heading.
    8. Do not become so focused on your own response to members' ideas that you think about what you are going to say while they are speaking. If you do, you will probably miss most of what they have to say.

Both speaking and listening are important for effective communication and team interaction.

Learning to admit error. Many of us do not like to admit error. Those of us who are insecure often perceive such an admission as a challenge to our self-esteem. Others may view it as a loss of status or power. Regardless, very little good is ever achieved by arguing for an idea we know is wrong. Such arguments usually waste precious team time, wear down the patience of other team members, and eventually make the person arguing look foolish. When members of teams concede they are wrong (if they actually are), they usually gain greater team respect and are taken more seriously on other issues. The costs of admitting to being wrong in this situation are usually very low. It is doubtful that student members will use this admission in any way to hurt other members.

Handling ego challenges. A team member may be faced periodically with an ego challenge from another member. An ego challenge is the point at which **winning** an argument becomes more important than the issue or idea being argued. The member being challenged can choose to fight the battle or peacefully and respectfully withdraw. Carefully consider what is at stake for both members and the implications of doing battle. If the conflict is with an insecure and aggressive person who refuses to admit mistakes, then the battle could be prolonged and fruitless. If the disagreement is with someone who up to this point has been reasonable, then getting that person to focus on the idea may help eliminate the "ego" issue and resolve the argument.

In resolving ego challenges, it is necessary to allow the other member to exit from the argument gracefully and save face. This outcome can be achieved by conceding to the other member's views or by finding a compromise or integrative solution. Remember, during ego challenges the psychology of the argument itself becomes more important than the ideas being argued.

MANAGING TEAM PROBLEMS

The third major skill is managing team problems. Here, the focus is entirely on the team rather than the individuals within it. Major subskills in this area include the following:

- Involving members in discussions
- Managing "talkers"
- Protecting the weak and providing support
- Checking the meaning of silence
- Dealing with conflict
- Avoiding cliques.

Involving members in discussions. It is every member's responsibility to encourage everyone to participate. Too often teams are dominated by a few individuals who like to talk or who think they have all the answers. There is not always a strong relationship between knowledge and time spent speaking. Try to understand that not all members are comfortable voicing their opinions. As noted previously, some members are passive and insecure and are afraid to say anything. These individuals may be the ones, however, who have the knowledge or information needed to solve a case or prepare a report. A team's ability and desire to encourage all members to speak and to give each individual ample opportunity to do so will determine in large measure whether all team members participate.

Managing "talkers". When a few individuals with limited knowledge control the discussion, the team suffers. If the team fails to establish norms of equitable participation at the group's inception, it becomes difficult to control garrulous individuals or talkers. However, the team can use some management techniques. First, "talkers" may not realize that they are dominating discussions. Sometimes they are enthusiastic people with many ideas they want to share. Speaking privately to these individuals before a meeting might help. You can point out to them that some shy but knowledgeable members do not always get a chance to participate. Try to encourage "talkers" to solicit other members' opinions during meetings.

Convincing "talkers" who think that they know everything to share meeting time may be more difficult. Attempt to explain to them the points raised in the preceding paragraph. If this approach fails, try a round-robin technique to involve everyone and possibly limit and control the amount of time available for each member's contribution (see Chapter 6).

The final and most drastic solution for handling "talkers" is to censure them and consider limiting or dropping them from team discussions. Although this is not the most desirable solution, it may be necessary for maintaining the integrity of the team.

Providing support. Encouraging insecure and passive members to contribute to discussions can be instrumental to team effectiveness. Try to create an atmosphere in which these members do not feel afraid to contribute. Make it clear to them that their viewpoints and contributions are welcome and needed. Although some "stronger" members may view this approach as unnecessary handholding, you can explain to them that these quieter members are also a vital part of the team and have useful knowledge. Nothing will be accomplished by ignoring team members. These actions will neither change their personalities nor make them "tougher." Ignoring them will serve only to reduce the total number of members available to contribute.

If weak members who have good points are attacked during discussions, come to their aid. Try to defend their points of view and provide support. You do not want to create a battle in this situation, but you do want to demonstrate that all members, strong or weak, have a right to voice their views and not be steamrolled. If there are legitimate disagreements with any member's points, express them in a constructive manner. Disagreements can be voiced without attacking. Responding with "You have an interesting point, but I disagree," is more supportive than responding with "That's a really lousy idea." Think how members feel when leaving a discussion in which they have been attacked, and what their attitude will be toward contributing to the team in the future.

Checking the meaning of silence. Silence plays an important role during team meetings. However, it is not always clear exactly what that role is. How many times have you been involved in team discussions, made a point, expected a response and the other team members sat there in silence? Did you wonder what that meant, or did you interpret it as indicating that members agreed with you? Care has to be taken in interpreting silence because it can mean different things. Possible meanings include the following:

- Agreement
- Lack of understanding
- Lack of interest
- Disagreement
- Fear of responding.

Making the right interpretation is important, since it will determine how you should react and respond.

When silence exists, analyze it rather than assume its meaning. Ask members why they are silent or what the silence means. Some very simple probing may clarify this issue and serve to eliminate any misperceptions and misunderstandings among members. Also, do not assume that silence means the same thing for all members and at all meetings. Frequently different members will use it to convey different messages.

Dealing with conflict. Sometimes silence and related phenomena indicate conflict. As our discussion of devil's advocacy in Chapter 6 demonstrates, conflict can be very useful in evaluating and choosing high-quality assumptions and recommendations. However, conflict also has a destructive side. When conflict is left unmanaged, it frequently results in petty arguments or in-fighting among team members. Too often what begins as legitimate disagreements over ideas escalates into personal attacks. If disagreements become heated, team members should attempt to de-escalate the conflict by dropping the discussion and allowing a "cooling off" period. Emotionally-charged arguments rarely accomplish anything constructive. If conflict shifts from arguments over ideas to personal attacks, attempts should be made to refocus the discussion. It is inevitable that when participants in an argument use critical statements such as "You don't know what you are saying" rather than "I disagree with that idea," the potential for destructive conflict intensifies. Remember, keep the argument focused on ideas, not personalities.

When involved in arguments, it is helpful not to take comments personally. Individuals involved in heated arguments frequently make emotionally-charged statements that are not really directed at anyone in particular, and they usually regret them afterwards. Having a "thick skin" and avoiding becoming defensive can avert or minimize destructive conflict.

Avoiding cliques. Finally, you should be sensitive to the formation of cliques or informal subgroups within the team. Cliques can easily destroy cohesiveness and disrupt the ability of team members to work together toward common goals, especially if the cliques become adversarial and uncooperative.

Teams can remain productive if cliques do not interfere with the exchange of information and communication among members. When cliques interfere with these activities, the benefits of having teams and pooling multiple resources are eliminated. Cliques should be avoided when possible. Try to work and interact with all team members to maximize personal learning and productive team outputs.

In summary, it is important that you learn how to assume individual responsibility, interact effectively with team members, and manage team problems. Admittedly you will still run into problems that neither you nor your other team members can solve completely. Still, possessing these three major skills -- and the many subskills related to them -- will greatly increase your own effectiveness and that of your team.

TIPS TO REMEMBER

7.1   Assume responsibility for managing personal time and commitments.

7.2   Avoid time traps and prioritize responsibilities.

7.3   Negotiate equitable solutions with other team members when team deadlines and meetings conflict with personal commitments.

7.4   Contribute high-quality work on all team projects.

7.5   Avoid dominating or withdrawing from team discussions.

7.6   Ensure that other members understand what you are saying and that you understand what they are saying.

7.7   Admit to being wrong when you realize an error.

7.8   Keep disagreements focused on issues rather than personalities.

7.9   Involve all team members in discussions.

7.10   Check the meaning of silence when it occurs.

7.11   Avoid creating destructive cliques.

ACTION EXERCISES

7.1   This exercise helps to identify your major responsibilities and determines whether sufficient time is being allocated to them. On form 1 below, list your major responsibilities. Include those related to work, school, family, and your strategic management team. Beside each responsibility, indicate the percentage of time you allocate to it and the amount of time you think you should. In assessing time that you should allocate, consider how these responsibilities fit with both your short- and long-term goals.

    After you complete Form 1, list your major responsibilities on Form 2. Next to each responsibility, list the steps that you are willing to take to adjust your allocation of time and the dates by which you hope to carry them out.

Form 1 - Major Responsibilities

Responsibilities	Percentage of Time Spent	Percentage of Time That Should be Spent
1. Team projects		
2.		
3.		
4.		

Form 2 - Responsibility Action Steps

Major Responsibility	Corrective Step	Date of Action

----

1.   1.

2.

3.

4.

2.   1.

2.

3.

4.

3.   1.

2.

3.

4.

4.   1.

2.

3.

4.

5.   1.

2.

3.

4.

7.2   This exercise provides an opportunity to learn about team interactions. Observe any team that will allow you to do so. **Do not** participate in the team activities. While observing, answer the following questions.

1. Were all members of the team encouraged to participate?

2. How were they encouraged to do so?

3. How were disagreements resolved?

4. How were "talkers" dealt with?

5. Was there any evidence of cliques forming?

Identify those activities that either facilitated or inhibited the team from interacting effectively. What changes would you make to eliminate negative activities and why?

SUGGESTED READINGS

7.1   Hall, J., Communication Revised. *California Management Review*. 15,
       pp. 56-67, 1973.
              This article focuses on interpersonal style and the communication process.
       Particular focus is given to the Johari Window, a technique used for assessing
       interpersonal relationships and the communication process.

7.2   MacKenzie, R. A., *The Time Trap*. New York: McGraw-Hill, 1972.
              This book provides a complete discussion of time traps encountered in
       organizations and solutions for eliminating them.

7.3   Rogers, C. R., and Farson, R. E., Active listening. In D. A. Kolb, I. M. Rubin,
       and J. A.McIntyre (Eds.), *Organizational Psychology: Readings on Human
       Behavior in Organizations*. Englewood Cliffs, NJ: Prentice Hall, 1984.
              This article provides an overview of active listening and discusses how to
       listen and problems encountered in listening.

Chapter 8

Writing Strategic Management Reports

MAJOR SKILLS

- ORGANIZING YOUR REPORT
- DEVELOPING A WRITTEN ARGUMENT
- WRITING PERSUASIVELY
- USING FIGURES AND TABLES
- DRAFTING YOUR REPORT
- USING A RATING FORM

You have spent many hours, possibly weeks, working on your analysis. You may have collected data from various secondary sources, interviewed managers in the company or industry you have chosen to study, and you have constantly categorized the information. In fact, you may have spent too much time on such activities, particularly if you short change yourself by writing your final report in a hurried manner. Thus, in writing your report, the first skill you must master is managing your time so you have a sufficient amount of it to produce a thoughtful, well-researched, and well-written report.

This chapter discusses six skills that can help you write a high quality report. Remember, the ability to write clearly and persuasively is directly related to your effectiveness and success as a manager. These six skills are directly transferable to the actual world of managerial work.

ORGANIZING YOUR REPORT

There are basically two types of reports generated in a strategic management or business policy course: a stategic analysis and plan and an industry analysis. Sometimes, an instructor will require each student to complete a separate report, although generally a team of three to five students must work together on a case or industry analysis. Whether you write the report alone or with a group, the method of organizing the final report is essentially the same.

Writing a case analysis. Appendix 8.1 contains a sample table of contents for a case analysis and plan report, annotated with examples drawn from the Levi Strauss and Co. case (see Part 2). Let us assume that the instructor wants a lengthy report of 15 or 20 pages or more. In this instance, the written report should contain an exective summary and a table of contents with page numbers for the five capitalized headings shown in Appendix 8.1. All of the headings and subheadings provided in Appendix 8.1 are typically used in a case report. They logically show how the plan and final recommendations were derived. For example, the Strategic Profile discusses the performance of a firm, the firm's culture, and the firm's current mission and strategic thrust. This section of the report is logically followed by an Internal Analysis describing key organizational capabilities and comparing these to critical organizational abilities that are required for success. The purpose of this section is to identify gaps that must be closed.

A lengthy report should also contain an Executive Summary, generally no more than one single-spaced page. That summary should include major elements of your strategic plan and specific recommendations. Space permitting, the executive summary should also include the major idea or ideas found in each of the capitalized headings in Appendix 8.1.

Sometimes, your instructor will ask you to provide a shortened case analysis of only seven to ten pages. In this instance, an executive summary is unnecessary. Your goal is to expand the descriptions provided in Appendix 8.1. Even in a brief report, however, it is important to use full sentences and other techniques described here in order to ensure that your meaning is clear.

Writing an industry analysis. Your instructor may also assign an individual student or a team of students to complete an industry analysis. Such an analysis usually includes a definition of the industry and a description of its product lines, selling and marketing techniques, and competition. A forecast of the industry's future is then made. See Appendix 8.2, which is an outline of an industry analysis of the electronic component distribution industry

The extended industry analysis (as well as the extended case analysis) should include a number of figures and tables, called exhibits. For example, our sample industry analysis in Appendix 8.2 would include nine exhibits.

Admittedly there are many variations that could be used to structure your final report. However, Appendixes 8.1 and 8.2 reflect in a sequential and logical fashion the major issues that need to be addressed. You may vary the structure of your report when you are unable to include important issues within the headings and subheadings described or when your instructor provides you with alternative suggestions.

Further, it is important for you to determine your primary reader and try to anticipate his or her ideas, biases, and points of view. Generally, the primary reader will be your instructor. In some instances, however, graduate students or business executives may also grade your report.

Finally, organizing your report is a two-step process: grouping similar ideas together and ordering the groups logically. You may well be overwhelmed by the amount of information that you must synthesize and condense in order to make your final report logical and persuasive. Hence, you may want to write ideas, key data, and related information on 5-by-8 cards as you read the material necessary to complete your report. You can then categorize these cards by the major headings and subheadings found in Appendixes 8.1 and 8.2, and rearrange them as necessary. This process will help you complete both steps of the organizing process effectively.

DEVELOPING A WRITTEN ARGUMENT

Thus far we have described the structure that you should use in your report. However, the structure is merely a hollow shell if it is not fleshed out with logical and persuasive arguments. In order to accomplish this objective, you must spend a considerable amount of time applying the skills described in previous chapters, especially Chapters 2-5.

It is essential that you become intimately familiar with the firm and/or the industry of which it is a part. In fact, analyzing the firm and/or industry generally will be the most difficult part of your project. For the case analysis, examine the firm's financial ratios, its profit margins, rates of return, and its capital structure. You should also examine marketing, production, and related issues, including managerial competence. You must complete similar (but, of course, somewhat different) analyses for an industry analysis.

We assume here that you possess the functional knowledge in marketing, accounting, finance, and management necessary to complete a case or industry analysis effectively. If you are working with a team, the group should attempt to match assignments and the strengths of members; for example, students majoring in marketing should examine the product life cycle (see Chapter 6). If you feel that your functional knowledge is deficient or that you have forgotten some key information, first review a basic textbook in that area of expertise before attempting to complete the analysis.

Once the analysis has been completed, you can start to write your portion of the paper. Begin to develop an argument supporting your conclusions and the overall conclusions in the final report. One simple way to do that is to list the reasons supporting your recommendation and then refute or rebut any opposing reasons or objections.

Similarly, you can develop an argument effectively if you avoid jumping to conclusions by recognizing the difference between a fact and a "non-fact". Such non-facts include inferences, opinions expressed by you and others, your value judgment, and so forth. Along the same line, when you make an assertion, indicate the inference you expect the reader to draw from it. For example, since Apple Computer exists in a highly volatile industry, you should state clearly that you expect this firm to experience some difficulties purely because of the nature of the industry. Also avoid the following:

- *Overgeneralizing.* Don't say "all companies" when you really mean "some companies" or "most companies."
- *Faulty causation.* Building more plants does not necessarily mean that a firm will sell more of its products.
- *Exaggerated significance.* Some commentators have expressed the unquestioned belief that Steve Jobs' departure from Apple Computer will automatically lead to this company's ruination.
- *An overly-simplified model of causation.* Don't include only two or three explanatory factors to interpret a particular company's situation when, in fact, many more factors are influential.
- *Historical bias.* It is important to note that a company has been successful in the past, but remember that this fact alone does not guarantee its success in the future.

Now you are ready to make recommendations and develop goals and plans. Through logical reasoning and evaluation, identify the recommendation with the least risk and/or the greatest potential reward. You must be able to argue that the recommended actions solve the problem (or threat); build upon opportunities; optimize profits and costs; and are feasible, given existing functional relationships among top-level managers and the availablity of resources. Your conclusions and recommendations should follow directly from your analysis. That is why we have emphasized the importance of structuring your report in the manner described in Appendixes 8.1 and 8.2. In other words, your conclusions and recommendations should be supported by analysis and reasoning, for without such support your written report will not be very persuasive.

WRITING PERSUASIVELY

Your overall objective is to convince the reader that your team has completed a thorough analysis and that your recommendations are logically consistent, creative, and forceful or persuasive. Hence you want to write persuasively. Sometimes an excellent analysis is seriously down-graded because the writer does such a poor job of persuading the reader that the recommended course of action is appropriate.

If you have drafted your report following the suggested formats or variants of them, looked for structural faults, and developed transitions, you have already begun to write persuasively.

A very persuasive way of writing is to use the active rather than the passive voice for verbs. An active verb (action word) tends to be preceded by a noun; for example, "Our team suggests that this firm do the following...." A passive verb is one that is preceded by a form of the verb "to be." For example, "It was suggested by our team that this firm do the following...." Many times, the passive voice obscures meanings. For example, if "by our team" is inadvertently dropped from the preceding sentence, it may well be hypothesized that the individuals making the suggestion know little if anything about the firm. Also, it is much more difficult to read sentences in the passive voice simply because the pace or tempo of the narrative is slow and uneven. Thus using the active voice helps you to say what you mean, a key ingredient of persuasive writing.

Another effective technique is to use examples that enliven your writing and add specificity to the analysis. It is also helpful to elaborate on the unusual if it is of major significance either in the analysis section of the report or in your set of recommendations. Highlighting the unusual makes it easier for the reader to remember your major points.

Try to avoid the following common errors:

- *Acronyms and abbreviations.* The full title of any organization should be spelled out the first time it is used, with the acronym or abbreviation placed in parentheses immediately after it.
- *Sexist language and ethnic or racial slurs.*
- *Misspellings.* (The reader will believe that you are a careless person if there are too many of them.)
- *Jargon, vogue words, and journalese.*
- *Unnecessary or redundant words, adjectives, and sentences.*

All of these common errors reflect directly and unfavorably upon the writer. They can be avoided easily if you spend even a small amount of time focusing on them. In contrast, you **should** use the following:

- Simple words and phrases
- Short and familiar words (whenever possible)
- Short sentences and paragraphs.

In addition, you should arrange issues or ideas from the most important to the least important, as the reader tends to assume that the first ideas are the most important ones. Similarly, you should tend to arrange your recommendations from the least controversial to the most controversial, as the reader is more likely to accept the more controversial recommendations after already accepting the less controversial ones. Additionally, make sure your recommendations are logically related to one another, even though the most important ones are presented first.

Finally, we must return to the issue of structuring your final report. Today many people speed-read, and they tend to read only the first or last sentence in a paragraph. Hence you should put your main idea in the first or topic sentence, or in the last sentence if necessary. Similarly, you should start each section of the report with a topic paragraph; it indicates what is in the section and how it will be presented. Through such techniques, you can persuade readers that your arguments and recommendations are logical and valid.

USING TABLES AND FIGURES

As you begin to develop your arguments, identify tables and figures that will help to support them. When constructing your exhibits use the following guidelines:

- Make one major point in each exhibit.
- Keep the exhibit as simple as possible, but provide enough information for the reader to feel confident in your analysis.
- Eliminate any information the reader does not need. Round off numbers, shorten exhibit headings, and so forth.
- Make the exhibit self-contained so that the reader can draw his or her own conclusions, but tie it directly into the text by describing the main point or points that it is designed to illustrate.
- Make sure any scale you use is appropriate. For example, the scale distance between 1 and 9 should be equal to that between 10 and 19.
- Use the heading to tell the reader why the exhibit is important, for example, "Dollar Sales from 1975 to 1985 -- New record in 1985 topping $2 million."

Frequently a table will contain a large number of figures and percentages. This may be unavoidable. However, if you can express that data more simply, you will minimize the risk of misinterpretation. Attempt to use simple figures such as a bar chart or trend line. They may make your point more clearly than a list of numbers. Although tables imply relationships, they do not clearly show them, particularly growth or decline relationships. For example, sales may have increased in 8 of 10 years from 1975 to 1985, but a reader may choose to focus on the two discrepant years. Presenting a trend line for 1975 to 1985 will demonstrate clearly that growth is positive.

The following guidelines can help you decide when to use various types of figures (See Figure 8.1).

- **Use** a pie chart when you want to show the relative size of components of a whole.
- **Use** a bar chart when you are showing parts a whole and or comparing several wholes and their parts.
- **Use** a bar chart when you want to compare or rank several items in one time period.
- **Use** a step chart (a vertical bar chart with columns connected) to show change over time in one or several variables.
- **Use** a line chart when you are relating changes in one item over time or comparing two items over time.
- **Use** a dot chart when you are showing the relationship between variables such as income and research investments. You should draw a line through the dots to show the pattern.

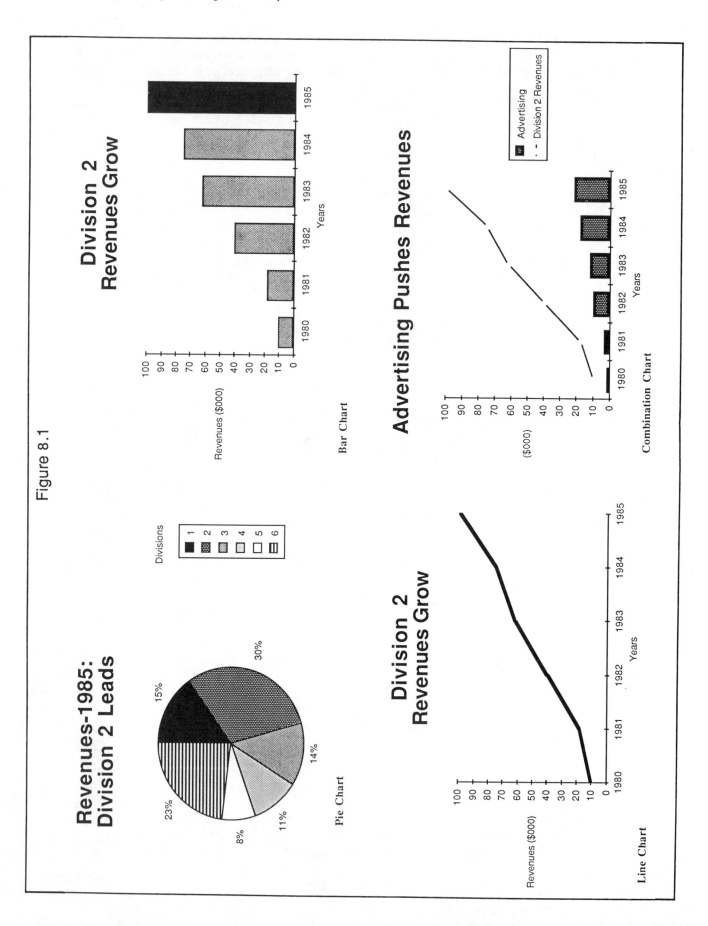

Figure 8.1

DRAFTING YOUR REPORT

Let us assume that you and your team have spent countless hours analyzing data related to a company or industry, and that you feel comfortable with the material. If you have followed the guidelines discussed in the previous section of this chapter, drafting your report should be relatively easy. However, as noted previously, it is important that you leave sufficient time to draft the report. Avoid working under the constraint of short deadlines, if possible. Try to determine right at the start approximately how much time it will take to draft and finalize the report. Excellent and exhaustive analyses are often ruined because the team does not have a sufficient amount of time to write effectively. When time is short, it's easy to omit information or make spelling mistakes.

Your draft should follow the outlines, or variants of them, shown in Appendixxes 8.1 and 8.2. If you have difficulty writing, or tend to procrastinate, use the "Swiss cheese" approach of beginning to work immediately, telling yourself that you will make little dents in the final product. Frequently you will continue to write after having made one or a few dents. Confidence in your analyses will strengthen your resolve, and enable you to finish a solid and respectable draft of the final report without too much difficulty.

If possible, do not revise the draft for at least one day. If you are under deadline pressure, overnight will be sufficient. Alternatively, someone else on a team may be assigned the task of rewriting your draft. If you are working alone on a report or industry analysis, it is helpful to have a devil's advocate comment critically on it before putting it into final form (see chapter 6). Usually such an advocate is a friend, and so you should strongly encourage the person to be as critical as possible. The natural tendency is to withhold criticism, which is of little, if any, value to you. The objective is to have a "fresh eye" critically examine and rearrange the material.

It is possible to speed up the writing process by using a word processor. It allows all team members to make changes without unduly burdening the typist.

Revising the draft is a two-step process:

- Reviewing for structural or organizational faults
- Correcting language.

We have already discussed the issue of using appropriate language and making corrections. Reviewing for structural faults should answer the following questions:

√   Can you quickly identify the major point or points in the report?
√   Is the organization of the paper logical?
√   Is the reader motivated rather than forced to continue reading the report to the end?
√   Are the paragraphs well-organized?
√   Do the transitions make easier reading?

Transitions are particularly important, as they help the reader see the connections between the arguments you develop. One rule is to use transition words at the beginning of paragraphs -- and sentences -- if they are related to one another. Such connective transition words are: In addition, further, similarly, furthermore, concomitantly, also, hence, thus, in consequence, consequently, then, and so forth.

You can also employ disconnective transition words if the paragraphs -- and even the sentences within paragraphs -- stand in marked contrast to one another or are unrelated. Some disconnective transition words are: In comparison, in contrast, however, but, still, and so forth.

The final section of a report often includes recommendations. Transition words such as "in summary" or "succinctly" appear in this section. The transition to summary recommendations should follow from the development of arguments that you identified through the use of connective and disconnective transition words throughout the report.

Further, make sure the headings and subheadings you use are as consistent as possible. You may want to review the sample headings and subheadings in Appendixes 8.1 and 8.2. Headings and subheadings should:

- Stand alone, that is, be understood by themselves
- Be parallel, that is, use the same format and express items of equal importance or that logically unfold in the report
- Create expectations so that the reader will want to continue reading your report.

If you would like to consider an alternative format to the headings in Appendixes 8.1 and 8.2, you could employ the pattern found in many articles and textbooks. Major "A" headings are capitalized, underlined, and centered above the text paragraphs. "B" subheadings are flush with the left margin, underlined, above the text, and with the first letter of each word capitalized. The third level, "C" subheadings, are underlined and indented, with the first letter of each word capitalized. They are placed on the same line as the paragraph, which continues immediately after the period separating the subheading from the text.

USING A RATING FORM

Many instructors use a rating form to evaluate your final report. Figure 8.2 is a sample rating form that allows you to evaluate your report. There are naturally many variations of such forms, but the intent here is to emphasize the skills we have highlighted in this and previous chapters.

Figure 8.2

WRITTEN PRESENTATION RATING FORM

Writing Style

Audience	vague				clear
Active voice	rarely				usually
Jargon	rarely				usually
Topic sentences	vague				clear
Examples	weak				strong
Transitions	weak				strong

Presentation Content

Argumentation	weak				strong
Persuasion	weak				strong
Analysis	weak				strong
Organization	weak				strong
Tables & Figures	weak				strong

Presentor _____

TIPS TO REMEMBER

8.1   Leave sufficient time to write the report.

8.2   Understand the biases and viewpoints of your primary reader.

8.3   Have at least one member of the team -- or, if working alone, someone other than the writer -- read the report and serve as a devil's advocate.

8.4   Use 5 by 8 cards to collect information and arrange it in the various parts of the report.

8.5   Make the exhibits clear and simple. Use the proper type of exhibit to demonstrate different types of relationships.

8.6   Use the "Swiss Cheese" method to begin writing the draft report. Start immediately and try to bite off small pieces.

8.7   Write clearly but persuasively, emphasizing the use of transition words, examples, and active verbs.

ACTION EXERCISE

8.1   Before you hand in your final report, ask the instructor or someone else to grade your draft using the rating form in Figure 8.2 or a similar rating form. Use this form to grade yourself. Then compare the instructor's ratings on the various aspects of this form to the ratings you assigned yourself.

SUGGESTED READINGS

8.1   Holcombe, M., and Stein, J., *Writing for Decision Makers*. Belmont, CA: Lifetime Learning Publications, 1981.
        This book clearly summarizes the various issues confronting anyone preparing a report that will be used as an input to managerial decision making. The emphasis is upon the preparation of a report that can be easily understood by managers who must make a decision.

8.2   Shurter, R., Williamson, J. P., and Broehl, W., *Business Research and Report Writing*. New York: McGraw-Hill, 1965.
        A classic treatment of business research and report writing, this book addresses such topics as the principles that should be followed when writing and the techniques for identifying and satisfying the primary readers.

8.3   Strunk, W., and White, E.B., *The Element of Style*. New York: Macmillan, 1978.
        Another classic, this book is an excellent but short introduction to the elements of style and what it takes to write effectively.

8.4   Zall, P., and Franc, L., *Practical Writing in Business and Industry*. North Scituate, MA: Duxbury Press, 1978.
        This book takes a nuts-and-bolts approach to busines writing, focusing not only on the long report but also on the business letter and short memorandum.

APPENDIX 8.1

Outline for Levi Strauss & Co. Strategic Analysis and Plan - 1981

I.   Executive Summary

II.   Strategic Profile

    A. *Assessment of Company Performance and Success.* Outstanding.

    B. *Cause of Performance and Success.* Levi Strauss and Co. has achieved its success by being very responsive to customer needs and by aggressively seeking diversification.

    C. *Structure.* Levi Strauss and Co. is a multinational conglomerate with largely autonomous profit centers.

    D. *Mission.* Provide people high-quality clothing products.

    E. *Goals.* Levi Strauss seems to be pursuing two main goals: 10% rate of growth and diversifying in clothing related businesses.

    F. *Strategic Thrust.* Levi Strauss and Co. can be described as an aggressively diversified market leader in the production of a wide variety of clothing and fashion products.

    G. *Strategic Actions.* Levi Strauss is: (1) emphasizing the sale of women's ware and activeware products; (2) providing clothing products for all ages through continued diversification.

III. Internal Analysis

    A. *Key Organizational Capabilities.* Levi Strauss and Co. operates efficient production facilities and possesses the ability to withstand economic downturns because of diversification.

    B. *Assessment of Organizational Abilities.* This section analyzes the gap between actual and needed capabilities, e.g., Levi needs a large number of seasoned executives if it is to expand.

IV.   Environmental Analysis

    A. *Strategic Forecast.* This section is a brief strategic forecast. Levi Strauss must be concerned about the aging of the population and increased competition from low-cost importers.

    B. *Opportunities* (Timing, Likelihood). What opportunities exist in the external environment, how likely are these opportunities, and how long will it take before these opportunities can be realized? E.g., Levi Strauss and Co. clearly sees that a demand exists for leisure wear (short-term timing and highly likely).

    C. *Threats* (Timing, and Likelihood). The analysis is similar to that for opportunities, e.g., Levi Strauss and Co. faces increased competition from imports and declining margins (medium term and highly likely).

    D. *Relative Significance of Opportunities and Threats.* This section should discuss opportunities -- and then threats -- in sequential order, listing the most important ones first. Thus Levi Strauss and Co.'s most significant opportunity seems to be foreign markets.

V.   Recommended Strategic Plan

    A. *Mission and Objectives.* No change.
    B. *Performance Targets.* Specific performance targets that Levi
        Strauss should achieve in such areas as net sales and net income.
    C. *Strategic Thrust.* Levi Strauss should emphasize the strategy
        of continued diversification and should aggressively defend
        market share in each of its respective markets.
    D. *Strategic Actions.* Major actions during planning horizon organized
        by major product lines.
    E. *Implementation Issues.* Include organization design issues.
    F. *Resource Allocations.*

VI.   Summary

    Levi Strauss and Co. has a dominant market position in a highly competitive market. It should continue to avoid far-flung diversification and commit its internally generated capital to what it knows best: clothes. Levi Strauss must keep its production costs low by seeking geographic locations with an abundant supply of workers and a favorable industrial relations climate, and by adopting the latest production technology. Finally, Levi Strauss and Co. should ensure that growth proceeds smoothly by expanding its number of line and staff personnel so that effective control of operations is maintained.

VII.   Appendixes -- including pro forma financial statements.

APPENDIX 8.2

Outline of Electronic Components Industry Analysis

I. Definition of the Industry

Companies in this industry distribute semiconductors, connectors, and other electronic parts purchased from component manufacturers to a wide range of commercial and industrial customers in the U.S. and overseas.

II. Functions Performed by Distributors

A. Hold and manage inventories.
B. Hold and manage accounts receivable.
C. Provide fast service in meeting orders.
D. Servicing of small orders. The typical distributor has an average order size in the range of $150 to $250.

III. Product Lines

A. Active components: components having a specific effect on the electrical component passing through them. They are :
1. Vacuum tubes, 2. transistors, 3. integrated circuits, 4. large-scale integrated circuits, 5. microprocessors.
B. Passive components: components influencing the behavior of active components, for example, connectors. Major types are easy to produce, have been on a technical plateau for many years, and are "off-the-shelf" items.
C. Product life cycle analysis.

IV. Customer Profile

Customers tend to be diverse and knowledgeable. Three buyer groups:

A. Large professionally managed companies with purchasing department.
B. Medium-size firms without an independent purchasing department.
C. Small companies.

V. Selling and Marketing

A. Distributor operations. Few economies of scale seem to be possible, since the bulk of the distributors' order-processing functions are handled by clerical-level personnel and many of the orders are small, averaging $150 to $250.
B. Distributor-Supplier Relations. Tend to be poor in the active-components' sector of the industry, as many buyers are individuals trained as scientists and not managers. Interview data indicated that distributors felt that they are treated as necessary evils. The opposite situation exists in the passive-components' sector.

VI.   Competition

This industry consists of a few national firms in addition to hundreds of small companies serving narrow regionalized markets based on personal business contacts.

VII.   Competitive Strategies

A range of competitive strategies has been adopted by firms in this industry. Jaco Electronics carried a limited product line consisting almost entirely of passive components. Cramer Electronics, the second largest component distributor in the U.S., serviced all segments of the market.

VIII.   Recent Recession Experience

A. Distributors believed the 1974-75 recession had run its course, and a sales increase of 15% or more was predicted.
B. Distributors were concerned about the large number of newly franchised entrants into their market that had been spawned by the recession.

IX.   Future Outlook

A. Availability of capital. Interest rates are projected to be high for a number of years, so the industry must generate its own capital if it is to expand.
B. Supplier integration. Some buyers such as Texas Instruments have begun to move toward a system of company-owned and operated distribution centers.
C. Services. Distributors want to provide more services, particularly in the area of microprocessing.
D. Management infrastructures. There is a movement toward developing modern computerized management information systems.
E. Effects of foreign competition. The Japanese are planning to compete directly with American firms, particularly in microprocessing.

X.   Exhibits

Nine figures and tables describing such relationships as sales projections over time, a profile of the top 25 distributors, and so forth.

You can read about this industry in 1976 in Michael Porter's book *Cases in Competitive Strategy,* in "A Note on the Electronic Component Industry" (see Suggested Reading 2.2). This outline is derived from that industry analysis.

Chapter 9

Making a Formal Oral Presentation

MAJOR SKILLS

- ORGANIZING THE PRESENTATION
- MANAGING PRESENTATION STRESS
- CONTROLLING YOUR VOICE
- CONTROLLING GESTURES
- SPEAKING FROM NOTES
- PERSUADING YOU AUDIENCE
- CONSTRUCTING VISUAL AIDS
- USING VISUAL AIDS
- RESPONDING TO QUESTIONS
- USING A RATING FORM

Customarily, managers submit a written report before making a formal oral presentation, although sometimes the oral presentation is given prior to completing the written report. Whatever the procedure, you should treat a formal oral presentation as a separate major task, since its success hinges upon the use of a distinctive set of skills. Your mastery of speaking and formal oral-presentation skills will influence your effectiveness as a manager and your career success.

Although this chapter focuses on team oral presentations, you may be asked to "go solo" and make an individual presentation. Whatever the presentation format and speaking assignment, the following skills are appropriate - in fact necessary - for most types of oral business presentations. For purposes of simplicity and clarity, we limit our discussion to a popular approach, the team presentation.

ORGANIZING THE PRESENTATION

Most teams try to allocate speaking time equally among members. Sometimes the most skilled speakers are given additional time for their presentations. The role of the first speaker is critical, as he or she sets the stage for what is to come. Hence this speaker should describe the objectives that the team is seeking to accomplish in its presentation, why these objectives are important, how the argument will be developed, and what the general conclusions and recommendations will be. This speaker should also introduce the other members of the team, identify what each of them will discuss, describe the purpose of various analyses, and show how all of the presentations are related.

Sometimes, the first speaker will also serve as the last speaker. This approach can provide continuity and can be an effective way to organize the presentation. If the time allocated for the presentation is limited, then this approach may result in too much rapidity in the changing of speakers. Also, if the first speaker is to play such a major role, then that should be noted initially. Speakers need to provide a clear roadmap. The rule is **no surprises**.

The middle speaker or speakers will present the detailed parts of the analysis. These speakers should be allocated meaningful and distinct topics to present. They are providing the foundation for the final persuasive speech. The final speaker will present major conclusions, recommendations, and a systematic summary of the entire presentation.

It is important that each member of the team speak approximately the same length of time. Otherwise the audience and instructor may downgrade the team's performance because only one or two of the speakers dominated the presentation. To plan time allocations and the content of individual presentations, each speaker should talk through his or her assigned part of the presentation. Then 10 percent more time should be added to the final figure for changing speakers, manipulating visuals, and dealing with the usual interruptions.

Finally, on the day of the presentation, some physical organization of the presentation setting is usually required. Team members should have planned in advance what arrangement of chairs, flip charts, etc. will best suit their needs. Team members should arrive at least 10 minutes before the scheduled presentation time to set up visuals, rearrange chairs, make sure that the visuals can be seen by all, and handle any last-minute details without becoming frazzled.

MANAGING PRESENTATION STRESS

It is quite typical for students to be nervous before and during an oral presentation. A certain amount of nervousness is to be expected, and it may even be helpful. However, too much stress creates problems, and so you should learn to manage it.

There are three steps in managing presentation stress: psychological preparation, mechanical preparation, and physical action. Psychologically, you can desensitize yourself by mentally visualizing the presentation. Fantasize that you have made the presentation effectively. Convince yourself about the importance of the subject and how well-prepared you are. In addition, try to shift the focus from yourself to the audience by responding very positively to the following types of questions:

√ Isn't the audience lucky to be here, listening to me address an
   important topic about which they are very concerned?
√ Do members of the audience really understand the material and its
   importance? Maybe I'd better patiently explain it to them.

Mechanical preparation focuses specifically on rehearsing. Know your material, how to deliver it, and how to use visuals effectively. Rehearse until you feel comfortable with the material. Usually, three rehearsals are more than adequate for a formal presentation: once by yourself in front of a mirror, once with the team, and once with the team in front of observers, preferably in the room where the presentation will be made.

Physical action refers to such activities as jogging or swimming a few hours before the presentation. Don't drink coffee or other stimulants. Before going to the podium, take two or three deep breaths and wet your lips. Arranging the presentation setting so that you walk a few steps to the podium helps. If a stress attack should strike you when you are presenting, move around, get a drink of water, walk to a visual aid and look at it, or otherwise distract the audience until you regain your composure.

If you feel very unsure of yourself, use complete notes for the first two minutes of the presentation. Then discuss a figure or table for the second two minutes. By this time, you should feel relaxed enough to proceed naturally, glancing occasionally at your outline but consistently establishing contact with the audience.

CONTROLLING YOUR VOICE

Even if you are able to manage stress effectively, your presentation may be less than optimal if you cannot control your voice and its pitch effectively. Many people tend to speak too fast and with a high pitch. Some people are also careless in articulating and projecting words: sounds are imprecise or garbled, and vowels are distorted. Some individuals possess a soft voice and/or speak in a monotone. A high-pitched individual who speaks too fast, too softly, and does not articulate and project words is usually viewed as very ineffective.

Fortunately it is possible to use specific skills to overcome these problems. The best correction for a squeaky or high-pitched voice is to relax. Breathe deeply, especially until your presentation begins. Diaphragmatic breathing helps you to feel natural and control your pacing. During the presentation, attempt to breathe deeply so you can feel and even see your stomach stretch.

A comfortable rate of speaking ranges from 100 to 125 words per minute. **Time yourself.** In addition, **listen to yourself speak**. Try speaking with one hand cupped over an ear, which is a technique commonly employed by singers and actors. With your left hand, push your ear forward and press it against your head so that it is almost closed. Now read your material aloud. This approach can be supplemented by tape recording your presentation and playing it back so that you can listen to how others hear you.

If you have a soft voice, it is imperative that you avoid a monotone speaking style. Although a soft voice can be hard to correct, you can overcome this problem by emphasizing words and phrases periodically. Speaking softly can also help you emphasize points in a speech. Even silence can be effective, as it punctuates your presentation and, if used effectively, signals the audience that you are in complete control.

Perhaps the most common problem in voice control is the use of slang words and repetitive phrases, particularly "you know" at the end or beginning of sentences. Many speakers also say "um" or "uh" throughout the presentation when they are searching for time or a thought. It is much better to practice being silent during such times, for as we have noted, silence can be an effective device in an oral presentation. To minimize such problems, force yourself to stop at the end of each sentence, particularly when you practice. Gradually the "ums," "uhs," and "you knows" will disappear.

Do not attempt to compete with distracting noises. If the noise is outside the room, stop, comment on it, then continue. Do not try to ignore it or speak louder, unless it is a single loud noise, such as a backfire. A light or humorous comment in this instance is appropriate and tends to create a sense of identification between the speaker and the audience.

If distracting noise is created by side conversations in the room, stop and look at the offenders with a smile until they stop. Then continue. If it happens again, stop once more. Further, if the members of the audience are simple unruly and no one makes an effort to control them, you may want to say, "There are some conversations going on in this room, and I would be grateful if you would discontinue them so that we can finish our presentation."

Finally, nervousness and a resultant dry throat may well inhibit your presentation. Take along a plastic cup or pitcher of water. Taking a drink of water not only helps to wet the throat but gives you time to collect your thoughts and control nervousness.

CONTROLLING GESTURES

The presentation is going well: You are not (or only slightly) nervous, and your voice firmly commands the audience's attention. If you control your gestures and movements effectively, you significantly increase the probability that your presentation will be highly successful.

You must control your body language. Don't fold your arms, as this technique makes you look stilted and rigid. It also seems to encourage slouching. Further, don't assume a relaxed, both hands-in-the-pocket pose. You may look like a kangaroo. Also, putting your hands on your hips or clasping them behind your back should be avoided unless you want to look like a priest or minister.

It is important that you stand straight and do not slouch. Practice improving your posture by standing up straight with your back to a wall. It is preferable to stand with one foot slightly in front of the other foot during the presentation, as this approach seems to make the speakers more confident and looks natural to members of the audience.

When gesturing, use your whole arm rather than just your forearm and wrist. It is more forceful and also more visible to those in the back of the room. Gesturing can be completed in many ways -- such as moving the whole body, and nodding the head -- but it is typical to rely primarily on the hands and arms for this activity. Further, it is generally preferable to gesture with both hands rather than with one hand. You seem more confident because you appear to be in total control of your body. Many speakers control their hand gestures by keeping the third and fourth fingers of the gesturing hand or hands slightly touching. This technique seems to allay any nervousness or signs of it.

Practice movements and gestures before the actual presentation is made, but do not appear to be rigid, artificial, or overly practiced. Use the gestures you like, and when rehearsing, ask other team members if they are effective. At the same time, avoid overusing gestures, as they can become distracting.

Finally, one movement that you must avoid at all costs is turning your back to the audience. This action is rude and members of the audience tend to resent it.

SPEAKING FROM NOTES

Most speakers use notes when making presentations. How you use them frequently determines whether the members of the audience perceive you as effective. Remember that whatever you write down for the presentation must be readable. Otherwise you will look foolish if you cannot read your own writing.

Don't even consider memorizing. Instead, learn to use notes unobtrusively. If you are using index cards, write clearly or type them, number them to ensure that they do not get out of order, and leave some space in which you can write additional ideas you may have forgotten to put down. It is generally best to write down only main ideas. Above all, don't walk around with the cards: **Keep the cards on the podium.** Walking with cards tends to be distracting; you are liable to drop them, and in the process bring on a stress attack.

If you want more prompting than is possible using cards, develop a script that can be written clearly or typed on regular 8 1/2- by 11-inch paper. In this instance, you can include more than main ideas. You may even decide to write out the entire presentation. If you prepare a complete script -- and we would not recommend this approach -- write the script in an informal, speaking manner rather than as a duplicate of your formal written report.   You are supposed to be speaking, not reading a report.

The following rules apply to the preparation of scripts:

- Use 8 1/2- by 11-inch paper.
- Use extra-large print or typed capital letters.
- Double space between lines.
- Do not split a paragraph between two pages.
- Number the pages at the bottom in case they get out of order.
- Allow space on the top of the first page to add notes.
- With a red pencil, insert pacing marks and underline major words.

Finally, remember the cards or the script should stay on the podium, and that it is usually awkward to hold them with one hand and gesture with the other hand. Further, clutching cards or papers with two hands clearly signifies to your audience that you are nervous and perhaps even terrified, even if you are not.

PERSUADING YOUR AUDIENCE

Things are going well in the early stages of your presentation because you have used many of the guidelines we have described. Still, you want to be sure that you strongly influence the members of the audience and persuade them that your point of view is logical and acceptable. For this reason it is important that you **establish** and **maintain** contact or rapport with the audience. If the audience identifies with you, you will tend to feel very comfortable, and that increases the probability that your presentation will be successful and that the audience will accept your point of view.

One very effective method of achieving rapport is to establish and maintain eye contact with members of the audience. If at all possible, try to look directly into the eyes of everyone in the audience at some point. In effect, you are saying to the members of the audience: "I can see that we are communicating effectively." Then focus on those people who respond with a nod or a smile rather than focusing on those who seem bored or hostile. There is nothing so reassuring to a speaker than an individual who smiles or nods frequently.

However, if eye contact with everyone is difficult because of the size of the group or some uneasiness on your part, select three or four individuals in widely scattered positions, preferably individuals who will nod affirmatively or smile at you. Move your attention from one of them to the other regularly. This will force you to look at all sections of the audience. If such eye contact is unnerving to you, look at a spot in the center of the forehead of each target person. Gradually your uneasiness will disappear.

Remember to **establish** and **maintain** eye contact. Some speakers do well at the beginning of a presentation, only to lose contact with members of the audience by staring too intently at their notes, looking only at a visual, or focusing on a spot high on the back wall. You will lose audience support very quickly if you engage in such activities, even if there was some initial rapport.

Do not hide behind the podium. A presenter who hides behind and holds the po-dium is terrified, and everyone knows it. Some speakers merely read their presentations from that supposedly secure position. Nothing destroys rapport with the audience faster than this approach. Particularly annoying is the tendency of speakers to use the podium as a resting place behind which they can slouch.   However, you must be careful when moving about the room during a formal presentation. Don't look like a caged tiger. To guard against moving too much or too little, stop moving each time you make a major point. By pausing, you can emphasize the importance of the point you are making.

When walking away from the podium, it is frequently helpful to take a few steps toward the audience. Start at the podium, walk away from it and point to a visual, then take a few steps toward the audience, then return to the podium. Just the act of walking toward the audience can help establish rapport between you and its members.

However, you must be careful. You do not want to make members of the audience uncomfortable by invading their physical space. For example, a tall speaker who approaches within inches of his audience and leans forward is expressing dominance rather than friendliness, and members of the audience will tend to react negatively to this ploy. Still, taking a few steps toward the audience helps your presentation enormously, and you should practice this approach until you feel comfortable.

But persuasion involves more than such techniques as establishing eye contact and gesturing correctly. You must analyze the audience and structure your presentation accordingly. Questions to answer include:

√ Will only students and your instructor be present?
√ Will your instructor invite some businessmen or women to evaluate the presentations?
√ Can you profile the audience in terms of such factors as sex composition, socioeconomic status, political beliefs, and so forth?

If you can develop such a profile, you will become sensitive to the types of statements that you can and cannot make in order to be persuasive.

Further, when you speak before an audience, its members expect you to exercise the authority that comes with the word "expert." In this instance you are the expert. Apologies, slumping shoulders, poor posture, and related deficiencies all signal a lack of confidence. Avoid them. You can create an aura of authority by reiterating points and using different types of statements such as "most authorities agree..."; "major companies such as IBM are moving in a similar direction..."; and so on.

Dressing appropriately can also create an aura of authority. There is no need to be ostentatious; in fact, such a ploy can seriously harm your presentation. The standard business dress remains dark suits and white or blue shirts for men and conservative suits or dresses for women. You should adhere to the standard business dress code when making your presentation.

The process of persuasion is also strenghtened if you attempt to be both formal and informal simultaneously. Admittedly, this is a difficult task, as you do not want to be so informal that you are not taken seriously. However, a statement such as "Jim, Bob, and I conducted our strategic analysis in the following way" is much more effective than "The three of us conducted the strategic analysis in the following way."

Along these lines, changing your presentation to fit the manner in which the audience is responding is a highly desirable skill that some very persuasive speakers possess. If you feel sufficiently confident, make such adjustments. But be careful if you do. Even the best speakers can drift away from the core of their presentations. Further, you may interfere with the other team speakers following you. Hence it is advisable to make adjustments if you feel comfortable, but do so very conservatively.

Finally, as we have already suggested, your gestures and movements can be very persuasive. They provide breaks in the action and help you to emphasize points so that you can move smoothly from one subject to another. Similarly, silence is a powerful tool. Dramatic pauses ram home ideas. A slightly longer pause -- for example, taking a drink of water -- can be used to indicate a change of approach.

In short, you can persuade the audience not only by establishing and maintaining eye contact but also by such techniques as establishing your authority and effectively using gestures and movements.

CONSTRUCTING VISUAL AIDS

In the previous chapter, we discussed guidelines for using particular types of tables and figures, such as the pie chart and the line chart. These guidelines also apply to the oral presentation. However, even greater care must be exercised in the oral presentation than in the written report, as deficiencies in your visuals are readily apparent to members of the audience.

Whatever the choice, you must remember that only simple tables and figures are appropriate for an oral presentation. Because most presentations involve numerical data, you should probably use line, bar, and pie charts, although maps and diagrams are also helpful at times. If the figures and tables in your written presentation are complicated, try to simplify them for the oral presentation.

If you construct your own charts, make sure that they can fit easily on an easel provided by the instructor. Alternatively, you can bring along masking tape to the presentation and have another member of the team post them at appropriate junctures of your presentation, instructing him or her to take each chart down as soon as you are finished talking about it. If there are more than 20 people in the audience, you must use highly visible exhibits or transparencies, which are appropriate for groups of up to 100. In constructing text visuals for your presentation use the following:

- No more than 4 to 6 lines of text
- Phrases rather than sentences
- A special large typewriter
- Both upper and lowercase type
- A simple typeface
- Bullets or Arabic numerals for listings
- Color, boldface, or large-size type for emphasis
- Approximately 40 characters per line
- Headings above rather than below the body of the exhibit
- Active verbs in headings, which should be twice as large as any other type in the visual
- Rounded numbers.

If you construct your own exhibits, you can use color, which in moderation is an effective way to keep audience attention. Shade part of a graph, highlight a number, or use a colored arrow. Use the brightest colors to attract attention to your main point, but use red sparingly. Contrasting colors suggest contrasting concepts or a major change. Two shades of the same color suggest a minor change.

In designing transparencies, take advantage of the natural, horizontal form of the overhead and work within a 7 1/2 x 9 1/2 inch space centered on the page. Anything outside these borders will not be clearly visible. Also, when overheads are completed, secure them in cardboard frames with transparent tape. This technique blocks out any extraneous light, and the transparencies will not stick together or slither away from your grasp and fall to the floor. You should also number your transparencies in the event that they do get out of place.

If by chance you have someone on your team skilled in calligraphy, take advantage of that skill. Neat, hand-lettered visuals are generally more attractive than typewritten ones, whether they are on poster board, transparencies, or flip charts.

It is essential that your visuals be consistent. Avoid using disparate types of lettering, widely varying artistic styles, or inconsistent formats. Similarly, don't make spelling mistakes or use poor grammar in your visuals. Lack of consistency and sloppiness, as manifested in poor spelling or grammar, create the impression that you are not well prepared.

Finally, you can use other techniques such as dry-transfer letters, gum-backed letters, and lettering templates. However, they tend to be expensive and/or time-consuming, and they may not be effective if you do not have a sufficient amount of skill to use them effectively. Given the time pressures normally associated with the oral presentation, we would generally recommend that you do not consider such alternatives.

USING VISUAL AIDS

There are some simple guidelines for using visual aids. These guidelines ensure that your presentation is professional.

If you decide to use poster board charts, don't hold them in your hand. Either use masking tape or place the charts on an easel. After discussing a chart or a transparency, either take the chart down or turn off the projector.

It is important that you practice using the visual aids prior to the presentation. You may discover that the charts do not stay on the easel or that the overhead projector does not work, but you still have time to correct the problem.

Don't become overly dependent on visuals. You should generally spend about two minutes on each visual, and include from four to six visuals in a 15-minute presentation.

Try to position yourself so that you can point to a chart or screen without turning your back toward the audience. A pointer can be very helpful to your presentation. Practice using it, however, as there is a tendency for inexperienced speakers to swing it wildly about. A recessed pointer is particularly helpful, as you can fold it up after pointing to a specific visual. Put the pointer in the hand nearest the screen and point at the visual while maintaining eye contact with the audience. If you point with your hand use the same procedure.

If you use transparencies, be sure that neither you nor the projector block anyone's view. Also, use a pencil or pointer rather than your finger to note a detail on a transparency, and write on a transparency only if you are very confident and experienced. Otherwise, you are liable to distort the basic message you are seeking to convey.

It is generally preferable that you operate the projector yourself. Also, do not dim the lights in the room.

When using a chart or transparency observe the following rules:

- Never talk about a topic different from that addressed in the chart.
- Never explain it in detail, as it should reinforce rather than substitute.
- Never cover a portion of it.

Finally, tell your audience the purpose of a chart or transparency before displaying it. In this way, the audience knows what is coming and does not become confused because you have hurried the use of your visuals.

RESPONDING TO QUESTIONS

If possible, leave time for questions and encourage them. Answering questions effectively can be very persuasive. However, questions should be asked only after all team members have completed their presentations. The questions should be addressed to specific members of the team to avoid confusion. Remember, the more involved the audience is with your presentation, the better they will accept your message.

Do not hurry your response to a question. It is quite appropriate to rephrase the question to ensure that you understand it. If the questioner indicates that there is a discrepancy, it is his or her responsibility to clarify the meaning of the original question.

But there are some dangers in accepting questions. Sometimes questioners will become verbose and/or repetitive, thus using up valuable time. More important, some individuals ask hostile questions designed to trip you up. Your response, however, should not be confrontational unless you are really pushed to the extreme. Rather, answer the question politely and then ask, "Does my answer resolve your problem?" If the answer is affirmative, you can then be conciliatory and say that you appreciate the individual's concern and willingness to express it openly.

In summary, although questions can be dangerous, there are many more advantages than disadvantages associated with responding to them, provided that you follow the simple quidelines we have described.

USING A RATING FORM

Fig. 9.1 is a rating form that you and your team can use to evaluate your performance either before the presentation or during it. We suggest that you complete evaluations both before and during the presentation in order to obtain additional feedback on your performance. Using a rating and evaluation form can help you master oral presentation skills.

TIPS TO REMEMBER

9.1   Organize your presentation and practice until you feel comfortable with what you are saying.

9.2   Manage presentation stress: visualize your ideal presentation, exercise a few hours before the presentation, and use complete notes for the first two minutes.

9.3   Practice controlling your voice, breathe deeply, and speak at a comfortable pace ranging from 100 to 125 words per minute.

9.4   Avoid using slang words and trite phrases such as "you know," "ah," and "um."

9.5   Always face your audience.

9.6   Do not hide behind and hold the podium.

9.7   Persuade your audience through establishing and maintaining eye contact, walking away from the podium periodically toward the audience, understanding the biases of your audience, and dressing correctly.

9.8   Use simple rather than complex charts and exhibits.

9.9   Use either charts or transparencies. Do not use both types of visuals.

9.10   Arrive early at the room where the presentation is to take place to iron out any last minute difficulties.

9.11   If possible, respond to questions, but only after all team members have completed their presentations.

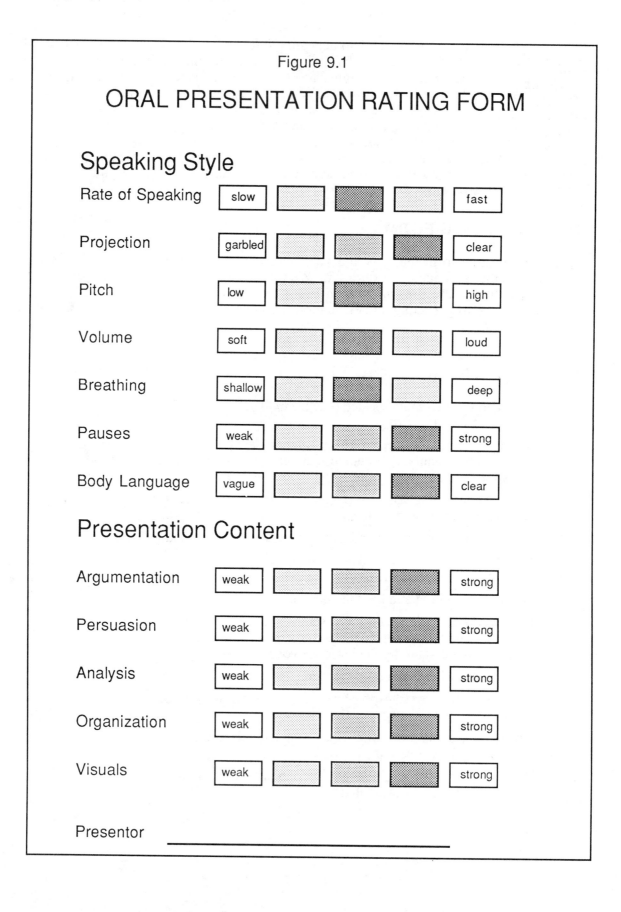

Figure 9.1

ORAL PRESENTATION RATING FORM

Speaking Style

Rate of Speaking	slow				fast
Projection	garbled				clear
Pitch	low				high
Volume	soft				loud
Breathing	shallow				deep
Pauses	weak				strong
Body Language	vague				clear

Presentation Content

Argumentation	weak				strong
Persuasion	weak				strong
Analysis	weak				strong
Organization	weak				strong
Visuals	weak				strong

Presentor _____

ACTION EXERCISE

9.1   One effective technique for preparing for an oral presentation is to ask one or more friends to listen to you make an oral presentation on a subject that they suggest. Give yourself five minutes to outline your thoughts and then make a formal oral presentation in front of these friends. Repeat this exercise until you feel comfortable talking naturally before an audience.

SUGGESTED READINGS

9.1   Holcombe, M., and Stein, J., *Presentations for Decision Makers*. Belmont, California: Lifetime Learning Publications, 1983.

An excellent overview of issues associated with making oral presentations, this book discusses in detail such topics as analyzing the audience, designing and using visuals, and delivering the presentation.

9.2   Jeffries, J., and Bates, J., *The Executive's Guide to Meetings, Conferences, and Audiovisual Presentations*. New York: McGraw-Hill, 1983.

This book effectively complements Holcombe and Stein's book. Some important topics are discussed in greater depth, including constructing and using visual aids.

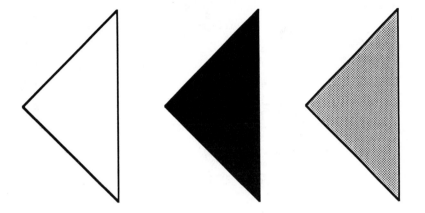

PART 2

Examples

3 Cases
Student Write-up

American Safety Razor Company (A)[1]

On the morning of October 1, 1977, John Baker, President and one of the new owners of the American Safety Razor Company (ASR), was trying to decide what strategies to follow with Flicker and Personna, ASR's two best selling product lines. He was also trying to decide what kind of company ASR should become over the next five years, particularly whether it should continue as a full-fledged competitor in the razor and blade industry.

Settling down to work was hard, for Mr. Baker was elated on his first day as ASR's largest stockholder. He was a little edgy as well. After planning ASR's liquidation for Philip Morris, he and eight fellow executives had bought their company with extremely leveraged financing. Cash threatened to be a problem, for the new owners were taking control in the slowest quarter for razor sales. Flicker, for example, usually produced $1 million in cash in August, but only $300 thousand in December. Until Mr. Baker was sure that his cash flow was strong, some decisions would have to be more conservative than he preferred.

To focus his mind, Mr. Baker began jotting down some leading facts about his business:

Flicker women's shaver, 1976 sales	$10.6	million
Personna razors and blades	10.5	"
Single-edged razor blades	5.5	"
Private label razor blades	2.2	"
Other shaving products and toiletries	1.2	"
Export and Puerto Rican sales	3.4	"
Industrial blades	7.9	"
Surgical blades	1.9	"

PROFILE OF AMERICAN SAFETY RAZOR

History. ASR entered business in 1875 as the Star Razor Company. Organized by the Kampfe brothers of New York, Star manufactured the first safety razor to reach the market, effectively a segment of a barber's straight-edge clamped into a hoe-shaped handle. In 1919 Star joined with two younger manufacturers of single-edged razors, Gem and Ever-Ready, to form the American Safety Razor Company. The Pal Blade Company merged into ASR in the 1950's, and in 1960 Philip Morris purchased ASR as part of a diversification program.

Philip Morris invested heavily in new equipment and made ASR as modern a blade manufacturer as any in the industry, but it failed to improve the company's market position significantly. After buying Miller Brewing in 1969, Philip Morris lost interest in the razor industry and began trying to sell ASR. Although the company had disappointed Philip Morris, its sales had grown each year since 1972. Pertinent financial statements are shown as Exhibits 1 and 2 at the end of this case.

---

[1]This case was prepared by Dennis Schafer, Research Associate, under the supervision of Associate Professor Ralph Biggadike, as a basis for class discussion, and is not intended to illustrate either effective or ineffective handling of an administrative situation. Copyright 1979 by the Colgate Darden Graduate Business School Sponsors, University of Virginia, Charlottesville, Virginia. Reproduced by permission.

Current Situation. ASR had undergone enormous changes during the past ten months, as this rough chronology suggests:

-   December 31, 1976. Bic Pen agrees to buy ASR from Philip Morris.

-   February 2, 1977. FTC challenges sale, arguing that it violates Clayton Act.

-   February 18, 1977. Unable to compromise with the FTC, Bic withdraws offer.

-   February 18, 1977. Philip Morris begins liquidation by cutting off all advertising, cutting sales force by two-thirds. Lays off one-third of factory workers by March 3.

-   April 29, 1977. Philip Morris agrees to sell to Baker and several associates if they can meet Bic's offer. Terms: $16.765 million as of December 31, 1976, minus any profits or surplus cash accumulated between that date and closing date. Baker group begins to seek financing.

-   September 29, 1977. Financing completed: $600 thousand equity; $6 million loan at 3% for 25 years from U.S. Economic Development Administration through Industrial Development Authority of Augusta County, Virginia; $250 thousand loan from Virginia Industrial Development Authority; $9 million in loans and credit line from Bank of Virginia.

-   October 1, 1977. Ownership transfers to Baker and eight associates.

THE RAZOR INDUSTRY

Although it was more often called the "razor industry," this industry was, effectively, the razor <u>blade</u> industry. Razors, the handle portion of the shaving utensil, accounted for sales of $40 to $50 million annually, but the industry treated them more as a promotional vehicle than as a product. With few exceptions, manufacturers made blades to fit one another's razors.

Exhibit 3 shows recent trends in razor blade sales and projections of future sales. The reason for the decline in number of blades sold despite a slight growth in the shaving-age population was the continuing conversion of shavers to longer lasting stainless steel blades. The reason for growth in dollar sales was the continuation of a trend begun by Gillette's Techmatic and Trac II shaving systems: conversion of shavers to more complicated, more expensive products, chiefly at the expense of double-edge sales (see Exhibit 4).

History. Until World War II, dozens of companies had competed in this industry and the largest, Gillette, had only an18% share of the market in 1938. The years between 1938 and 1950 bought large structural change to the industry, of which Gillette was both a primary cause and the leading beneficiary. By adopting improved production technology, by pioneering in advertising on sports broadcasts, and by winning contracts to supply razors and blades to the armed forces during World War II, Gillette made itself the industry's leader.

When the shakeout was over, only four significant competitors remained, all old soldiers of the industry: Gillette, American Safety Razor, Schick and the Pal Blade Company. Later, ASR purchased Pal. In the early 1960's Wilkinson Sword entered the industry with a stainless steel blade, and in 1976 Bic Pen began to compete with a disposable razor. In 1976 Gillette had 58% of the market, Schick 24%, ASR 9%, Wilkinson 7%, and Bic less than 1%.

Production. The production lines of all competitors were highly integrated. Razor blades were made from continuous bands of steel the width and thickness of a finished blade. The manufacturing process had six major steps: perforating, hardening, grinding (itself a three-step process), sputtering (the application of a preliminary tungsten-, platinum-, or chromium-ion coating to stainless steel blades), coating with plastic or silicone, and packaging. The difficulty of manufacturing blades is suggested by the fact that grinding tolerances were held to less than a millionth of an inch on machines that ground blades at the rate of 400 per minute.

In general, industry experts said, blade makers could expect manufacturing costs to run about 30% of the factory price to wholesalers. Costs broke about 60/40 between packaging and the other five steps of the manufacturing process. According to ASR's Vice President of Finance and former Vice President of Manufacturing, Gray Ferguson, "We all design our own machines, but each of the three American manufacturers has produced so many blades for so long that the learning curve might as well not exist for them." Mr. Ferguson said that while the established American companies could all produce blades equal in quality, the quality of Wilkinson blades was marginal (despite their reputation for high quality) and Bic's Greek blade was of inferior manufacture.

At first appearance, the capital investment necessary to compete in the razor industry seemed low-- a new competitor might enter with an $8-$10 million capital investment--but marketing costs for establishing a new brand were significant.

Marketing. Marketing in the razor industry was a complex blend of push and pull. The key points of competition were distribution channels, retail display space, promotional support, and advertising. Until Bic's arrival, no manufacturer had competed primarily on price. As a generalization, Gillette was the price leader, and Schick, ASR, and Wilkinson kept their list prices in fairly standard ratios to Gillette's. Schick generally matched Gillette's list prices to the penny; ASR's and Wilkinson's list prices ranged below Gillette's. The ratios differed from product to product, and Gillette was not even the price leader in all categories. Schick was the leader in injectors, for example, and all competitors sold their injectors at lower prices than Schick. Standard suggested wholesale prices in the industry were factory list price plus 20%; standard suggested retail prices were factory list price plus 2/3. But blades were usually sold on promotion, both to the trade and to the consumer, so price differentials and differentials in trade margins could be created or altered by subtle adjustments of promotional terms.

Channels, promotions, and merchandising. Blades reached retail outlets either directly from the manufacturer or through various wholesalers and independent merchandisers. Retail distribution rates, which measure marketing power in the channels, are shown in Exhibit 6. At retail, sales in 1976 divided among different kinds of retailers as shown below.

Kind of Outlet	Number of Outlets	Sales %
Food (Total)	193,600	53
Chains	39,300	33
Large Independents	19,400	11
Medium & Small Independents	134,900	9
Drug (Totals)	50,700	30
Chains	9,700	18
Large Independents	10,300	7
Medium & Small Independents	30,700	5
Mass Merchandise	5,100	17

Source: Company Records.

Retailers made the majority of their razor blade purchases in preparation for retail promotions. Since retailers treated blades as health and beauty aids, blades competed for retailers' promotional support against all health and beauty aids, not just against other blades. For several reasons, retailers had recently been running fewer health-and-beauty-aid promotions, so competition for promotional support, always fierce, was becoming fiercer. Razors and blades were normally displayed on pegboards in retail outlets. Taking all outlets together, Gillette controlled 40% of display pegs.

Advertising. Although an established brand could sustain profits without advertising at a market share as small as 1/2%, a much higher share was required to support significant advertising, and significant advertising was required to support a high market share. According to one industry expert, a company could count on putting $4 million a year against the total market (perhaps $2 million against the women's market) to keep a brand from losing share. To support that kind of advertising, a brand needed to hold at least a 5% share of the total market.

Exhibit 7 analyzes recent advertising expenditures in the industry.

Competitors and their postures. By 1977, Gillette had become a diversified manufacturer of toiletries, small appliances, pens, and cigarette lighters. Schick Safety Razor (a separate entity from Schick Electric Razor) was owned by Warner-Lambert. Wilkinson was a small manufacturer of gardening tools as well as razor blades. Bic Pen Corporation was the American subsidiary of Societe Bic, the French manu - facturer of disposable pens and cigarette lighters. Financial profiles of these companies are in Exhibit 8.

Schick and ASR competed as fast followers of Gillette, and both had product lines nearly as full as Gillette's (see Exhibit 9). Wilkinson's product line was less complete, but Wilkinson had been innovative, pioneering both stainless steel blades and bonded blades. Bic was concentrating on its disposable shaver, following the low price, high volume strategy that had succeeded in disposable pens and cigarette lighters.

Gillette, unquestionably the strongest competitor, was fiercely defensive of its market share and of its leadership in product development. If beaten on an innovation, Gillette responded aggressively. It introduced a slightly different version of the challenger's new product, it beat the challenger into national distribution if possible, and tried to convince consumers through advertising that Gillette's product was better. Using this tactic against Wilkinson, Gillette had established itself as the leader in stainless steel blades, and, with Trac II, in bonded blades--both of them product categories that Wilkinson had opened. In 1977, it was attacking Bic's disposable with its own Good News disposable.

Gillette handled razors and cigarette lighters with a sales force of 150, supported by a corporate merchandising staff. Warner-Lambert sold Schick blades, Listerine, and its other consumer products through a sales force of 100-plus, assisted in major markets by retail merchandisers. Wilkinson sold through Colgate's sales force of 250.

Market trends. For the present, industry eyes were on Bic's introduction of disposable razors, which had stirred a debate within the industry. Between them, Gillette's Good News and the Bic Shaver had over 5% of the market by the final months of 1976. Compared to the introductions of other new razor products, market share for disposables was rising fast. Some experts predicted that disposables would not catch on beyond small trial sales, arguing that they gave inferior shaves, that they were inconvenient for consumers to store, and that they would confuse trade channels and offer the channels insufficient margins. Others, seeing a travel market and some attraction in not having to fiddle with putting blades into a razor, believed that disposables would carve a small niche in the market, ten percent at the outside. Bic executives, on the other hand, argued that disposables would take over this market as they had the pen and lighter markets, and that Bic's own share would eventually reach 30% or 50%. It was too early to tell who was right, but if disposables captured a large portion of the market they would reverse the current market trends, shrinking industry dollar sales while expanding unit sales.

Industry analysts also wondered if the late seventies and eighties would see more segmentation of the razor market, as had happened in other consumer goods markets. To date little market segmentation had been attempted. Partly, the force of Gillette's market leadership was responsible for this situation. Gillette preferred to appeal to all segments with the same product or, when absolutely necessary, with minor var - iations on the same product. Partly, the inherent difficulty of segmentation was responsible. "The opportunity for segmentation is minimal," commented one authority, "because the desired end result is always the same: cutting hair close to the skin without cutting skin."

Traditionally, the razor industry thought of market segments as franchises belonging to various types of blades, single-edged, injector, double-edged, and so on. Some basic market division according to value had also been traditional in the industry. Wilkinson's introduction of stainless steel blades during the early sixties had demonstrated that a significant group of consumers was willing to pay a premium for technologically improved shaving products. Perhaps the most successful segmentation in recent years, however, had been by sex when ASR introduced Flicker in 1972.

Among men some obvious market segments had yet to be exploited. Fully eight percent of the male market suffered skin problems that made shaving particularly difficult, such as acne or the slack, wrinkled skin of old age. Even among men with normal skin and beard, shaving requirements varied significantly, according to the toughness of the shaver's skin, the thickness of his beard, and his preference for a close shave over a comfortable shave or vice versa.

ASR's RAZOR OPERATION

Production. ASR produced razor blades in a 307,000 square foot factory near Staunton, Virginia. Although the plant had room for doubled capacity, it was operating at 70-80% of machine capacity. Because most of ASR's grinding machines were used for several different products, both razor and non-razor, production scheduling became complicated at times. Moreover, decisions to drop or add a product, or to expand or shrink sales of a product, required compensating adjustments in the production levels of products sharing the same equipment.

Marketing. In a normal year, ASR spent roughly one-third as much on advertising as on promotion. Since February 1977 it had spent nothing on advertising except through cooperative programs with retailers. In the spring of 1977 ASR had reduced its sales force from 100 people to 30. Since this reduction, ASR had emphasized selling at headquarters and paid most attention to the largest 995 accounts, which previously had represented 80% of sales (see Exhibit 10). The sales people had no time to check retail stores, and ASR had no merchandising staff.

ASR had always fared worse in food stores than its competitors. Forty-nine percent of its volume was through food stores, compared to 58% for Gillette, and 53% for the whole industry. According to Alan Goldenberg, Vice President for Sales, the reasons for this performance were: (1) that food stores tended to buy on the basis of national market share and manufacturer's image, thus making advertising a more important factor than in drug and mass merchandise channels; (2) that food stores had fewer promotions for health and beauty aids than drug and mass merchandise outlets; and (3) that razor display boards were generally smaller in food stores, thus intensifying competition for display space.

ASR's RAZOR BLADES

Flicker. In 1976 Flicker was ASR's best performing product in both sales and profitability. Introduced in 1972, it was the first women's razor that was more than a men's razor with a few frills and a feminine name. The shaver was shaped like a powder compact--round, except for its cutting edge--and held five blades. When one was used, the next blade was rotated into postion; when all five were used, the entire razor was discarded. Flicker's disposability appealed to women and its shape distinquished it from men's razors, but its most important difference was a thin wire wrapped around the blade. By crossing the cutting edge at intervals, this wire held the cutting edge several thousandths of a inch from the skin, thus reducing the risk of nicking.

Gillette and Schick responded to Flicker in 1973 with Lady Trac II and Lady Super II, colored-handle versions of their male twin-bladed systems. Sensing that disposability and distinctive design were keys to Flicker's success, Gillette introduced Daisy in 1975, a disposable twin-bladed women's razor with a specially designed handle, packaged in a plastic cup rather than on a blister card. Early in 1977, Schick entered test markets with Personal Touch, a modification of Super II with an imitation tortoise-shell handle, packaged in an imitation tortoise-shell case. Exhibit 12 shows prices for Flicker and competing products.

From a peak in 1975, Flicker's sales and market share declined steadily. John Baker was uncertain just how to interpret this decline: 'The trend is down, but is that because the market has matured, or because we've been harvesting share as an unintended result of the decision to liquidate? We know that not advertising for the last seven months has hurt sales, but we don't know whether it's too late to grow Flicker's share again by resuming advertising.

Strategic Options for Flicker. As a signal to the trade that Flicker was alive and well, and as a way to increase consumer trial rates, ASR's new owners were about to market the Flicker Single, a one-bladed version of Flicker to be used mainly for promotions. Beyond this measure the owners had identified three possible strategies for Flicker.

1. Milk the product: cut advertising and promotion to a minimum and treat Flicker as a product that has passed the peak of its life cycle.

2. Resume full advertising and promotion following earlier plans. Treat Flicker as a product that has yet to reach its full potential.

3. Reposition the product: resume full advertising and promotion, but in a direction that gives Flicker greater strength in the competition with Gillette's Daisy and Schick's Personal Touch.

As they selected a strategy for Flicker, the owners faced three major tasks: understanding Flicker's success accurately, reconciling an inherent dilemma in its positioning, and improving distribution.

ASR knew Flicker had been successful, but didn't know quite how to define the market it served and so didn't know quite how to evaluate its success. Women purchased 20% of all wet-shaving products exclusively for their own use. Many women shared razors and even blades with their husbands, so although the women's segment was more than 20% of the total market, its exact size was impossible to determine. If, to evaluate Flicker, ASR defined the market as all users of razors and blades, men and women alike, Flicker was a minor but profitable force. If the market was all women who shaved with razor and blade, Flicker's share was between 20% and 30% but Flicker was outsold by male products like Trac II. If, however, the market was women who used products designed especially for women, Flicker's share was well over 50%.

The positioning dilemma arose because Flicker was positioned against the whole women's segment, even though the product's qualities suited it best for a narrower segment, women who nicked easily. Other women were likely to consider Flicker an inferior product because it didn't shave as closely as conventional razors. By positioning Flicker too narrowly, ASR would lose some sales to non-nickers who liked Flicker anyway; by positioning it too broadly, ASR risked losing sales by hurting the razor's reputation. ASR had no data on the size of the nicking segment.

Two solutions to this problem were possible: first, marketing one Flicker, positioned for safety, to the nicking segment, and another, with a finer guage of wire around its blade to deliver a closer shave, to the general women's market; or second, switching to a finer guage of wire and marketing only to the general women's market. A razor aimed at the general women's market would need to be repositioned, for although Flicker was currently aimed at the general market (with a strong appeal to young girls, in order to engender loyalty to the product early) its slogan emphasized safety--"Don't be a nicker, be a Flicker." Flicker's new position would need to account for the position of Daisy, whose appeal was the femininity of its pink, flower-embossed handle, and for the position of Personal Touch, whose name implied intimacy and whose tortoise-shell handle and case suggested elegance.

ASR also faced distribution problems with Flicker. Although Flicker had won over the more sophisticated channels (97% distribution in mass merchandise outlets by June 1976, 97% in drug chains, and 92% in food chains), it had not been very successful at penetrating small and medium-sized independent food stores (10% and 35% distribution, respectively). Even in the channels that accepted Flicker, ASR met resistance to stocking heavily for summer to meet the seasonal peak for women's shaving products.

Personna. Under the name Personna, ASR sold a full razor-and-blade line (the Double II), a specialty double-edged blade (Face Guard), and three kinds of refill blades (double edges, injectors, and twin injectors).

Personna blades were positioned against the entire male wet-shaving market, but ASR executives believed that their users were generally over forty and of average to lower income. Although Gillette, Schick, and ASR blades did not differ substantially in quality, consumers considered Personna blades inferior to Gillette, Schick and Wilkinson blades. Personna blades were sold through the same channels as competitor's blades. They fared substantially worse in food stores (25% of Personna's sales versus 50% or more of competitors' sales) and substantially better in drug stores, an older channel for shaving products (40% versus 25%).

Double II. In effect a double-edged, twin-bladed razor, Personna Double II was ASR's only full line of razors and blades. It represented ASR's only recent attempt to compete head-to-head with Schick and Gillette in the mainstream of the male shaving market. Introduced in 1973 as an improvement on Gillette's Trac II and Schick's Super II, the line consisted of the Double II razor, the Lady Double II razor, a razor-and-blade set, a 49 cent temporary trial razor, and a refill dispenser with five blade cartridges. The Double II blade fit no competitor's handle, and no competitor made refill blades for the Double II.

The Double II had long been controversial. Even with strong advertising support, it had failed to gain significant share and it consistently lost money. Some executives had believed that Double II was ASR's most promising product and that with more support it would take off. In 1975, Double II's product manager had projected sales growth between 20% and 30% annually through 1978, based on the rapid growth of bonded systems and based on the conviction that ASR had designed a better razor than Gillette's and Schick's twin-bladed razors. Other executives believed that Flicker deserved increased support because Flicker had shown results, and because Flicker did not challenge Gillette in the Gillette mainstream. This debate had been rendered academic when Philip Morris stopped advertising, but the question of Double II's potential remained unanswered.

Face Guard. This blade, which fit convential double-edged razors, was a male analogue of Flicker. It had teflon bands across the cutting edge so it gave a comfortable shave at the expense of closeness--properties unique among all blades on the market. Introduced in 1972, just as Trac II began to cut away the sales of double-edged blades, Face Guard never managed to establish significant sales or distribution outside its test market on the west coast. It sold 3 million blades per year from 1974 through 1976 (a 0.2% national market share), and made a small contribution to profit and overhead each year.

Refill blades. Personna double-edged, injector and twin injector blades were all made to fit razors sold by competitors. Unless Double II were revived or succeeded by a new razor-and-blade line, refill blades would be the heart of the Personna business in the future.

ASR had learned from experience that, for Personna refill blades to compete, their prices had to be roughly 30% below Gillette's at retail. ASR's strategy was to maintain this 30% price differential (except on Face Guard and Double II, which had no direct competition) and to offer channels higher margins than competitors offered, both through slightly higher list margins and through heavy promotion. ASR did not advertise Personna refill blades.

Despite the fact that total double-edged and injector blade sales were declining rapidly as Gillette converted users of these blades to newer shaving systems, sales of Personna double-edged and injector blades rose slightly in 1975 and 1976, and margins for the products remained high. The two blades promised to settle eventually into the position of ASR's single-edged blades: obsolete blades that would continue selling for years to a small, loyal franchise, without advertising and with minimal promotional support. The two greatest problems for these two blades concerned distribution. As Gillette took support away from these categories (and Schick in the case of injectors), distribution tended to erode and competition for display pegs intensified.

Personna's Injector II was introduced as a defensive reaction to a marketing ploy by Gillette. In an effort to convert injector users to Trac II, its twin-bladed razor, Gillette introduced a twin-bladed injector system in 1973 and supported it heavily with advertising. To capitalize on Gillette's advertising, to protect their own injector sales, and to get in early on any trend toward twin-blade injector systems that might begin, ASR introduced Injector II early in 1974. Twin-injector systems aroused no strong interest among consumers, however, and distribution levels remained low for the product category. Sales for Injector II fell in every year following 1974.

This blade illustrated what Mr. Baker considered one important use for Personna refill blades: "Personna can serve as a control brand. We can be in each market with a commodity product. We won't advertise, just take what the market wants to give and smile."

Strategic options for Personna. Since the company lacked funds for advertising and promotion after Philip Morris's decision to liquidate, ASR's de facto strategy for Personna Double II was to harvest the brand. Its choices for the future were to continue harvesting it or to resume advertising and promotion in an effort to establish Double II as a major competitor against Gillette's Trac II and Schick's

Super II. ASR executives felt no need to reconsider their strategy for the Face Guard blade: the brand could continue its modest course without problem.

The strategic decisions about Personna that were the most pressing, ASR's executives said, con - cerned the refill line. Management was debating two strategies for Personna refills: discontinuing the line, or raising prices to improve margins at the expense of some lost sales. In a report to the other executives, Bill Robbins listed the pros and cons of discontinuing Personna refill blades:

Pros

1. We are near 100% capacity on double-edge grinding machines. Discontinuing Personna would free 37 days for grinding other products.

2. Capacity increases for non-double-edge products may be realized by converting certain machinery.

3. More effective use of G&A personnel.

4. Reduction of inventory.

5. Availability of additional warehouse space.

6. Elimination of production scheduling problems.

7. More effective and profitable capacity utilization.

8. More effective use of sales force time.

Cons

1. Adverse trade reaction concerning health and future of ASR as a full line razor blade manufacturer.

2. Possible morale problems with sales personnel; concern about job security and the future of the ASR sales force may have an adequate effect on our ability to sell the trade other products.

3. Little opportunity to reduce fixed manufacturing expenses, especially labor costs.

4. Sales force expenses will remain constant even with discontinuation of Personna. Allocation to Flicker will reduce Flicker's profitability seriously.

Mr. Baker believed the decision to continue or discontinue Personna should depend on the nature of ASR's financial requirements. "We are about to start making money on Personna, although ROI will still be very low," he said. "If cash is tight we may have to stay in the Personna business because Personna is a steady cash generator. If cash is not tight and growth is a goal, we should get out because getting out frees a lot of capital for other uses that can give us a higher ROI."

Mr. Robbins outlined a second possible strategy that involved raising prices for Personna refill blades. The basis for this strategy was the fact that at the same unit sales volume, each 1 cent increase in the price of all blade dispensers would yield $41,000 additional net income before tax. (This calculation assumes sales at the level projected for 1978 in Exhibit 13 and assumes seven blades to the average dispenser.) In addition to price increases, this second strategy involved following the leader on major new product introductions--preparing a refill blade for Gillette's Atra, for example.

Single edges. Single-edged blades, which had been on the market for over a hundred years, still represented a significant portion of ASR's sales and were second only to Flicker in profitability. ASR sold four brands of single edges. Their Gem Stainless Steel blade, the only one distributed nationally, accounted for a third of sales and half of brand contribution. Three budget carbon-steel brands, Treet, Pal, and Gem Blue Star, sold well regionally.

Market studies showed that ASR held a remarkably strong franchise with these blades, predominantly among older customers, predominantly in rural areas. Effectively, ASR had the single-edged segment of the market to itself. "Our strategy," explained John Baker, "is to do just enough to discourage competition, and to let these blades generate lots of cash." ASR realized the single-edge market would eventually dry up, but not for some time.

Private labels. ASR entered the private label business as a way of picking up factory overhead while increasing the company's importance to the channels that handled its branded blades. Sales of ASR's private label blades accounted for 2.9% of the blade market by unit and less than 1% by dollars.

ASR had only one competing supplier--UFI, now a division of Wilkinson--with whom they split the market about equally. UFI priced its blades below ASR's, but ASR executives considered that they offered better quality, better service, and more versatility than UFI. With few exceptions, ASR had the larger, more profitable accounts and UFI had the smaller, less profitable ones that ASR was not interested in pursuing.

All selling was done from headquarters by two members of ASR's managment, in contract negotiations with customers' headquarters. The key tasks of selling were to demonstrate that ASR's blades would be a profitable venture and a credit to the customer's private label program, and to plan merchandising with the customer. To avoid inventory problems from erratic orders and cancellations, ASR approached only prospects that already had well established private label programs. ASR had forty-two customers, including nearly all the national chains with private label programs. It only had twenty or thirty more pros - pects that met its criteria for size and seriousness, including two national chains.

ASR's other products. ASR made 275 different industrial blades, which generated $7.6 million of its sales in 1976. It was the industrial blade industry's price leader and at 25% had the largest or second largest market share. Because this industry was unmapped, ASR executives found it difficult to predict how fast their business would grow. "It's safe to assume demand will increase at the economy's growth rate," said Bill Kerr, manager of this business. Any very large growth, Mr. Kerr said, would come only if ASR learned new production methods for blades requiring different materials than ASR now used.

ASR held 30% of the $7.5 million surgical blade market, second only to the 50% share of Beckton Dickinson. Philip Morris had sold marketing rights for ASR surgical blades to Seamless Hospital Supply, a division of Dart Drug. Under the agreement with Seamless, ASR guaranteed quality and promised to develop new products as needed; Seamless guaranteed purchases at a specified level, currently $1.7 million annually. ASR was satisfied with the profit it made on this business, 20% before tax, but any decision to make the business grow belonged to Seamless, not to ASR.

ASR had four other products, Burma Shave shaving cream, the Every Ready shaving brush, Speak Easy spray breath freshener, and American Line tools, none of which represented an appreciable part of its sales. The American Line, a line of hobby and do-it-yourself cutting tools, excited several ASR executives, for the do-it-yourself market was large and growing fast. ASR was test marketing the line in food, drug, and mass merchandise outlets, but had not yet learned enough about how hardware and paint-and-sundry items reached those outlets to be confident of success.

CHOICES FOR A CORPORATE STRATEGY

ASR's executives agreed that they must decide on product strategies for Flicker and the Personna line soon, preferably before the new year. They agreed that the other businesses, single-edged razor blades, private label razor blades, industrial blades, surgical blades, Burma Save, Every Ready, Speak Easy, and American Line could run themselves for the present. Flicker and Personna, however, were the two largest components of ASR's sales and were the products most vulnerable to competition. Moreover, Personna's margins were unsatisfactory. ASR's strategic options for Flicker, to recapitulate, were: (1) milk the product; (2) resume full marketing support, retain the existing positioning and use the same campaign that was interrupted when the liquidation began; or (3) reposition the product and resume full marketing support. Its options for Personna Double II were to continue harvesting the brand or once again to try building it into a major competitor to Trac II and Super II. Its options for Personna refill blades were to discontinue the line or to raise prices in order to improve margins.

As part of the prospectus they prepared in the summer of 1977 to solicit financing for their purchase, ASR's management had outlined a marketing strategy for the five years, 1977-1981. The strategy they mocked up for the prospectus was a conservative one that assumed a significant drop in unit sales from the level of 1976 and assumed that the company would have little cash to spend on marketing. Although management did not feel committed to any of the strategic decisions implied in this prospectus, they used the sales and financial projections they developed for it as a base for estimating the results of those strategic options they were now debating. The unit sales projections, marketing budget, pro forma income statements, and pro forma balance sheets from this prospectus are reproduced in Exhibits 13, 14, 15 and 16. The specific assumptions about major product line strategies and resulting sales trends that were used for these projections are detailed in the note to Exhibit 13.

The hardest strategic questions facing ASR's new owners, and the first to be answered, was whether to continue competing in the razor industry and, if so, what posture to take. Broadly speaking, ASR could compete directly against Gillette and Schick in the mainstream of the industry or it could follow a segmentation strategy or some other strategy that took it out of the mainstream.

A mainstream strategy would require heavy emphasis on the Personna line, for male shaving products such as these were the industry's mainstream, and the only way to eclipse Schick or Gillette would be to beat them in head-to-head competition in male products. A mainstream strategy would also rquire that ASR have a full razor-and-blade system of its own, which meant either pushing Personna Double II hard once again or developing a new razor-and-blade system to compete with Gillette's and Schick's major systems. An industry rule of thumb was that putting a new blade on the market cost at least $3 million in machinery and marketing before the blade could be introduced.

Mr. Baker made these remarks about a segmentation strategy: "As an article of faith, segments are waiting to be discovered, but no one has a clear, simple way of discovering them. We have to do it the way a dog finds a hole in the fence--he runs up and down the fence, barking and barking, until he's on the other side." Should ASR fix on the suitable segment to serve, he said, the economics of a segmentation strategy would be as follows.

Assume a segment which is 15% of the total market, of which ASR could win 20% share, giving it the highest relative share within that segment. In the first six months the product could cost $350 thousand for fixed capital investments, $200 thousand for advertising, and $100 thousand for promotions. Over the first three years, advertising would cost $3 million; fixed promotions, $1 million; variable pro - motions, $500 thousand; and fixed capital investment, $750 thousand. Spending at this rate against 15% of the market would give the product an introduction comparable to Gillette's introduction of the Trac II.

Should ASR choose to leave the razor industry, the new owners were willing to consider entering other consumer goods markets to exploit their marketing skills, growing their current non-razor businesses, adding new products that would use their manufacturing skills, or entering new businesses by acquisition.

As he considered these choices--getting out of the razor industry, competing in its mainstream, and competing in its eddies--Mr. Baker kept in mind two goals for the business. First, and for the present most important, was continued profitability. By buying ASR the owners had saved it from liquidation, and they felt a strong obligation to their employees and to the residents of the Staunton area not to let the company fail. This obligation aside, the owners could not afford failure. All had drawn down their personal savings and several had taken second mortgages on their homes to make up their share of the purchase price. The second goal was growth. "There are nine owners," Mr. Baker said. "Our average age is 45. At 58 I'm an old man of the bunch, and everyone knows I won't retire, ever. For the moment we have our hands full getting our $40 million company running right. But if we're going to grow as people, in skill and responsibility, the company has to grow."

EXHIBIT 1

AMERICAN SAFETY RAZOR COMPANY (A)

CONSOLIDATED INCOME STATEMENTS 1972-1977

(000's omitted)

	1972	1973	1974	1975	1976
Operating Revenues	$26,300	$30,859	$34,915	$37,819	$42,412
Cost of Goods Sold	14,731	17,503	19,178	19,098	22,281
Marketing Expenses	9,025	9,411	11,033	14,320	15,206
G & A	1,560	1,658	1,730	2,075	2,117
R & D	732	729	820	896	1,065
Total Expenses	11,317	11,798	13,583	17,291	18,388
Operating Profit	252	1,558	2,154	1,430	1,743
Misc. Expenses	282	135	318	117	179
Pre-tax Income	(30)	1,423	1,836	1,313	1,564
Tax	----	713	916	653	782
Profit After Tax	$ (30)	$ 710	$ 920	$ 660	$ 782

Source: American Safety Razor

EXHIBIT 2

AMERICAN SAFETY RAZOR COMPANY (A)

BALANCE SHEETS
(Period Ending December 31, 1973-76)

	1973	1974	1975	1976
ASSETS				
Cash and Funds Surplus	$ 38	$ 70	$ 62	$ 374
Accounts Rec. (net)	2,761	3,718	4,002	4,664
Inventories	5,902	8,483	8,306	9,536
Other Current Assets	1,808	331	886	58
Current Assets	10,509	12,602	13,256	14,632
Net Property	7,083	6,917	6,463	6,458
Other Non-Cur. Assets	206	258	84	237
Total Assets	$17,798	$19,777	$19,803	$21,327
LIABILITIES & NET WORTH				
Accts. Payable	$ 200	$ 874	$ 460	$ 642
Other Cur. Liab.	1,024	1,411	1,195	1,755
Current Liabilities	1,224	2,285	1,655	2,397
Long-Term Debt	0	0	0	0
Total Liabilities	1,224	2,285	1,655	2,397
Common Stock	0	0	0	0
Retained Earnings	16,574	17,492	18,148	18,930
Net Worth	16,574	17,492	18,148	18,930
Liabilities & Net Worth	$17,798	$19,777	$19,803	$21,327

Source: American Safety Razor Company

EXHIBIT 3

AMERICAN SAFETY RAZOR COMPANY (A)

U.S. RAZOR BLADE SALES AT RETAIL, 1970-1981

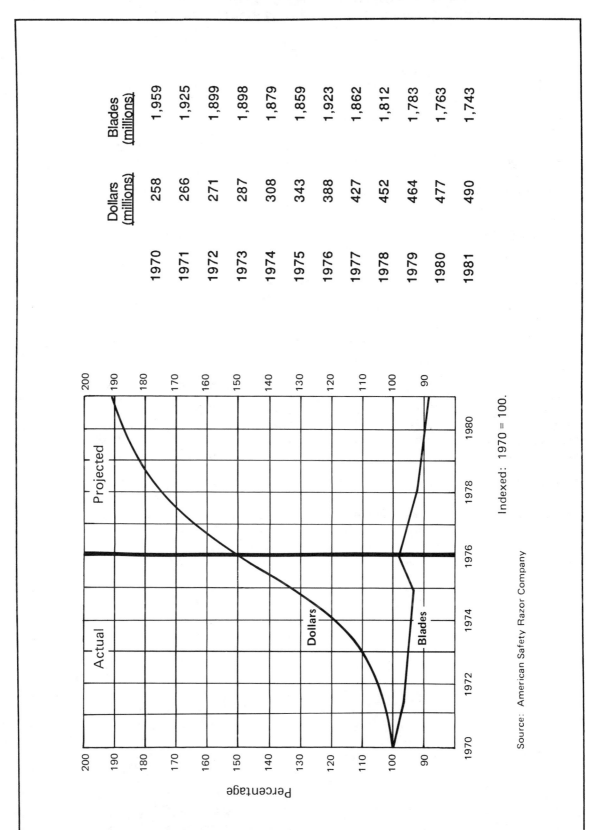

	Dollars (millions)	Blades (millions)
1970	258	1,959
1971	266	1,925
1972	271	1,899
1973	287	1,898
1974	308	1,879
1975	343	1,859
1976	388	1,923
1977	427	1,862
1978	452	1,812
1979	464	1,783
1980	477	1,763
1981	490	1,743

Indexed: 1970 = 100.

Source: American Safety Razor Company

EXHIBIT 4

AMERICAN SAFETY RAZOR COMPANY (A)

RAZOR BLADE MARKET BY CATEGORY OF BLADE
(Numbers represent percentage of industry sales at retail)

Dollar Basis

	Nov.-Dec. 1972	1973	1974	1975	1976
Twin:	20.0	26.7	35.4	40.8	42.9
Band:	13.0	10.9	7.7	5.6	4.2
Injector:	17.5	16.4	16.2	14.9	13.9
Double Edge:	44.1	39.3	33.2	28.7	25.7
Single Edge:	3.0	2.8	2.6	2.4	2.2
Women'sDisposable:	.9	1.7	3.2	5.4	5.8
General Disposable:	-	-	-	-	3.7
Private Label, other:	1.5	2.2	1.7	2.2	1.6

Blade Basis

	Nov.-Dec. 1972	1973	1974	1975	1976
Twin:	15.0	20.9	27.4	32.2	34.2
Band:	11.0	9.6	7.3	5.8	4.1
Injector:	15.9	15.1	15.1	14.5	13.9
Double Edge:	49.1	44.9	39.5	35.3	32.3
Single Edge:	5.3	5.1	4.9	4.7	4.6
Women's Disposable:	0.6	1.1	1.9	2.5	3.3
General Disposable:	-	-	-	0.5	2.5
Private Label, Other:	3.1	3.3	3.9	4.5	5.1

Source: American Safety Razor Company

EXHIBIT 5

AMERICAN SAFETY RAZOR COMPANY (A)

RAZOR INDUSTRY MARKET SHARES

DOLLAR SHARE OF MARKET*

		Nov.-Dec. 1972	1973	1974	1975	1976
Total	Gillette	58.4%	58.1%	57.0%	57.6%	57.7%
	Techmatic	11.1	9.6	6.9	5.2	3.9
	Double Edge	30.8	27.7	23.1	20.2	18.1
	Injector	3.1	3.2	4.2	3.7	3.0
	Trac II	13.4	17.6	22.8	27.1	27.7
	Good News	-	-	-	-	2.8
	Daisy	-	-	-	1.4	2.2
Total	Schick	22.7	23.2	23.7	22.6	23.7
	Band	1.9	1.3	.8	.4	.3
	Super II	2.2	4.4	7.1	8.0	9.7
	Double Edge	6.1	5.7	4.7	3.7	3.4
	Injector	12.5	11.8	11.1	10.5	10.3
Total	Wilkinson	8.6	8.3	7.9	7.5	6.9
	Double Edge	4.2	4.0	3.8	3.2	2.7
	Bonded	4.4	4.3	4.1	4.3	4.2
Total	Bic	-	-	-	-	0.2
Total	ASR	8.8	8.7	9.5	10.0	9.3
	Single Edge	3.0	2.8	2.6	2.4	2.3
	Personna Inj.	1.9	1.5	.8	.7	.5
	Personna D. E.	3.0	2.3	1.7	1.6	1.6
	Flicker	.9	1.7	3.2	4.0	3.7
	Personna Double II	-	.4	1.2	1.3	1.2
Private Labels, Other		1.5	1.7	1.9	2.3	2.2

*At retail

Source: American Safety Razor Company

EXHIBIT 5 (continued)

AMERICAN SAFETY RAZOR COMPANY (A)

RAZOR INDUSTRY MARKET SHARES

<u>**UNIT SHARE OF MARKET**</u>

		Nov.-Dec. 1972	1973	1974	1975	1976
Total	Gillette	58.0%	57.2%	56.4%	56.4%	55.5%
	Techmatic	9.4	8.3	6.3	5.1	3.8
	Double Edge	36.1	32.9	28.8	26.0	23.4
	Injector	2.9	3.0	3.7	3.5	3.0
	Trac II	9.6	13.0	17.6	21.3	22.1
	Good News	-	-	-	0.5	2.3
	Daisy	-	-	-	-	0.9
Total	Schick	20.1	20.5	21.3	20.8	22.3
	Band	1.6	1.3	1.0	.7	.3
	Super II	1.7	3.1	5.3	6.2	8.2
	Double Edge	5.8	5.5	4.6	3.7	3.6
	Injector	11.0	10.6	10.4	10.2	10.2
Total	Wilkinson	8.0	8.0	7.9	7.5	6.9
	Double Edge	4.4	4.3	4.3	3.8	3.3
	Bonded	3.6	3.7	3.6	3.7	3.6
Total	Bic	-	-	-	-	0.2
Total	ASR	10.7	10.2	10.2	10.9	10.6
	Single Edge	5.3	5.1	4.8	4.7	4.6
	Personna Inj.	2.0	1.5	1.0	.8	.7
	Personna D. E.	2.8	2.2	1.7	1.8	1.9
	Flicker	.6	1.1	1.9	2.6	2.4
	Personna Double II	-	0.3	0.8	1.0	1.0
Private Labels, Other		3.2	4.1	4.2	4.4	4.7

Source: American Safety Razor Company

EXHIBIT 6

AMERICAN SAFETY RAZOR COMPANY (A)

RETAIL DISTRIBUTION RATES, JANUARY-FEBRUARY 1977
(Percentage of outlets reached)

Product	Kind of Retail Outlet		
	Food	Drug	Mass Merchandise
Gillette (total)	98	99	N.A
Trac	95	99	N.A.
Techmatic	90	95	N.A.
Double Edge	97	98	N.A.
Injector	86	90	N.A.
Good News	84	96	N.A.
Daisy	68	79	92*
Schick (total)	96	97	N.A.
Super II and Band	89	95	N.A.
Double edge	72	93	N.A.
Injector	95	97	N.A.
Wilkinson (total)	92	95	N.A.
Bonded	88	93	N.A.
Double edge	52	87	N.A.
Disposable	5	5	N.A.
Bic Shaver	20*	43*	29*
ASR (total)	97	99	N.A.
Flicker	79*	86*	94*
Single edge	89*	96*	72*
Personna injector	29*	47*	N.A.
Personna double edge	45*	72*	N.A.
Personna Double II	54*	79*	79*

* Starred numbers are national distribution rates. All other numbers are distribution rates for the east-central region. These regional distribution rates approximate national rates fairly closely. East-central rates for Bic's disposable shaver, whose test market was in that region, were 64% in food channels and 84% in drug channels.

Source: American Safety Razor Company

EXHIBIT 7

AMERICAN SAFETY RAZOR COMPANY (A)

ADVERTISING EXPENDITURES, 1975 and 1976

Spending by Company ($000)

	1975	1976
ASR	$ 2,424	$ 3,056
Gillette	11,082	11,773
Schick	7,072	8,383
Wilkinson	3,234	2,925
Total	$23,812	$26,137

Share of Advertising vs. Dollar Market Share

	1975 %Adv./SOM	1976 %Adv./SOM
ASR	10.2/10.0	11.7/9.3
Gillette	46.5/57.6	45.0/57.7
Schick	29.7/22.6	32.1/23.7
Wilkinson	13.6/7.5	11.2/6.9

Advertising Media

	1975	1976
Television	18,548	21,116
Spot television	2,174	2,969
Magazines	2,649	1,526
Newspaper	342	572
Radio	109	–

Source: Company Records

EXHIBIT 8

AMERICAN SAFETY RAZOR COMPANY (A)

FINANCIAL PROFILES OF ASR'S COMPETITORS

	Total Sales[1] (millions)	Net Income[2] (millions)	ROI	D/E Ratio[3]	Payout Ratio	R&D[4]
Gillette	$1,491	$78	7%	32%	58%	2.3%*
Warner-Lambert	$2,349	$160	8%	21%	49%	3.4%
Wilkinson**	N.A.	N.A.	N.A.	N.A.	N.A.	N.A.
Bic Pen	$123	$10	11%	5%	23%	9.2%

* Competitors estimated that Gillette spent as much as 80% of its R&D budget on the razor division.

** Because Wilkinson was a British company, its financial records were not public.

[1] Total Sales for all product & divisions

[2] Net Income after Tax

[3] Debt/Equity Ratio

[4] R&D Expense/Sales all products & divisions

Sources: Various

EXHIBIT 9

AMERICAN SAFETY RAZOR COMPANY (A)

COMPETITORS' PRODUCT LINES

Product Categories

	Auto.	Disp.	Twin Inj.	Twin	Band	Inj.	DE	SE
Gillette	s	sw	s	sw	sw	s	sw	--
Schick	--	--	s	sw	sw	s	s	--
ASR	--	w	s	swp	--	sp	sp	s
Wilkinson	--	--	--	sp	--	p	sp	p
Bic	--	sw	--	--	--	--	--	--

Code: s = standard version; 2 = women's version; p = private label version

Product categories:

SE. Single edge. An early blade design. Blade has one cutting edge and a reinforced spine for locking into razor. Introduced 1875 by ASR.

DE. Double edge. Dominant blade design until 1970's. Blade has two cutting edges, one on either side of blade. Introduced 1903 by Gillette.

Inj. Injector. A single-edged blade, narrower than conventional single edges and without reinforced spine. It is injected into razor by a special dispenser. Introduced 1920 by Schick.

Band. A razor "system" with a single cutting edge. Cutting edge is a continuous band that can be advanced when a portion of it has dulled. Introduced 1965 by Gillette. Example: Gillette Techmatic.

Twin. Twin-bladed system with two parallel blades bonded into a plastic cartridge that attaches to razor handle. Introduced 1971 by Gillette. Examples: Gillette Trac II, Schick Super II, Wilkinson Bonded II, Personna Double II.

Twin inj. Twin injector. An injector system with two parallel blades. Introduced in 1973 by Gillette.

Disp. Disposable razor. Bonded blade (or bonded twin blades) and plastic handle are one unit. Whole unit thrown away when blade has dulled. Introduced 1976 by Gillette. Examples: Gillette's Good News, Bic Shaver, ASR's Flicker disposable women's shaver introduced 1972.

Auto. Automatically adjusting razor system. A twin-blade bonded razor system with a "floating" head that keeps the blades at the proper shaving angle to the face. Only Gillette Atra currently available. Introduced 1977.

Note: Single-edge, double-edged, and injector blades were available in both carbon steel and stainless steel, and with a variety of ionic coating--platinum, tungsten, chromium, etc. Blades made of different steel or having different coatins were treated as separate brands by their manufacturers. Newer products--twins, twin injectors, disposables, and automatics--were all made of stainless steel; brands were distinguished by design, not by blade composition.

EXHIBIT 10

AMERICAN SAFETY RAZOR COMPANY (A)

ASR ACCOUNT CONTRIBUTION, 1976
($000's)

Top Accounts	$ Sales (All Brands)	% Sales	% Accounts
199	$13,643	50.0%	2.3%
398	17,425	63.9	4.6
597	19,496	71.5	6.9
796	20,888	76.6	9.3
995	21,867	80.2	11.6
1,194	22,583	82.8	13.9

Sales Through Top 995 Customers, by Brand

Brand	Total Sales	Top 995 Sales	% Sales
Flicker	$10,591	$8,505	80.3%
Personnal Double II	5,405	4,302	79.6
Single edge	5,540	4,293	77.5
Personna refills	4,677	3,845	82.2
Other branded products	1,063	922	86.7

Total Sales Branded Products $27,276
Total Number of Accounts   8,600

EXHIBIT 11

AMERICAN SAFETY RAZOR COMPANY (A)

RAZOR BLADE SALES AND CONTRIBUTIONS, 1976
(000's)

	Flicker	Double II	Faceguard	Refill Blades	Total	Single Edges	Private Label
			Personna				
Units Shipped	10,637	20,610	2,713	40,133	63,456	91,769	55,086
Net Sales	$10,591	$5,405	$349	$4,716	$10,470	$5,450	$2,199
Marginal Contribution	$ 8,235	$3,176	$218	$3,608	$ 7,002	$3,610	$ 918
Direct Marketing:							
Advertising	$1,274	$1,355	-	-	$1,355	-	-
Promotion	$2,229	$2,403	$107	$2,568	$5,078	$ 200	$ 17
Other	$ 129	$ 83	$ 5	$ 34	$ 122	$ 74	$ 7
Total	$3,632	$3,841	$112	$2,602	$6,555	$ 274	$ 24
Brand Contribution	$4,603	$ [665]	$106	$1,006	$ 447	$3,336	$ 894

EXHIBIT 12

AMERICAN SAFETY RAZOR COMPANY (A)

PRICES OF REPRESENTATIVE WOMEN'S SAVING PRODUCTS

Product	Retail	Price per package Wholesale	Factory	Factory Price per blade
Women's Shavers				
Flicker (5 blades)	$1.69	$1.21	$1.01	$.20
Gillette Daisy Shaver 2's	1.19	.86	.71	.35
Schick Personal Touch refill 4's	1.59	1.15	.96	.24
Schick Personal Touch razor kit				
(razor, 4 blades, and case)	2.15	1.54	1.29	--
General Disposables				
Gillette Good News 2's	.60	.43	.36	.18
Bic Shaver	N.A.	N.A.	N.A.	N.A.
Males Products Commonly Used by Women				
Gillette Trac II 5's				
(also fit Lady Trac II razor)	1.70	1.22	1.02	.20
Schick Super II 5's				
(also fit Lady Super II razor)	1.70	1.22	1.02	.20

Source: American Safety Razor Company

EXHIBIT 13

AMERICAN SAFETY RAZOR COMPANY (A)

UNIT SALES FORECAST, APRIL 5, 1977
DOMESTIC SHAVING BLADES (000's)

	1976	1977	1978	1979	1980	1981
Flicker	10,640	7,550	9,000	10,000	10,500	10,750
Personna Double II	23,260	10,765	8,300	6,000	–	--
Personna Face Guard	2,680	1,680	1,500	1,500	1,500	1,500
Personna Refill Blades	39,800	30,800	29,000	30,500	36,000	40,000
Single Edge	91,570	63,450	74,000	71,000	68,000	65,000
Private Label	55,420	69,750	71,000	74,000	73,000	72,000
Total	223,370	183,995	192,800	193,000	189,000	189,250

Source: Company Records

Note: These projections were prepared as part of a prospectus used to seek financing for the purchase of ASR. They do not reflect firm strategic decisions that management accepted as of October, 1977. The major product line strategies and assumptions about product line sales that were used for these projections were as follows:

Flicker. Introduction of a single-blade version; resumption of advertising and promotion, but at a lower rate than before 1977. Initial drop in sales due to uncertainty in the channel's about ASR's future; quick return to sales levels of 1976 and slight growth thereafter.

Personna Double II. No advertising or promotion. Discontinuation of razors after 1978; of blades after 1979.

Personna Refill Blades. Return to pre-1976 promotional levels; still no advertising. Steady decline in sales from double-edged and injector refills through 1978 due to competition from twin blades, then leveling of sales. Introduction of Personna twin-bladed refill in 1978 will bring steady growth to 20,000 units by 1981.

Single Edges. No change in strategy. Immediate drop in sales due to reduced sales coverage; resumption of historical rate of slow decline thereafter.

Private Label. No change in strategy. Sales growth due to introduction of twin-bladed cartridge.

EXHIBIT 14

AMERICAN SAFETY RAZOR COMPANY (A)

DOMESTIC SHAVING BLADES MARKETING
$000's - 4/5/77

	1976	1977	1978	1979	1980	1981
Advertising	2,633	1,512	900	1,000	1,000	1,000
Other Selling	508	403	500	550	575	600
Promotion	7,208	5,482	5,441	5,653	5,629	5,999
Field Force	2,871	2,071	2,087	2,282	2,498	2,733
Market Research	165	81	--	--	--	--
Marketing Administration	407	83	--	--	--	--
Total Marketing	13,792	9,632	8,928	9,485	9,702	10,332

Source: American Safety Razor Company

Note: See Note to Exhibit 13 for an explanation of the assumptions behind this budget. These figures, pre-pared in April 1977, project lower levels of marketing expense than are projected in Exhibit 15, prepared in August 1977.

EXHIBIT 15

AMERICAN SAFETY RAZOR COMPANY (A)

PRO FORMA INCOME STATEMENT, 1977-1981
($000's)

	1977	1978	1979	1980	1981
Net Sales	37,622	41,391	44,397	47,852	51,734
Cost of Sales	21,054	22,771	24,968	27,396	29,994
Gross Proft	16,568	18,620	19,429	20,456	21,740
Marketing Expenses	11,051	10,700	11,354	11,698	12,492
G&A R&D	1,552	2,781	3,059	3,372	3,701
Depreciation	1,431	1,154	886	699	800
Operating Profit	2,534	3,985	4,130	4,687	4,747
Severance & Royalties	1,322	135	50	50	50
Interest Expense	190	872	783	748	766
Net Before Tax	1,022	2,978	3,297	3,889	3,931
Income Tax	511	1,489	1,649	1,945	1,966
Net Profit (Loss)	511	1,489	1,649	1,945	1,966
Purchase Adjustment	19,100	0	0	0	0
Cash Flow[1]	7,186	(240)	246	257	269

[1]Cash Flow = Net Profit - Change in Working Capital - Change in Net Property

Sales Breakdown

	1977	1978	1979	1980	1981
Domestic Blades					
Flicker	7,717	9,159	10,778	11,338	12,403
Personna Double II	3,136	2,648	1,914	--	--
Personna Face Guard	226	226	226	250	250
Personna Refills	4,066	4,307	4,775	6,479	7,406
Single Edge	3,837	4,976	4,774	5,332	5,224
Private Label	3,304	3,705	3,936	4,624	4,615
Total domestic blades	22,286	25,021	26,403	28,023	29,898
Exports and Puerto Rican Sales	4,063	4,134	4,514	4,959	5,420
Toiletries and Miscellaneous shaving products	372	475	509	542	578
Industrial and Surgical Blades	10,901	11,761	12,971	14,328	15,838
Total Sales	37,622	41,391	44,397	47,852	51,734

Note: See note to Exhibit 13 for explanation of assumptions behind this statement.

Source: American Safety Razor

EXHIBIT 16

AMERICAN SAFETY RAZOR COMPANY (A)

PRO FORMA BALANCE SHEETS, DEC. 31, 1977-1981
($000's)

	1977	1978	1979	1980	1981
ASSETS					
Cash	750	830	890	960	1,035
Accounts Receivable Net	4,175	4,662	5,000	5,390	5,830
Inventories	8,000	8,826	9,566	10,410	11,400
Other Current Assets	51	54	57	60	63
Current Assets	12,976	14,372	15,513	16,820	18,328
Net Property	5,608	5,154	5,068	5,569	6,369
Other Non-Current Assets	100	100	100	100	100
Total Assets	18,684	19,626	20,681	22,489	24,797
LIABILITIES & NET WORTH					
Short Term Borrowings	4,022	3,138	2,603	2,580	3,103
Current Maturities	399	151	245	256	269
Accounts Payable	560	618	670	729	798
Accrued Income Tax	85	372	412	486	491
Other Current Liabilities	1,500	1,500	1,500	1,500	1,500
Current Liabilities	6,566	5,779	5,430	5,551	6,161
Term Loan - 10.5%	2,592	0	0	0	0
Mortgage 20 Yrs. 10%	0	2,924	2,866	2,802	2,732
EDA Loan 3%	6,000	5,908	5,721	5,528	5,330
State Virginia 3%	250	250	250	250	250
Purchase Discount	2,335	2,335	2,335	2,335	2,335
Total Liabilities	17,743	17,196	16,602	16,466	16,808
Common Stock	600	600	600	600	600
Retained Earnings	341	1,830	3,479	5,423	7,389
Net Worth	941	2,430	4,079	6,023	7,989
Liabilities & Net Worth	18,684	19,626	20,681	22,489	24,797

Note: See note to Exhibit 13 for an explanation of the assumptions behind these balance sheets.

Source: American Safety Razor Company

Anheuser-Busch Companies, Inc.[1]

For Anheuser-Busch Companies, Inc., 1983 was the best year in the company's history. Sales were up 28 percent to $6.7 billion and earnings increased 16.1 percent to $348 million. According to a 1983 Fortune poll, Anheuser-Busch Companies was one of "America's Most Admired Corporations," ranking eighth among all U.S. corporations and number one in the beverage industry. In terms of overall size, A-B ranked 55th on the 1983 *Fortune* listing of the 500 largest industrial corporations in the United States (up from a ranking of 77 in 1982).

During 1983, the company's brewing subsidiary, Anheuser-Busch, Inc., sold an all-time industry record of 60.5 million barrels of beer--more than 23 million barrels above its nearest competitor and the largest leadership margin in its history. Already the world's largest brewer for 27 consecutive years, Anheuser-Busch achieved a 2.4 percent increase in barrelage over 1982--a year in which total industry sales growth was only 1.5 percent. The company's 1983 market share in beer was 32.5 percent.

COMPANY HISTORY AND BACKGROUND

Anheuser-Busch Companies, Inc., was formed originally through the acquisition of the failing Bavarian Brewing Company in St. Louis, Missouri. Eberhard Anheuser, a successful soap manufacturer and Bavarian's major credit, purchased the nearly bankrupt brewery in 1860. But Adolphus Busch, Anheuser's son-in-law was responsible for many of the innovations which put Anheuser-Busch on the road to industry prominence.

During Adolphus Busch's tenure as president, he created a network of railside ice houses to cool beer being shipped long distance, pioneered a new pasteurization process, and established the industry's first fleet of refrigerated freight cars. He developed both the Budweiser and Michelob brands of beer. Busch's talents also extended to the promotional side of the business. He made the St. Louis brewer a showplace for the public, insisted that only the finest horses pull the Anheuser-Busch delivery wagons, and initiated one of the company's most successful promotions of all times--the distribution of large reproductions of the painting, *Custer's Last Fight.*

Using his skills as a brewer and promoter, Adolphus Busch pushed the company towards becoming a national factor in an industry where local breweries and local beers were still the industry norm. In 1901, annual beer sales exceeded the million-barrel mark.

Busch's descendants continued his strategy of creating innovations to meet demand. August A. Busch Sr., assumed control of the company after his father's death in 1913 only to face three major crises in succession--World War I, Prohibition, and the Great Depression. To survive, he focused the company in new directions--the production of corn products, baker's yeast, ice cream, commerical refrigeration units, and truck bodies. The company also produced carbonated soft drinks and a nonalcoholic malt-derived beverage, BEVO. It was during this period that the Budweiser Clydesdales were acquired to celebrate the ending of one crisis--passage of the 21st Amendment. The Clydesdale horses pulling an Anheuser-Busch beer wagon soon became one of the company's symbols and trademarks, a tradition which continues today.

As times became more stable, August Sr.'s successors carried on his policy of growth and expansion through diversification and vertical integration. Adolphus Busch III, who became president in 1934, led the company's effort to become the leading producer of baker's yeast in the United States. August A. Busch, Jr., who served as president and chief executive officer from 1946-75, extended the company's diversification efforts to include family entertainment (Busch Gardens), real estate, can manufacturing,

[1]Prepared by Prof. L. Sharon Topping, The University of Alabama. Reprinted with permission from A. J. Strickland III, and Arthur Thompson, Jr., *Cases in Strategic Management (2d ed.),* Plano, TX: Business Publications, Inc., pp. 288-314, copyright © 1985.

also flourished--eight breweries were constructed; the Busch brand of beer was introduced; and annual beer sales were increased from 3 million barrels in 1946 to 34 million barrels in 1975.

In 1976, August A. Busch III became the fifth Busch to assume control of the company. Under his leadership the company expanded its brewing capacity, increased its vertical integration capabilities, and continued to extend its diversification efforts. And it was during his presidency that Anheuser-Busch had to cope with a significant change in the competitive environment of the brewing industry and a virtual revolution in the way beer was marketed.

Exhibit 1 contains a 10-year financial and operating review.

THE CHALLENGE OF THE SEVENTIES

It was 1957 when Anheuser-Busch seized the industry leadership from Schlitz Brewing Company and, with the triumph, began more than a decade of unchallenged rule. During this period the company experienced strong demand for its products; according to a former manager, Anheuser-Busch found it was "running out of beer every summer."[2] Consequently, top management saw no real need for aggressive marketing. August Busch, Jr., who was in his 70s, was even more reluctant to take on additional debt to increase capacity. The prevailing philosophy seemed to be, "Why spend money when you are selling all you can?"

Meanwhile, a significant acquisition occurred. Miller Brewing Company was acquired by Philip Morris, Inc., and, shortly afterwards, started receiving infusions of capital and marketing savvy from the new parent. Between 1970-77, Miller expanded capacity fivefold. Its media advertising budget rose from $8.4 million to $42.4 million, much of which went toward the purchase of advertising spots on TV sports programs. By the end of 1977, Miller sponsored 70 percent of all the network ads on TV sports programs.

Miller's television commericals were part of an aggressive marketing campaign based on market and product segmentation and target advertising and promotion, techniques new to the beer industry. Miller was the first brewer to use image-building, rather than price, to sell beer. Featuring young men engaged in manly labors, such as cutting trees and then cooling off with beer, Miller's TV ads created a new image for its flagship brand, Miller High Life. With "Miller Time," this premium beer was repositioned to attract a broader market base and, thereby, compete directly against Anheuser-Busch's Budweiser brand.

Using the same advertising technique, Miller launched one of the most successful promotions ever, the introduction of its low-calorie beer, Miller Lite. From marketing research, the company found that a significant proportion of the beer market was composed of young to middle-aged male sports fans who dreamed of athletic prowess. By using retired athletes still known for their speed and quickness, the advertisements conveyed the message that with one third fewer calories, rugged men could drink lots of Lite yet remain fast. The image was one of athletic ability not weight control.

By the mid-1970s, Miller posed a serious threat to Anheuser-Busch's industry leadership, Anheuser-Busch had no low-calorie beer to compete in this fast-growing new market segment. Capacity had not been expanded since 1972, and its marketing organization was outdated and in need of an overhaul. From 1972-76, Anheuser-Busch's average per barrel advertising expense was 55.8 cents while Miller spent triple that amount. During the same period, Anheuser-Busch's sales volume grew approximately 5 percent annually compared to Miller's annual volume growth of over 30 percent.

Miller's challenge for industry leadership came when Anheuser-Busch was in the middle of a major transition in management from the domineering style of August Busch, Jr., to that of his son. Moreover, the company was involved in a 100-day strike in 1976, which kept Anheuser-Busch's products off retailers' shelves during the peak summer season. As a result, Budweiser lost market share--from 18.0 percent in 1974 to 13.8 percent in 1976 (see Exhibit 2). After the strike, the sales of Budweiser were slow to recover against the fierce competition of Miller High Life (Miller's total market share increased steadily between 1970-77--from 3.4 percent to 15.4 percent by 1977). With Budweiser constituting more than 60 percent of Anheuser-Busch's total revenue, its leadership slippage became a serious matter, and the company was forced into action to defend its position as number one in the industry.

---

[2]As quoted in *Business Week*, July 12, 1982, p. 52.

EXHIBIT 1
Financial Summary, Anheuser-Busch Companies, Inc., 1974–1983 *($ million, except per share and statistical data)*

	1983	1982	1981	1980	1979	1978	1977	1976	1975	1974
Sales and earnings:										
Barrels sold	60.5	59.1	54.5	50.2	46.2	41.6	36.6	29.1	35.2	34.1
Sales	$6,658.5	$5,185.7	$4,409.6	$3,822.4	$3,263.7	$2,701.6	$2,231.2	$1,753.0	$2,036.7	$1,791.9
Federal and state beer taxes	624.3	609.1	562.4	527.0	487.8	442.0	393.2	311.9	391.7	378.8
Net sales	6,034.2	4,576.6	3,847.2	3,295.4	2,775.9	2,259.6	1,838.0	1,441.1	1,645.0	1,413.1
Cost of products sold	4,113.2	3,331.7	2,975.5	2,553.9	2,172.1	1,762.4	1,462.8	1,175.0	1,343.8	1,187.8
Gross profit	1,921.0	1,244.9	871.7	741.5	603.8	497.2	375.2	266.1	301.2	225.3
Marketing, administrative and research expenses	1,220.2	752.0	515.0	428.6	356.7	274.9	190.4	137.8	126.1	106.7
Operating income	700.8	492.9	356.7	312.9	247.1	222.3	184.8	128.3	175.1	118.6
Interest expense	(111.4)	(89.2)	(89.6)	(75.6)	(40.3)	(28.9)	(26.7)	(26.9)	(22.6)	(11.9)
Interest capitalized	32.9	41.2	64.1	41.7	—	—	—	—	—	—
Interest income	12.5	17.0	6.2	2.4	8.4	11.7	7.7	10.3	10.9	9.9
Other income (expense), net	(18.8)	(8.1)	(12.2)	(9.9)	5.4	.7	4.1	1.7	1.9	4.9
Loss on partial closing of Los Angeles Busch Gardens	—	—	—	—	—	—	—	(10.0)	—	—
Gain on sale of Lafayette plant	—	20.4	—	—	—	—	—	—	—	—
Income before income taxes	616.0	474.2	325.2	271.5	220.6	205.8	169.9	103.4	165.3	121.5
Income taxes	268.0	186.9	107.8	99.7	76.3	94.8	78.0	48.0	80.6	57.5
Income before cumulative effect of an accounting change	348.0	287.3	217.4	171.8	144.3	111.0	91.9	55.4	84.7	64.0
Cumulative effect of change to the flow-through method of accounting for the investment tax credit	—	—	—	—	52.1	—	—	—	—	—
Net income	348.0	287.3	217.4	171.8	196.4	111.0	91.9	55.4	84.7	64.0

EXHIBIT 1 (cont.)

Per share—primary:										
Income before cumulative effect of an accounting change	6.50	5.97	4.79	3.80	3.19	2.46	2.04	1.23	1.88	1.42
Cumulative effect of change to the flow-through method of accounting for the investment tax credit	—	—	—	—	1.15	—	—	—	—	—
Net income	6.50	5.97	4.79	3.80	4.34	2.46	2.04	1.23	1.88	1.42
Per share—fully diluted	6.50	5.88	4.61	3.80	4.34	2.46	2.04	1.23	1.88	1.42
Cash dividends paid:										
Common stock	78.3	65.8	51.2	44.8	40.7	37.0	32.0	30.6	28.8	27.0
Per share	1.62	1.38	1.13	.99	.90	.82	.71	.68	.64	.60
Preferred stock	29.7	—	—	—	—	—	—	—	—	—
Per share	3.60	—	—	—	—	—	—			
Average number of common shares	53.5	48.1	45.4	45.2	45.2	45.1	45.1	45.1	45.1	45.1
Balance sheet information:										
Working capital	175.1	45.8	45.9	26.3	88.1	223.7	175.4	182.1	255.4	132.4
Current ratio	1.2	1.1	1.1	1.1	1.3	1.8	1.8	2.0	2.5	2.1
Plant and equipment, net	3,204.2	2,988.9	2,257.6	1,947.4	1,461.8	1,109.2	952.0	857.1	724.9	622.9
Long-term debt	961.4	969.0	817.3	743.8	507.9	427.3	337.5	340.7	342.2	193.2
Total debt to total debt plus equity	31.9%	35.4%	42.4%	43.4%	36.0%	36.4%	33.4%	35.8%	36.8%	26.7%
Deferred income taxes	573.2	455.1	357.7	261.6	193.8	146.9	119.1	93.0	74.6	60.1
Common stock and other shareholders' equity	1,766.5	1,526.6	1,206.8	1,031.4	904.3	747.9	673.9	611.9	587.1	531.2
Return on shareholders' equity	18.0%	19.9%	19.3%	17.8%	16.9%	15.6%	14.3%	9.2%	15.2%	12.5%
Total assets	4,330.2	3,902.8	2,875.2	2,449.7	1,926.0	1,648.0	1,403.8	1,268.1	1,202.1	931.4
Capital expenditures	428.0	355.8	421.3	590.0	432.3	228.7	156.7	198.7	155.4	126.5
Depreciation and amortization	187.3	133.6	108.7	99.4	75.4	66.0	61.2	53.1	51.1	45.0
Total payroll cost	1,350.8	853.3	686.7	594.1	529.1	421.8	338.9	271.4	268.3	244.4
Effective tax rate	43.5%	39.4%	33.1%	36.7%	34.6%	46.0%	45.9%	46.4%	48.7%	47.3%
Price/earnings ratio	9.6	11.0	8.9	7.3	7.1	9.8	9.8	18.8	18.1	17.1
Percent of pretax profit on gross sales	9.3%	9.1%	7.4%	7.1%	6.8%	7.6%	7.6%	5.9%	8.1%	6.8%
Market price per common stock:										
High	77	70¾	44⅛	31¼	27⅛	27¾	25¼	38⅝	39⅝	38
Low	58½	38⅝	27⅝	21	19⅜	17½	18¾	20¾	24½	21

Source: Anheuser-Busch Companies, Inc., *Annual Report,* 1983, and *Standard & Poor's Stock Report,* 1984.

EXHIBIT 2

**Market Share, Sales Volume, and Advertising Expenditures per Barrel
for Anheuser-Busch, Inc., and Miller Brewing Company, 1974-1983**

Year	Market Share		Sales Volume (millions of barrels)		Advertising per Barrel	
	A-B	Miller	A-B	Miller	A-B	Miller
1974	23.2%	6.2%	34.1%	9.1%	$0.36	$1.33
1975	23.4	8.6	35.2	12.9	0.55	1.62
1976	20.9	12.1	29.1	18.2	0.89	1.58
1977	23.3	15.4	36.6	24.2	1.24	1.74
1978	25.1	19.3	41.6	31.3	1.52	2.06
1979	26.4	20.7	46.2	35.8	1.89	2.10
1980	28.2	21.0	50.2	37.3	1.87	2.37
1981	30.4	22.5	54.5	40.3	2.05	2.31
1982	32.0	21.9	59.1	39.3	2.63	3.04
1983	32.5	20.0	60.5	37.5	2.72*	4.22*

*Estimate

Source: *Beverage Industry Annual Manual, Standard & Poor's Industry Surveys. Modern Brewery Age,* and *Beverage World.*

A MARKETING OVERHAUL

In 1976, August A. Busch III assumed full control of the company and declared all-out war on Miller. According to a former Anheuser-Busch division manager, "After the strike, Busch solidly installed his brand of leadership--attack, attack, attack."[3] To begin with, Busch totally revamped the company's marketing strategy--first, to regain market share and then, to fight off Miller.

As Michael J. Roarty, vice president of marketing of Anheuser-Busch, described it:

Realizing that the game had changed and the competition was getting tougher, Anheuser-Busch took stock of itself in 1977. Every market segment, every computer, every product, and every one of the market programs was analyzed. The result was a marketing overhaul--a renaissance, in retrospect--the likes of which the industry had never witnessed.[4]

To meet the challenge from Miller, Budweiser obviously had to lead the way. The first priorities following the strike were to beef up the marketing staff, build a strong brand management system and pinpoint where Miller had made its most damaging inroads. While industry analysts wondered whether a company that refused to recognize the opportunity for low-calorie beer could beat Miller at its own game of strategic marketing, Anheuser-Busch recruited new talent from such savvy marketers as General Mills and Procter & Gamble and set them to work breaking down the beer market into useful demographic segments.

Analysis of the demographics revealed that Budweiser's most serious losses were among young people and minorities. In response, the company hired about 100 recent college graduates and organized them into "Swat" teams to promote sales on college campuses and other centers of young beer drinkers. It also created new advertising campaigns aimed at the youth segment and blacks and Hispanics.[5]

---

[3]Ibid.

[4]Michael J. Roarty, *Marketing Communications,* November-December 1982, p. 47.

[5]As reported in *Dun's Business Month,* February 1982, p. 83.

As part of the revamped advertising strategy, Anheuser-Busch became the leading sponsor of sports events in the country. By 1982, the brewer sponsored 98 professional and 310 college events compared to 12 and 7, respectively, in 1976. These included pro football, major league baseball, basketball, hockey, racquetball, running, fishing, softball, horse racing, soccer, rodeos, and bowling.

Anheuser-Busch's entrance into auto racing exemplified the breadth of its sponsorship program. Through marketing research, auto racing was identified as the second-largest spectator sport in the country (surpassed only by football), with 85 percent of the fans drinking beer. Moreover, they were found to be the most responsive consumer group to advertisers who sponsor their events. This prompted Anheuser-Busch to increase its sponsorship of auto racing events to include:

The Paul Newman/Can-Am team and the entire race series.
The Budweiser King Funny Car on the drag-racing circuit.
The Busch Pole Award in every NASCAR race which automatically qualified the winner for
    the Busch Clash Stock Car Race.
The Natural Light Corvette in Sports Car Clue of America Class GT-1 events.
The Budweiser Rocket, the first manned vehicle to break the speed of sound on land with
    an acceleration from 1 to 143 in one second and a run of 739.6 mph.

Anheuser-Busch started to compete with Miller for network TV time. According to A-B's marketing vice president:

Budweiser's brand managers also realized that one of Miller's most powerful weapons was its aggressive purchase of television sports programming in the early 1970s. Miller had locked up 70 percent of TV sports, the most efficient media vehicle for reaching men aged 18 through 44, the primary target for most beer advertising. Between 1976 and 1981, the Budweiser media budget was more than tripled as its admen scrambled to find sports sponsorships.[6]

In 1982, Anheuser-Busch bought spots on ABC-TV's Monday Night Football, long an exclusive Miller domain. The company became the official and exclusive brewer for the 1984 Summer Olympics and the U.S. Olympic Team. As a major corporate sponsor ($10 million), Anheuser-Busch had the right to use the Olympic symbol in conjunction with its various corporate and brand logos.

With competition intensifying throughout the industry, Anheuser-Busch aggressively pursued market and product segmentation. First, the national market was broken down into various geographic segments to identify the different growth trends associated with each. This analysis showed that, in the South, demand for beer was growing faster than any other region in the nation (Exhibit 3). Furthermore, the five states with the fastest-growing beer consumption per capita over the past 40 years (1940-1980) were in the South.

California led the country in total beverage consumption with 605.7 gallons. During the 1970s, beer sales grew more rapidly in Florida and Texas than in any other states:

State	*Million Barrels* 1970	1980	Volume Change 1970-1980
Florida	4.8	9.0	89.0%
Texas	8.2	15.4	86.9
U.S. Total	122.6	168.8	37.7

Given the geographic analysis, Anheuser-Busch concentrated its marketing efforts in the western and southern regions of the country, with particular emphasis on Florida, Texas, and California. The company expanded its breweries in Houston and Los Angeles. Advertising was increased in these areas, with promotions specifically geared to the Hispanic markets. By 1980, Anheuser-Busch had captured the biggest market share in both Texas and California.

---

[6]Ibid.

From 1976-82, Anheuser Busch expanded its brand offering from three to eight. The new lineup included three low-calorie beers-Natural Light, Michelob Light, and Bud Light. Michelob Classic Dark, a premium beer, and Wurzburger Hofbrau, a German import, were added, as well. Budweiser, Michelob, and Busch completed the offering but with new advertising campaigns and packaging.

Exhibit 4 summarizes the Anheuser-Busch marketing strategy.

EXHIBIT 3

The South's Per Capita Consumption Growth, in Gallons, 1940-1980

Region/ State	1940	1970	1980	Percentage Change 1940-1980
South Atlantic:				
Delaware	12.9	18.7	25.5	97.7%
Florida	8.1	18.4	29.4	263.0
Georgia	1.7	12.7	19.5	1,047.1
Maryland	19.0	21.1	25.2	32.6
North Carolina	2.6	11.7	19.4	646.2
South Carolina	2.8	12.7	21.1	653.6
Virginia	6.7	18.2	21.8	225.4
West Virginia	9.0	14.4	17.5	94.4
East South Central:				
Alabama	2.3	9.6	16.4	626.1
Kentucky	6.9	15.3	18.5	168.1
Mississippi	1.6	12.9	19.0	1,087.5
Tennessee	3.9	14.3	19.3	394.9
West South Central:				
Arkansas	2.7	11.6	17.5	548.2
Louisiana	6.9	18.8	23.4	239.1
Oklahoma	4.1	13.0	19.8	382.9
Texas	7.5	21.1	30.1	301.3
Total South	5.7	16.3	23.3	308.8
Total United States	12.1	18.6	24.3	100.8

Source: United States Brewers Association's Brewers Almanac, as reported in *Beverage World*, November 1982, p. 128.

EXHIBIT 4

The Anheuser-Busch Marketing Game Plan, 1977-1982

The Actions	The Results
Completely restructured marketing and production operations functions	Sales volume increased 86 percent between 1977 and 1981
Renewed emphasis on brand management teams, employing top package goods marketers in key positions.	During the same period, sales increased 25.4 million barrels while the industry as a whole gained only 22.8 million barrels.
Replaced or revamped all advertising campaigns, and quadrupled the marketing budget.	A-B's industry lead expanded to a record 14.2 million barrels at the end of 1981, the widest margin ever.
Introduced two light beers: Natural Light and Michelob Light. A third light brand, Budweiser Light, was introduced nationally in 1982.	
Beefed up the field sales force, adding 500 people at various levels.	
Revised the packaging graphics, and added something on the order of 600 new packages.	
Acquired many new sports venues-- both broadcast properties and promotional programs-- and became the largest sports sponsor in the United States, if not the world. The recent acquisition of half the ABC-TV Monday Night Football package-- formerly an exclusive property of a major competitor-- is a most significant addition to the company's athletic arsenal.	

Source: Michael J. Roarty, vice president of marketing of Anheuser-Busch, *Marketing Communications*, November-December 1982, p. 47.

Budweiser. Bud was Anheuser-Busch's flagship brand and the largest-selling premium beer in the United States. The premium market consisted of beer drinkers who were semi-cost conscious but still discriminating tastewise. This medium-priced category was a significant part of the industry since it consisted of nearly 50 percent of the total volume.

With Bud's slippage in 1976, Anheuser-Busch concentrated its efforts on stopping the decline. Advertisements and promotions were directed at those segments showing the greatest loss. The advertising slogan was changed in both 1977 ("When Do You Say Budweiser?") and 1978 ("Welcome Home"). Yet, the "King of Beers" still felt the threat from Miller, so Roarty's marketing staff went into action:

> In the spring of 1979, interim advertising was shelved in favor of a new campaign which saluted various segments of the working public, saying in a variety of ways, "America, This Bud's For You. . ."

> The national umbrella campaign was extended to various ethnic segments and age groups. In order to salute consumers of Hispanic descent, localized versions which Latin consumers could relate to were produced. Young adults, those in the minimum age to 24 bracket, presented special problems. With different viewing and listening habits than the other beer consumers, they did not respond well to conventional commercial messages. With that in mind, an ensemble of zany Bud lovers called the "Tastebuds" hit radio. The Tastebuds did their job and then some.[7]

---

[7] Roarty, *Marketing Communications*, pp. 47-48.

Anheuser-Busch planned to continue the "salute" campaign by incorporating it into the promotion around the Olympics. Commericals were aired in 1983 saluting the workers, coaches, and trainers who prepared the site and trained the athletes for the games. "This Bud's for You... The Team Behind the Team."

The "salute" campaign revitalized Budweiser. Sales grew at double-digit rates between 1979-1981, but slowed to 4.4 percent in 1982 and 5.0 percent in 1983. This was attributed to the introduction of Bud Light and the subsequent cannibalization of regular Bud's sales. By the end of 1983, Bud's share of the market was 22.8 percent, with sales reaching 42 million barrels. Miller High Life, Bud's closest competitor, continued to lose market share, prompting Miller to increase advertising support from $36.9 million in 1980 to $96.5 million in 1982. Anheuser-Busch spent $83 million on advertising in 1982 for Budweiser.

Michelob and Michelob Classic Dark. Both Michelob and Michelob Classic Dark were positioned as super-premium beers and marketed as "top of the line" to customers wanting a smooth, rich taste without regard to price. In 1982, the super-premium segment accounted for 6.1 percent of the total industry volume with an estimated annual growth rate of 6-8 percent. Michelob's share of the super-premium segment was approximately 75 percent.

In the late 1970s, the Michelob advertising campaign focused around the theme, "Weekends Are Made For Michelob." Sales increased during that time, but 1980 brought a slowdown in growth. Michelob's sales stalled at 8.3 million barrels for the next three years. Part of this was attributed to the economic situation and the consumer's proclivity to trade down to cheaper beer. Others believed that it was due to competition from the increasing number of new super-premium brands being introduced, such as Miller's Special Reserve and Stroh's Erlanger.

As a result of the slowdown, the advertising and packaging of Michelob were revamped in an attempt to increase sales. This involved a more product-oriented push with commercials highlighting Michelob in bottles and glasses. The only spoken words were the new slogan, "Some Things Speak For Themselves." Anheuser-Busch extended this campaign to the 1984 Olympics through advertisements relating the excellence of Michelob to the excellence portrayed in Olympic competition.

The advertising budget for Michelob was $47.6 million or $5.73 per barrel in 1982, up from $13.6 million in 1980. Sales of Michelob slipped 13.3 percent in 1983; as a result, Michelob lost its position as the number five top-selling beer in the country to Pabst (Exhibit 5). Lowenbrau, Michelob's closest competitor in the super-premium category, managed to achieve a slight sales increase in 1983, but its market share remained under 1 percent.

Michelob Classic Dark was introduced nationally in 1981 and was available in draught only. While a super-premium beer like regular Michelob, it was promoted as "the ultimate in dark beers." In 1983, Anheuser-Busch began distribution of Michelob Classic Dark in 12-oz nonreturnable bottles on a limited basis in California.

Busch. Positioned as a popular-priced beer, Busch was introduced in 1955 to compete directly with subpremium regional beers. In 1975, sales of the Busch brand totaled 4.5 million barrels, but declined over the next three years. To stop the decline, Anheuser-Busch reduced its price and began to emphasize Busch's smooth, slightly sweeter, lighter taste using the advertising slogan, "Head for the Mountains." Additionally, Anheuser-Busch expanded distribution of Busch to 35 states. In 1983, distribution was expanded again to include Pennsylvania, southern New Jersey, and West Virginia.

In 1979, Busch's advertising budget doubled (from $4.2 million in 1978 to $8.0 million in 1979) and during the following year, reached $10.5 million. Even with a new package, a new image, and increased advertising and promotion, Busch continued to lose sales and, by 1981, it was no longer one of the top-10 best-selling beers in the country (edged out by Michelob Light). Busch faced even more serious competition in 1983 when Miller introduced two popular-priced brands, Meister Brau, and Milwaukee's Best.

EXHIBIT 5

1983 Top 10 Beer Brands

Brand	1983 Market Share	1983 Volume (mil. bbl.)	1982 Volume (mil. bbl.)	1983 Brand Growth
1. Budweiser	22.8%	42.0	40.0	+5.0%
2. Miller Lite	9.7	17.9	17.2	+4.1
3. Miller High Life	9.5	17.6	20.0	-12.0
4. Coors	5.2	9.6	8.4	+14.3
5. Pabst	4.3	7.9	8.1	-2.5
6. Michelob	3.9	7.2	8.3	-13.3
7. Old Milwaukee	3.7	6.9	5.9	+16.9
8. Stroh	3.1	5.7	5.6	+1.8
9. Old Style	3.0	5.6	5.5	+1.8
10. Bud Light	2.1	3.8	3.3*	+15.2
Top 10	67.3	124.2	122.3	+1.6%
Other brands	32.7	60.3	59.5	+1.3%
Total Industry	100.0	184.5	181.8	+1.5%

*Nine-month total.
Source: *Beverage World*, March 1984, p. 38.

EXHIBIT 6

Beer Sales for Anheuser-Busch and Miller Brewing, by Major Brands, 1977-1982 (millions of barrels)

Year	Bud	Miller High Life	Busch	Michelob	Natural Light	Michelob Light	Bud Light	Miller Lite
1982	40.0	20.0	3.3	8.3	1.4	3.2	3.3	17.2
1981	38.3	23.6	3.1	8.3	1.9	3.2	-	15.0
1980	33.9	23.8	2.8	8.3	2.5	2.6	-	13.2
1979	30.0	23.6	3.2	8.0	3.0	2.0	-	11.2
1978	27.0	20.8	3.5	7.5	2.5	1.0	-	9.5
1977	25.0	17.3	3.3	66.2	1.9	-	-	7.5

Source: *Beverage Industry Manual*, *Beverage World*, and *Standard & Poor's Industry Survey*.

Low-Calorie Beers: Natural Light, Michelob Light and Bud Light. Low calorie or light beer represented nearly 20 percent of the industry sales in 1983. Miller Lite was the top-selling light beer, a position it had held since its introduction in the 1970s. Anheuser-Busch had three brands positioned to address each of the three price segments, yet none had been able to catch up with Miller Lite (Exhibit 6). The three brands together totaled approximately 23-24 percent of the light market, and one half of this was Bud Light. Both Michelob Light and Natural Light were behind the number three selling brand, Coors Light.

Natural Light. Anheuser-Busch's first low-calorie beer was Natural Light. Introduced in 1977 as a premium-priced brand, it was developed to go after Miller Lite and steal market share. Sales amounted to 1.9 million barrels in the first year, grew to 3.0 million barrels in 1979, but declined over the next three years to 1.4 million barrels.

In response, Natural Light was repositioned as a popular-priced brand. Distribution was shifted to supermarket accounts, where the customer was more price sensitive and women were the traditional buyers. The new advertising campaign aligned Natural Light with food. "The Beer with a Taste for Food" promoted lightness as a counterpart to heavy food. The advertising budget was $16.5 million in 1982. Busch sales continued to fall in 1983, but much of this loss was attributed to the introduction of Bud Light.

Michelob Light. Introduced in 1978, Michelob Light was Anheuser-Busch's first super-premium light beer. At first, it was promoted in close association with its namesake, but five years later, was repositioned on its own. The hub of the advertising campaign was amateur sports. Using the theme, "Michelob Light for the Winners," most commercials featured young men and women in hotly competitive games, with Michelob Light as the ultimate reward. Anheuser-Busch spent $21 million in 1982 in advertisements and promotions, mostly in TV spots.

During its first year, Michelob Light sold 1 million barrels. By 1982, sales reached 3.2 million barrels and it was fourth in the light beer market.

Budweiser Light. With Natural Light and Michelob Light only moderately successful, Anheuser-Busch introduced Bud Light in 1982. As a premium-priced light beer, it was positioned directly against Miller Lite. At the end of its first year (9 months), Bud Light sold 3.3 million barrels to make it the number two best selling light beer. Anheuser-Busch spent between $35-40 million to introduce Bud Light. By 1983, sales reached 3.8 million barrels; volume growth was 15.2 percent. In less than two years, Bud Light bumped Schlitz as the 10th best-selling beer in the United States by gaining 2.1 percent of the total beer market. It was considered by the industry as the most formidable challenger to Miller Lite.

With the advertising slogan, "Bring Out Your Best," Anheuser-Busch made the statement that Bud Light was the finest light beer on the market. The advertising campaign tied Bud Light closely to regular Bud. Anheuser-Busch's premium light brand was described as "having a clean, crisp, real beer taste with only 1/3 the calories of regular Bud." A series of commercials were developed around the Triathlon event in Hawaii, the Iron-Man contest, in which people were featured doing their very best in sports competition and winning. Bud Light also sponsored a 12-event U.S. Triathlon series across the country. The image of the best in beer and the best in competition was extended to the Olympics in 1983 advertisements and promotions.

Anheuser-Busch's management believed that there was only minimum cannibalization of the regular Bud market but that the effects on Natural Light were much greater. Bud Light was believed to have contributed to Miller High Life's sales decline in 1983 and to Miller Lite's slower growth in sales. Growth in Lite sales declined from 14.6 percent in 1982 to 4.1 percent in 1983.

Imported Beer: Wurzburger Hofbrau. Wurzburger Hofbrau was a rich, full-bodied beer with a hearty European taste which was positioned in the growing luxury beer market. To maintain freshness, this beer was imported from West Germany in 500-gallon stainless steel drums and bottled in Anheuser-Busch's Newark, New Jersey, plant. Testing of Wurzburger Hofbrau began in 1979 in New England, but sales never reached the 100,000 barrels mark. By the end of 1982, Anheuser-Busch had pulled out of the test markets, and the bottling capacity in New Jersey was to be used for the Anheuser-Busch brands. Advertising support during the testing period was never more than $500,000.

Many of the major U.S. brewers marketed at least one foreign brand (e.g., Heileman's Beck's), but the leading imports were sold by companies with no competing brands in this country. Heineken, in the number-one position by a large margin, had a 38.5 percent share of the U.S. import market with sales reaching 68.7 million gallons. Following in second place was Canadian-brewed Molson. Both market leaders have given up market share in recent years to Beck's, Labatt, and Moosehead. One particular problem with import beers was their high price, making their sales highly susceptible to an economic slowdown.

THE INTERNATIONAL BEER MARKET

Anheuser-Busch was the first U.S. beermaker to push into the international market. This strategy was explained by an Anheuser-Busch executive:

> Less than 1 percent of our total volume presently is sold internationally--and the world beer market is four times larger than that of the United States. Moreover, our research tells us, as the world comes closer together in a travel and communications sense, tastes change, too. We think that will augur well on a long-term basis for American malt beverages, and we are taking steps now to be in a position to take advantage of such opportunities.[8]

Anheuser-Busch's push into Europe, the biggest non-U.S. market, started in Sweden and, by 1981, had moved into Britain, Germany, and France. The company's strategy was the same each time -- to link up with the top distributor in the country and alter the product to local tastes, if necessary.

In Sweden, Bud in 16-oz. cans was imported from the United States to Rock Polar Corporation, the exclusive purveyors. At the end of the first year, sales were estimated around 300,000 cases. Distributors of alcoholic beverages in Sweden faced numerous, uncompromising regulations and restrictions which discouraged their sales. Bud could not be associated even indirectly with sports or athletes; no one could be shown drinking it; and no posters or display ads could be used outdoors. To overcome these advertising restrictions, Rock Polar concentrated on the pro-American feeling in Sweden and the increasing number of Swedes traveling to the United States. Bud was promoted as a super-premium beer, using the slogan, "All the way from the U.S.A.--drink it cold."

After Sweden, Anheuser-Busch moved into the United Kingdom, but withdrew in 1982. The next year, the company signed a licensing agreement under which Bud could be brewed and sold in the U.K. beginning in 1984. Essentially, local brewing would decrease Bud's high price, which was the major reason for the poor sales showing earlier. Anheuser-Busch brands were introduced in France and Germany in late 1982.

Anheuser-Busch also went after the Asian market. In 1978, Bud was introduced in Japan, the biggest beer drinking country in Asia and the fifth largest beer market in the world. In less than five years, sales reached 1 million cases, making Bud the best-selling foreign beer in Japan. This rapid rise to the top was not immediate, however, but came after Suntory, Ltd., one of the country's largest liquor distillers, acquired the importing rights in March 1981. Because of their distribution clout, Bud was distributed widely in Japan.

Bud's success was due also to Suntory's slick promotional campaign emphasizing its American origin. Because of Japan's postwar love affair with American culture, Bud enjoyed good brand recognition long before it was imported. One obstacle that Suntory faced in marketing Bud was the perception of American beer as too watery for Japanese tastes. But Japanese youth, brought up on soft drinks and very much influenced by American things, showed a marked change in taste preference for lighter beers. Taking advantage of this trend, the company concentrated on Japan's postwar generation, stressing distribution in discos, pubs, and other nightspots. Ad spending for Bud was $1.4 million in 1982, with Suntory and Anheuser-Busch splitting evenly the cost.

Although sales of Bud were expected to grow in 1983 to 1.5 million cases, concern existed that this growth could not be sustained and sales would level off in the future. One reason for this was the high price that the Japanese customer had to pay for Bud. The average price charged for domestic beer was 79

---

[8]As quoted in *Advertising Age*, July 27, 1981, p. 46.

cents, compared to Bud's $1.28 per can. Another problem was the belief that Bud was not as fresh as Japanese beer since it came from overseas. Because of these two factors, imported beer accounted for less than 1 percent of the total beer consumed annually in Japan--1.24 billion gallons. Bud and Heineken together took 70 percent of the import market; the remainder was shared among 50 other brands from 20 countries.

To overcome the freshness problem and to maintain sales momentum, Suntory and Anheuser-Busch agreed in January 1983 to begin local production of Bud the next year. Beer yeast and production techniques were to be imported from the United States to Suntory's new plant for brewing. Local brewing allowed Bud's price to be cut to almost that of its domestic competitors. For Suntory to earn a return that would justify its additional investment, it needed substantially greater sales volume than before. According to Suntory's Mr. Shimizu, "To increase sales, we will have to change our marketing strategy from empahsizing the fashionableness of Bud to making it a part of every Japanese life and involve other generations other than the young. To carve out this new market, we will have to spend a little bit more money for Bud than comparative beer campaigns."[9] Furthermore, Bud faced additional competition in Japan since local production of Lowenbrau began in spring 1983. Suntory was aiming at a sales goal of 3 million cases during the first year of local production.

As part of its international expansion, Anheuser-Busch concentrated on countries closer to home, as well. In 1981, the company pushed Bud into Canada, and after a year showed a profit. By the end of 1983, Bud was the fifth best-selling brand there with 5 percent of the national market. Again, much of the success was due to the size and reputation of the Canadian partner, for Bud was brewed under agreement with Labatt Brewing Co. In 1982, Anheuser-Busch initiated export agreements with Argentina, Chile, Peru, the People's Republic of China, and Israel.

MANUFACTURING AND QUALITY CONTROL

Anheuser-Busch's brewing objective was to maintain the naturally brewed quality and superior taste of its brands. The company used a long natural process taking up to 30 days or longer. It was the only major brewery in the world to use the traditional beechwood aging process to age and naturally carbonate its beer. Most brewers added carbon dioxide instead of using a second fermentation. Instead, all Anheuser-Busch beers were transferred into lager tanks after the first fermentation and beechwood aging. This was done by spreading beechwood chips on the bottom of the tank to provide more surface area for the action of the yeast. After settling on the chips, the yeast was allowed to work until the beer was completely fermented. Every Anheuser-Busch beer was completely natural, without artificial ingredients, preservatives, or chemical additives.

The company insisted on superior ingredients--barley malt, hops, rice, or corn, yeast, and water. Anheuser-Busch used more malt per barrel than any other major brewer in the country. All Anheuser-Busch beers contained both two-row and six-row barley malt, while some major beer producers used no two-row in their beer. Being a choicer ingredient, the two-row barley malt produced a smoother-tasting beer; thus, the percentage used varied by brand. Michelob, for instance, contained the highest. The brewer's yeast used in all Anheuser-Busch beers were supplied from one carefully perfected and maintained pure-culture system. The hops were literally hand-selected. Even the water was checked, and, if necessary, treated to ensure exacting standards.

Quality control at Anheuser-Busch began with testing and tasting every batch of ingredients before the brewing even started. Numerous taste panels at each brewery and headquarters were used daily to judge aroma, color, and taste. Additionally, samples were taken randomly every two weeks from retail outlets and flown to St. Louis for taste evaluations. This insured that quality control did not stop after the beer left the brewery, but became part of the responsibilities of the beer wholesalers.

In the marketplace, beer freshness was maintained through a program of rotating beer stocks on retail shelves. This rotation program involved a can-coding system which electrostatically placed a date code on the botton of the can. The code identified the day, year, and 15-minute period of production plus the plant and production line. A similar process was used for bottles and kegs. Periodic inspections for "outdated" beer was conducted on a regular basis. Draught beer was considered outdated 45 days after the

---

[9]As quoted in *Advertising Age*, March 28, 1983, p. 23.

production date, while bottles and cans of Budweiser, Bud Light, Busch, and Natural Light was not outdated until 105 days. Michelob and Michelob Light were "old" 75 days after production. Anheuser-Busch beer distributors could lose their territorial franchise for not rotating beer stock according to those standards.

BEER PRODUCTION FACILITIES

Anheuser-Busch met the challenge of the 1970s with a commitment to expansion and modernization. Between 1977-83, the company invested $3.8 billion in a building program to increase capacity and lower production costs through operation efficiencies. By the end of 1983, Anheuser-Busch had a network of 11 breweries (capacity of 66 million barrels) strategically located throughout the United States operating at 98 percent capacity.

St. Louis, Missouri. The company's oldest and largest brewery was constructed in 1870. Due to various expansions since that time, the St. Louis complex covered 100 acres and had an annual shipping capacity of approximately 13 million barrels.

Newark, New Jersey. The first branch brewery, completed in 1951, was located adjacent to the Newark International Airport. It covered an area of 50 acres and had an annual shipping capacity of nearly 5 million barrels.

Los Angeles, California. In 1954, Anheuser-Busch completed construction of its third brewery on part of an 85-acre site in the San Fernando Valley. An expansion, completed in early 1982, nearly tripled the brewery's capacity to approximately 10.5 million barrels.

Tampa, Florida. In 1959, the company completed a brewery in Tampa. Located on part of a 273-acre site, the plant had an approximate shipping capacity of 1.8 million barrels.

Houston, Texas. The company's Houston brewery began shipping beer in 1966. The plant was located on a portion of a 126-acre tract of land and had an annual shipping capacity of approximately 3.7 million barrels. An expansion to be completed in 1985 would increase its capacity to 8.5 million barrels and bring the company's total operating capacity to approximately 75 million barrels.

Columbus, Ohio. In 1968, Anheuser-Busch opened its sixth brewery, located on part of a 252-acre site. The factility had an approximate annual shipping capacity of 6.3 million barrels.

Jacksonville, Florida. The brewery at Jacksonville began production in 1969 and had an annual shipping capacity of approximately 6.7 million barrels. The plant was situated on a portion of an 860-acre site.

Merrimack, New Hampshire. In the summer of 1970, the brewery in Merrimack was completed. The facility was located approximately 10 miles south of Manchester on part of a 3300-acre site and had an approximate shipping capacity of 2.8 million barrels.

Williamsburg, Virginia. The company's ninth brewery, built on a portion of 3,600 acres near historic Williamsburg, began shipping in early 1972. A major expansion project completed in 1980 increased the plant's shipping capacity to 8.3 million barrels.

Fairfield, California. Anheuser-Busch began shipping in 1975 from its 10th brewery, constructed on a 200-acre site which was 40 miles northeast of San Francisco. The plant had an annual shipping capacity of approximately 3.9 million barrels.

Baldwinsville, New York. In 1980, the company purchased the former Jos. Schlitz Brewing Company plant, which was located near Syracuse, for $100 million. After three years of extensive modifications (costing more than $100 million), the brewery opened with a shipping capacity of approximately 6 million barrels. A mini-expansion was to be completed in 1984 which would increase capacity to 7.2 million barrels.

Additionally, Anheuser-Busch exercised an option on a 1,130-acre tract of land in Fort Collins, Colorado, for possible construction of a brewery. In 1983, the company continued its expansion program by allocating more than $2 billion in capital projects over the next five years. Anheuser-Busch planned to dominate the beer industry by building huge, efficient breweries.

DISTRIBUTION

A vital component of Anheuser-Busch's marketing effort was its distribution system. Already one of the best in the country, the new plans called for even more intense involvement of the more than 960 independent and 16 company-owned beer wholesalers. "We were told that if we didn't get more involved in grassroots efforts in the marketplace, we would be washed away," recalled one president of a wholesale beverage company.[10] This meant participation in not only quality control but also local marketing efforts. Wholesalers were expected to capitalize on Anheuser-Busch's extensive outlays for advertising and promotions to gain a larger amount of shelf space for Anheuser-Busch products.

To aid in this, Anheuser-Busch conducted extensive training seminars for the wholesalers, covering such topics as financial management, merchandising, promotions, and warehousing. The brewer developed a computerized shelf-space management program to audit retail sales margins and turnover by brand and package. On a regular basis, field and headquarters staff evaluated each wholesaler's weekly and monthly sales of all beers. Anheuser-Busch believed that this attention was critical since most of the fight for future sales would be waged at the wholesale and field level.

With the focus at the grassroots level, open communication between top management and the wholesalers was a crucial concern. Any problems were to be dealt with immediately either through the breweries or directly through a hot line to St. Louis. The Anheuser-Busch Wholesaler Advisory Panel, which met with top management regularly, was a key communication link between headquarters, field personnel, and the individual wholesaler. The distributors were included also in the overall planning process. They were required to develop written strategic plans including demographic profiles of their customers.

The relationship between Anheuser-Busch and its wholesalers was built on years of mutual concern and cooperation. This unique relationship dated back to 1967 with the initiation of the Anheuser-Busch Wholesaler Equity Agreement. This agreement gave wholesalers a degree of security and ownership value never experienced before in the brewing industry. This was accomplished by:

> Granting the wholesaler the right to sell his or her business, subject only to Anheuser-Busch's approval of the proposed purchaser.

> Granting the wholesaler the right to transfer the business to his or her heirs upon death.

> Establishing an orderly termination procedure in instances of substandard performance by a wholesaler and eliminating the possibility of arbitrary, "overnight" terminations.

CORPORATE STRUCTURE AND ORGANIZATION

On October 1, 1979, a new parent corporation, Anheuser-Busch Companies, Inc., was established as a holding company, and Ahheuser-Busch, Inc., became a wholly owned subsidiary of the new company. Those divisions and subsidiaries of Anheuser-Busch, Inc. that were not directly involved in the brewery operation were reorganized as wholly owned subsidiaries of Anheuser-Busch Companies, Inc., as well. Each business was operated as a separate company (Exhibit 7).

The purpose of the reorganization was explained in the 1979 annual report:

> The new name and corporate structure are intended to more clearly communicate the increasing diversification of the corporation. In addition, the new structure will provide management with increased organizational and operational flexibilty and will help relieve the corporation's nonbeer business from certain restrictive laws and regulations that govern the brewing industry.[11]

The reorganization reflected the increasingly diversified nature of the operation and the long-range goals of the company. Anheuser-Busch's primary objective was well-planned and managed growth. In addition to continued volume and profit increases in the beer and beer-related businesses, the company was pursuing a strategy of growth through diversification. The major diversification efforts in the past involved vertical integration and the development of new businesses internally. However, the acquisition of Campbell Taggart, Inc., in 1982 was a significant diversification move.

---

[10]As reported in *Business Week*, July 12, 1983, p. 52.

[11]Anheuser-Busch Companies, Inc., *Annual Report*, 1979, p. 4.

EXHIBIT 7

Anheuser-Busch Companies, Inc., Corporate Structure

Subsidiaries	Year Established	Subsidiaries	Year Established
Brewing operations		Other diversified operations:	
Anheuser-Busch, Inc	1860	St. Louis Refrigerator Cars, Inc.	1878
		Manufacturers Railway Co.	
Beer-related operations:		St. Louis National Baseball	
Busch Agricultural Resources, Inc.	1962	Club, Inc.	1953
Metal Container Corp.	1974	Busch Entertainment Corp.	1959
Container Recovery Corp.	1978	Busch Properties, Inc.	1970
Metal Label Corp.	1979	Busch Creative Services	1980
Anheuser-Busch International, Inc.	1980	Civic Center Corp.	1981
		Anheuser-Busch Wines, Inc.	1982
Food products operations:		Sports Times	1983
Busch Industrial Products Corp.	1972	Anheuser-Busch/Interferon	
Eagle Snacks, Inc.	1979	Sciences	1983
Campbell Taggart, Inc.	1982		

Sources: *Anheuser-Busch Fact Book,* 1982, and Anheuser-Busch Companies, Inc., *Annual Report,* 1979, 1982, 1983.

BEER-RELATED OPERATIONS

Vertical integration activities had long been a strategic thrust at Anheuser-Busch. The purpose was to provide not only a source of growth but also control over quality, quantity, and cost of packaging and raw materials for the brewery operation. The beer-related operations included the following:

Busch Agricultural Resources, Inc. In 1983 this subsidiary established record sales of malt and milled rice to Anheuser-Busch, Inc. Operations included: two malt processing plants (supplied 32 percent of the brewer's requirement); rice handling and storage facilities; a rice milling plant completed in 1982 (to ensure brewing rice supplies and to open new business opportunities in domestic and export rice sales); grain elevator for barley (leased in 1983); and two nurseries involved in land application of brewery wastewater (acquired 1983).

Metal Container Corporation. Of Anheuser-Busch, Inc.'s total container requirement, this subsidiary produced 36 percent of the cans and 18 percent of the lids in 1983. Through technology, it was able to reduce the amount of metal in each can, thereby lowering the production costs of beer. All plants were capable of bimetallic production, affording flexibility if the price or availability of aluminum or steel changed.

Container Recovery Corporation. Established to lower container costs and express environmental concerns, Container Recovery operated aluminum can collection programs throughout the United States and container (cans and bottles) recycling process plants in three states. Collecting 180 million pounds of aluminum in 1983, it ranked second in the industry.

Metal Label Corporation. As part of a joint venture with a Belgian company, Metal Label produced metalized labels which required less than 1 percent of the aluminum formerly used in foil labels. Using unique technology pioneered in Europe, the Tennessee facility was the first fully integrated paper metalizing and printing plant in the United States. The metalized labels allowed increased operating speed on the brewery packaging lines.

Anheuser-Busch International, Inc. The company's international licensing and marketing subsidiary was formed to explore and develop export and licensed production markets outside the United States. In both Canada and Japan, locally brewed Budweiser was one of the largest-selling imported beers. Export agreements were initiated with other countries, such as Israel, Chile, and Peru.

DIVERSIFIED OPERATIONS

Besides vertical integration, Anheuser-Busch Companies pursued a strategy of diversification through the development of new businesses internally. Many of these were natural extensions of the brewery operation, often providing needed services. Additionally, as a means of building for the future, the company sought diversified activities which would further the use of its extensive beer distribution network. Two of these, Eagle Snacks and "Wine on Tap," were recent developments.

Eagle Snacks, Inc., was the company's internally developed snack food business. This food-related operation produced a full line of premium snack food and nut items for sale in the on-premise market sector (hotels, bars, restaurants). Distribution was through Anheuser-Busch wholesale network, mainly in the eastern United States. In June 1982, the company expanded distribution to include convenience stores and larger food store chains with the objective of nationwide distribution in two years. To support the growth in sales, steps were taken to increase the production capacity. This included the purchase and operation of plants in North Carolina and Alabama, with a third in Tennessee coming on-line in 1984.

In 1982, Anheuser-Busch Companies began to move into the "Wine on Tap" market with partner LaMont Winery, Inc. (a DiGiorgio subsidiary of Canadian brewer, John LaBatt, Ltd.). Under the agreement, the wine was produced in LaBatt's winery in northern California to be distributed to restaurants and taverns. Red, white, and rose wines under the Master Cellar's brand name were offered in much larger kegs than Almaden, Paul Masson, or Coca Cola's Wine Spectrum's bag-in-box containers. Using its wholesalers, Anheuser-Busch began distribution of the wine in parts of Colorado and California later in the year.

The diversified operations included:

Busch Industrial Products, Corp. Busch Industrial Products was one of three food-products operations (Eagle Snacks and Campbell Taggart being the others). As the leading producer of compressed yeast for the baking industry (50 percent of all baker's yeast in United States), this subsidiary set new production volume records in 1982 and 1983. It was the only producer of autolyzed yeast extract, a flavoring agent sold to food processors. In 1982, the subsidiary sold its corn refining plant since its contribution to the corn products industry was minor and offered limited growth potential.

St. Louis Refrigerator Car, Inc. A fleet of 700 specially insulated and cushioned railroad cars were operated exclusively for transportation of Anheuser-Busch beer. It also did commercial repair, building, maintenance and inspection of railroad cars. In the late 1970s, the subsidiary achieved record profits, but performance declined in 1982. Although the industry was in a slump in 1983, this subsidiary showed significant improvement.

Manufacturers Railway Company. This subsidiary operated a fleet of railroad cars (hopper cars and general-service) used by Anheuser-Busch and others. It also provided terminal rail switching services over its 42 miles of company-owned track to St. Louis industries. Truck cartage and warehousing services were provided at seven brewery locations. This subsidiary was profitable in 1983, as it had been for a number of years.

St. Louis National Baseball Club, Inc. The 1982 World Champion Cardinals set attendance records in St. Louis (2.7 million paid customers in 1982) and on the road. They finished fourth in the Eastern Division of the National League in 1983. The championship made 1982 the most successful in 15 years, but operating costs continued to increase (especially the players' salaries), resulting in net operating losses. However, Anheuser-Busch believed that, over the years, sales of its beer products had benefited from the ownership of the Cardinals.

Busch Entertainment Corp. This subsidiary operated two theme parks, a water park attraction, and two Sesame Place educational play parks. In 1983, four of the five reported good attendance--up at least 5 percent--except Tampa park, which decreased 6 percent (attributed to Disney's opening of its new EPCOT attraction at nearby Orlando). Although normally steady profit centers, these operations were hurt by recessions (poor performance in 1982 attributed to recession).

Busch Properties, Inc. Busch Properties developed residential and commerical properties. Kingsmill on the James, a 2,900-acre residential and recreational development near Williamsburg, Virginia, had record sales in 1983. In 1982, the first phase of the vacation homes sold in two weeks, but the sales of the residential homes were poor. Of its three Busch Corporate Centers, only the Fairfield, California, operation was having trouble.

Busch Creative Services, Inc. This multimedia and creative design service produced meetings and product promotional materials for Anheuser-Busch. It began to acquire outside clients in 1983 and added a video services department. Due to its success, future plans included expansion on a national level.

Civic Center Corp. The Civic Center Corporation was formed in the early 1960s to redevelop 43 blighted downtown blocks. Anheuser-Busch originally owned 25 percent, but became sole owner in 1981. Civic Center owned Busch Stadium, four parking garages nearby, and 2 3/4 undeveloped downtown city blocks in St. Louis. Successful operations and marketing of the stadium resulted in a new attendance record in 1983.

In addition to these diversified operations, Anheuser-Busch in 1983 began a $6 million three year research and development program with Interferon Sciences, Inc. (ISI), to produce interferon and related biological products. Using ISI's genetic engineering technology and Anheuser-Busch's yeast fermentation technology, this project produced by year's end the highest concentration of genetically manufactured Interferon in the industry. As part of the agreement, Anheuser-Busch owned options to purchase 3 million shares of ISI common stock during the next seven years. The company would receive royalties on any commerical products that resulted.

Campbell Taggart, Inc. Anheuser-Busch made a significant diversification move away from the beer industry with its 1982 acquisition of Campbell Taggart, Inc., the country's second-largest commercial baker. August A. Busch III stated in his letter to the shareholders:

> For some time we have stated that significant diversification was needed to provide an additional base for future growth in sales and earnings. It has been emphasized in the past that any major diversification would be predicated on a solid, integrated business plan and on economic justification consistent with the company's future business goals and growth objectives.
>
> Anheuser-Busch Companies decided that its first major acquisition should have a relatively low down-side risk, while at the same time provide up-side growth potential. Campbell Taggart met that objective and other criteria which have been established for an acquisition. The combination of Campbell Taggart with Anheuser-Busch Companies will allow us to capitalize on the strengths within our organization and benefit from synergies between the business operations of the two companies.
>
> Campbell Taggart is a well-managed, quality company with a good record over the years. It is the second-largest producer of fresh baked goods in the country, and it is the leader among large baking companies in terms of profitability and return on capital. Moreover, it has demonstrated an ability to successfully expand its existing business and to move into new product lines--such as high margin sweet goods, variety breads and dinner rolls--which have become the fastest growing segment in the baking industry.[12]

The Dallas-based Campbell Taggart operated 58 wholesale bakeries primarily in the Midwest and the Sunbelt, four refrigerated dough plants, three variety bread and snack food plants, two cookie and cracker plants, and a refrigerated plant producing El Charrito Mexican frozen foods. It had international subsidiaries in Spain, France, and Brazil. Under its Merico brand, Campbell Taggart was the nation's largest maker of private-label dough. Consistent with the Eagle Snacks, Inc., expansion, this acquisition provided an enlarged distribution system--mainly supermarket delivery--for the food snacks and nut items.

With annual sales in excess of $1.3 billion, Campbell Taggart was acquired for cash and stock valued $579 million. Anheuser-Busch paid $36 a share in cash for approximately half of the 15 million Campbell Taggart shares outstanding and issued a new convertible preferred stock for the reminder. The acquisiton was applauded by industry analysts on grounds that Anheuser-Busch got--for a relatively cheap price--an extremely profitable bakery in a super-growing region of the country where industry competition was minimal. According to a report in *Dun's Business Month*, "The acquisition will increase Anheuser-Busch's earning from nonbeer operations from less than 5 percent currently, to almost 20 percent next year." [13] (see Exhibit 8).

---

[12]*Anheuser-Busch Companies, Inc., Annual Report,* 1982, pp. 2-3.

[13] As reported in *Dun's Business Month,* December 1982, p. 48.

EXHIBIT 8

Business Segment Information, Anheuser-Busch Companies, Inc., 1982-1983
(in millions of dollars)

	Beer and Beer-Related	Food Products	Diversified Operations	Eliminations	Consolidated
1983:					
Net sales	$4,907.7	$1,320.4	$150.2	$344.1	$6,034.2
Operating income*	649.9	47.3	3.6		700.8
Depreciation and amortization expense	129.5	40.3	17.5		187.3
Capital expenditures	348.1	54.8	25.1		428.0
Identifiable assets	2,994.1	768.6	143.7		3,906.4
Corporate assets					423.8
Total assets					$4,330.2
1982:					
Net sales	4,488.1	282.8	145.1	339.4	4,576.6
Operating income*	464.1	23.5	5.3		492.9
Depreciation and amortization expense	110.8	8.8	14.0		133.6
Capital expenditures	310.1	23.4	22.3		355.8
Identifiable assets	2,758.1	779.3	148.9		3,686.3
Corporate assets					216.5
Total assets					$3,902.8

*Operating income excludes other income and expense which is not allocated among segments.
Source: Anheuser-Busch Companies, Inc., *Annual Report*, 1983

In 1983, Anheuser-Busch approved a major capital expenditure program to modernize existing facilities and expand the Colonial Bakery in St. Louis. Also significant changes were made in the marketing effort, including brand management teams in the bakery operations. The new marketing strategy involved differentiation of brands by quality as a means of developing consumer loyalty. Earth Grains, for instance, was positioned as a premium variety bread using advertisements and promotions based on the slogan, "The Promise of Earth Grains... Bread at Its Best."

Exhibit 9 contains a 10-year financial and operating summary for Campbell Taggart, Inc.

FUTURE DIRECTIONS

As stated in the 1982 annual report, Anheuser-Busch was committed to long-term growth:

> Anheuser-Busch Companies, Inc.'s philosophy is to maintain a growth posture through contined beer expansion and through future development of other diversified activities. The company is not managed for the short term. A long-range planning process has been developed to prepare for change rather than simply reacting to it. Any new endeavor undertaken by the company must be compatible with existing business operations and consistent with the company's basic business philosophy. Consistent with that philosophy, the company is dedicated to excellence in everything it does, determined to be a leader, and wherever possible, to be number one in everything it undertakes. The company's long-term strategies show this commitment to continued managed growth.[14]

---

[14]*Anheuser-Busch Companies, Inc.*, *Annual Report*, 1982, p. 6.

Dun's Business Month reported from an interview with President Busch that prospects for future acquisitions

> will be confined to companies in recession-resistant segments of the consumer products area. However, Busch is looking to not only acquisitions but internal expansion to fuel future growth. Profits from the company's international beer operations and snack food line are still a drop in the barrel. But Busch believes their growth potential is greater than that for the domestic beer business.[15]

The goal was to increase the nonbeer contribution to earnings.

Despite the industry warnings of a slowdown in beer consumption growth, the primary objective for the beer operations was to increase market share to 40% by 1990. Anheuser-Busch planned to stay in the number one place in the industry. According to Vice President Roarty this involved the following actions:[16]

> Increased production capacity with the prospect of a new plant in Colorado.

> Expansion of current brands.

> Increased entry into the international market.

> Constantly redefining marketing strategies and action plans to keep up and ahead of competition.

Already, Anheuser-Busch planned to introduce in 1984 a light-alcohol beer (LA). Playing on the public concern with alcohol abuse, this beer had an alcohol content of less than 2 percent, compared with 4 percent in regular and light. It was priced as a premium beer like Bud and targeted at the on-premise consumer. LA was expected to lure drinkers of light beer, but it was not anticip[ated to hurt Anheuser-Busch as much as Miller. However, both Heileman and Stroh were planning to produce low-alcohol beers, and other brewers could be expected to do so if the product proved successful.

Anheuser-Busch had faith in its ability to grow in the future. The company believed that its goal could be achieved by simply redoubling its efforts: building huge, efficient facilities; spending on advertising and promotion; maintaining price leadership where a commanding share of the market was held; and decreasing prices when needed to gain business. However, Anheuser-Busch faced a highly competitive, hostile environment in 1983. Several large competitors had merged; major regional breweries had expanded into new geographic regions; and the growth in beer consumption had slowed. Although it had been a very good year, Anheuser-Busch ended 1983 with the slowest growth in a nonstrike year in two decades.

---

[15]As reported in *Dun's Business Month*, December, 1982, p. 49.

[16]Roarty, *Marketing Communications*, p. 48.

EXHIBIT 9

Financial Summary, Campbell Taggart, Inc., 1972–1981 *(in thousands of dollars, except per share data)*

	1981	1980	1979	1978	1977	1976	1975	1974	1973	1972
Sales and earnings:										
Net sales	$1,257,514	$1,113,147	$1,007,360	$881,619	$787,420	$743,221	$707,928	$624,498	$486,538	$395,638
Costs and expenses	1,164,529	1,031,981	933,345	819,464	722,866	686,207	656,082	580,246	453,434	361,127
Interest expense	10,672	8,690	8,147	6,231	5,663	4,918	4,262	4,327	2,525	1,748
Income before income taxes	82,313	72,476	65,868	58,924	58,891	52,096	47,584	39,925	30,579	29,763
Provision for income taxes	36,645	32,604	29,795	28,815	29,558	26,596	24,860	19,776	15,195	15,029
Income before minority interests	45,668	39,872	36,073	30,109	29,333	25,500	22,724	20,149	15,384	14,734
Minority interests in income of subsidiaries	3,984	3,625	3,194	461	3,393	2,451	2,707	3,685	2,480	2,239
Net income	$ 41,684	$ 36,247	$ 32,879	$ 29,618	$ 25,940	$ 23,049	$ 20,017	$ 16,464	$ 12,904	$ 12,495
Cash flow	$ 87,001	$ 74,898	$ 68,010	$ 58,050	$ 56,156	$ 48,368	$ 43,555	$ 37,750	$ 31,520	$ 28,697
Balance sheet information:										
Current assets	180,659	154,753	144,406	129,651	104,803	91,335	90,471	85,507	67,756	53,119
Current liabilities	119,762	110,864	108,802	107,228	72,517	64,968	67,677	61,069	42,153	27,408
Working capital	60,897	43,889	35,604	22,423	32,286	26,367	22,794	24,438	25,603	25,711
Current ratio	1.51:1	1.40:1	1.33:1	1.21:1	1.45:1	1.41:1	1.34:1	1.40:1	1.61:1	1.94:1
Net value of property, plant, and equipment	292,199	277,976	267,733	241,582	210,756	196,682	168,402	149,026	127,668	114,813
Total assets	514,753	443,601	423,168	381,625	323,523	295,547	267,226	242,521	198,955	169,648
Long-term debt	125,462	70,739	77,270	61,718	54,620	55,062	41,712	37,438	26,480	20,223
Deferred income taxes	21,757	17,996	15,856	13,347	12,311	9,638	8,333	6,593	5,678	4,665
Minority interests in subsidiaries	22,754	21,321	21,597	20,708	24,885	22,764	21,742	23,307	21,374	20,938
Stockholders' equity	225,018	222,681	199,643	178,624	159,190	143,115	127,761	114,113	103,270	96,414
Additions to property, plant and equipment	43,429	45,732	56,163	58,094	40,953	50,404	38,962	38,969	28,772	32,303
Per share information:										
Net income	2.50	2.18	1.98	1.80	1.60	1.42	1.23	1.01	0.79	0.76
Cash dividends	0.90	0.80	0.72	0.64	0.59	0.50	0.41	0.35	0.31	0.31
Book value	14.09	13.38	12.00	10.75	9.81	8.82	7.87	7.04	6.36	5.87
Average common shares outstanding during year	16,706,328	16,637,858	16,629,230	16,499,662	16,225,609	16,223,655	16,217,304	16,220,953	16,344,849	16,430,497
Common shares outstanding at year-end	15,974,687	16,642,921	16,634,446	16,625,103	16,228,359	16,226,350	16,221,315	16,214,329	16,241,329	16,430,497
Number of stockholders	6,507	5,612	5,960	5,908	3,916	2,525	2,428	2,386	2,401	2,293

Source: Campbell Taggart, Inc., *Annual Report*, 1981.

Student Strategic Analysis and Plan (1985-1989) [1]

Anheuser-Busch Companies, Inc.

This document contains a proposal for a strategic plan for Anheuser-Busch Companies, Inc. This proposal is the result of (1) an assessment of the current status of the company, (2) in-depth analyses of the internal and external environments, and (3) a strategic forecast. These steps are covered in the first half of the following study; the second half of the report details recommendations for a five-year strategic plan which will ensure the continued growth and success of Anheuser-Busch Companies, Inc.

STRATEGIC PROFILE

The mission of Anheuser-Busch Companies, Inc., has evolved and broadened over time. The brewery intially focused on the production and nationwide distribution of high-quality beer; this remains true although the scope of the brewing subsidiary's activities has now become international.

Over time, Anheuser-Busch became increasingly involved in beer-related and other diversified operations. In recent years there has been a clear shift of emphasis from vertical integration to diversification as demonstrated by the reorganization which took place in 1979 and by the 1982 acquisition of Campbell-Taggart, Inc. Today, Anheuser-Busch Companies, Inc. is a holding company with multiple mission statements which reflect the variety of activities in which it is engaged.

Traditionally, the goals of the company have been to achieve excellence and growth. To meets these objectives, the strategy of the brewing operations has had to change over time. Initially, the company stressed technical innovation. This enabled the company to enjoy economies of scale and to establish a national presence at an early stage. In the 1950s and 1960s the strategy of the company--and of the other growing national brewers--was built around three components: (1) the production of a quality beer with mass appeal, (2) nationwide distribution, and (3) advertising. This last factor assumed prominence in the 1970s after Philip Morris entered the market with its acquisition of Miller Brewing Co. and quickly gained market share by revolutionizing beer marketing.

In fact, savvy marketing and heavy advertising explain Anheuser-Busch's success in recent years. In 1983, sales from beer and beer-related operations increased 9% despite the fact that total beer consumption declined. This means that, in effect, Anheuser-Busch stole market share from its competitors and strengthened its leadership position. By the end of 1983 its market share was 32.5%.

The overall strategy of Anheuser-Busch Companies, Inc. is to attain well-managed growth through diversification. In fact, total sales increased 28% after the acquisition of Campbell-Taggart, Inc. (a baked goods company) from $5.2 billion to $6.7 billion; and in 1983, the percentage of sales from operations other than beer and related operations was 24%.

In summary, Anheuser-Busch Companies, Inc. is a successful company. This is mainly attributable to the excellence of its management team which has demonstrated expertise, the ability to

---

[1]This Student Strategic Analysis and Plan was prepared by four University of Maryland MBA students: Karen J. Freeto, Sherry L. Greenwald, Christine Lemyze, and Robert E. Walton in April 1985. Daniel J. Power edited the manuscript. This strategic analysis and plan is included here to provide an example of such a document. This is only one example; it has both good and bad characteristics (see Chapter 8). This document was used with their permission.

respond and adapt to the environment--as it did in the 1970s when the company was threatened by Philip Morris' agressive marketing--and a strong commitment to strategic planning.

INTERNAL ANALYSIS

Anheuser-Busch has many characteristics that contribute to its success.

Beer and beer-related operations. Past and current concentration trends in the beer industry have allowed the remaining participants to achieve economies of scale. Further, products do not differ significantly in quality or taste among brewers. Thus it follows that the key to success in the beer industry today is marketing: specifically, market segmentation, advertising, promotion, and distribution.

Anheuser-Busch is strong in these areas as demonstrated by the following:

• **Market segmentation.** The company has pursued market and product segmentation since the late 1970s. It concentrated on the Western and Southern regions of the country (where beer consumption was growing the fastest) and expanded its brand offerings from three to eight between 1976 and 1982 (see Exhibit 1).

• **Advertising.** Anheuser-Busch has the largest advertising budget of all national brewers ($165 million in 1983) and competes successfully with Miller for network TV time.

• **Promotion.** The company has become the leading sponsor of sports events in the country; of particular significance was Anheuser-Busch's entrance into auto racing which is the second largest spectator sport in the U.S. Furthermore, Anheuser-Busch was the official and exclusive brewer for the 1984 Summer Olympics and the U.S. Olympic Team.

• **Distribution.** The excellent distribution system of the company has benefited from extensive training seminars for its wholesalers and an emphasis on communication.

In addition, due to a commitment to expansion and modernization--$3.8 billion invested in a building program between 1977 and 1980--Anheuser-Busch can boast of new and cost effective production facilities. Finally, the company has been consistently profitable (Return on equity has averaged 17% annually over the past five years) and is financially strong as exemplified by its current ratio, increase in working capital and relatively low debt/equity ratio.

The only area in which a weakness can be identified is the marketing of light beer. Anheuser-Busch was slow in entering this segment and has yet to gain a significant share: Natural Light, its first light beer, has been slipping for the past 4 years, and Bud Light and Michelob Light have been only moderately successful. Miller Lite is undeniably the leader in this category with a market share of 48% in 1983.

Food products operations. Recent changes in consumer demand--notably a decline in the demand for white bread--have resulted in increased competition and price cutting in the baked goods industry. Successful companies are those able to respond to changing consumer tastes and introduce and market new products.

Campbell-Taggart, Inc. has some clear competitive advantages in this environment:

• **Innovation.** The company has successfully moved into new product lines (sweet goods, variety breads, and dinner rolls).

• **Marketing.** A new marketing strategy focusing on brand management was implemented in 1983. Campbell-Taggart can be expected to benefit further from Anheuser-Busch's marketing expertise.

• **Production facilities.** A major capital expenditure program was undertaken in 1983. Campbell Taggart's modernized production facilities will result in increased cost efficiency.

Further, Campbell-Taggart is a well-managed company which has consistently grown and been profitable over the past decade and thus enjoys a strong financial position. However, conflicts between Anheuser-Busch's and Campbell-Taggart's management styles will have to be resolved if the past level of performance is to be sustained in the future.

In conclusion, Anheuser-Busch Companies, Inc. is a successful holding company which has been able to (1) achieve congruence between general corporate goals and the diversification moves it undertakes, and (2) identify the keys to success in each of the industries it has entered.

ENVIRONMENTAL ANALYSIS

The environment is generally favorable for Anheuser-Busch. However, a number of trends and threats and opportunities must be noted and acted upon.

Strategic forecast. U.S. Economic Outlook: the annual rate of growth of the economy will be moderate over the next five years (estimates vary between 2% and 4%).

A. Beer industry

1. Growth will be affected by a number of environmental factors and will be minimal (between .5% and 2% annually). However, the light beer and luxury segments of the market will experience significantly higher rates of growth (7% and 5% respectively).
2. There will be no ban on TV advertising of beer and wine. This prediction is based upon our belief that strong lobbying efforts from broadcasters will prevent passage of the proposed bill. Furthermore, the current administration has not supported increased governmental regulation. However, the legal drinking age is most likely to be raised in most states.
3. The consolidation moves which have occurred within the industry in recent years will not continue; this is because additional mergers among the dominant brewers would constitute a violation of antitrust laws.

B. Baked goods

1. Growth in sales of bakery products is forecasted to remain moderate (approximately 2% annually) until the end of the decade.
2. Demographic changes--a 1.5% increase in the population aged 20 to 49 between now and 1990--will spur cracker consumption. However, cookie sales are likely to suffer from a yearly decline in the 5 to 19-year-old age group.
3. Demand for variety breads will continue to increase. However, growth in demand will likely slow as firms continue to reformulate white bread.

C. Frozen foods

1. The outlook for frozen foods is promising as the current trends are expected to continue into the 1990s. Demand--especially in the area of low-calorie, nutritional entrees--will be fueled by the increase of affluent two-income and single households.

Threats and opportunities. We view the following environmental trends as potential threats to the growth and success of Anheuser-Busch.

A. Beer and beer-related industries

1. The consumption of beer in the United States has been declining for the past two years. Prior to 1982, the average yearly rate of growth was 1.83%. This decrease in consumption is attributable to (1) a change in consumer tastes and attitudes towards health and (2) new legislation which restricts the availability of alcohol to people under 21 (who are among the heaviest beer drinkers). This may **raise marketing costs and reduce profits.**

2. Anti-alcohol groups have been lobbying for a ban on advertising of beer and wine on television. Television advertising is a crucial element of the marketing strategy of Anheuser-Busch; thus passage of this bill would seriously **hurt the company's sales.**

3. The trend in the beer industry is toward increased concentration as shown by the large number of mergers that took place in the past four years. Although this is not threatening Anheuser-Busch's leadership position, it might make it **difficult for the company to increase or even maintain its market share.**

B. Baked goods industry

1. Competition and price cutting have been increasing in the industry; this has already **reduced the profitability of Campbell-Taggart.**

2. The industry is experiencing a low rate of growth which might **threaten Campbell-Taggart's desired expansion and reduce profits.**

Finally, many industries in the United States are mature industries which are experiencing slow rates of growth. Thus attaining growth through diversification will become increasingly challenging for Anheuser-Busch. Nonetheless, some opportunities exist:

1. The world beer market is four times as large as the U.S. market. Anheuser-Busch could **expand its beer operations abroad** in order to **increase its total sales.**

2. Some product segments in the beer industry have been growing, specifically the luxury-priced imports, super-premium beers, and light beers. An increased effort in these areas might provide **increased market share** for Anheuser-Busch.

3. Sales of white bread have been enhanced by recent efforts to alter the formulation of the product. Demand for variety breads is increasing. Campbell-Taggart might be able to **develop new products** and exploit these trends.

4. Sales of frozen foods--specifically of frozen food entrees, vegetables, fruits-- have shown positive gains since 1979. This might provide an opportunity for **internal product expansion.**

STRATEGIC PLAN

The mission and goals of the company should remain essentially the same. We feel that an average annual growth rate of 15% over the next five years is a realistic goal for Anheuser-Busch (see Exhibits 2 and 3). This projection is based upon the company's past performance and current market opportunities. In order to accomplish this objective, we believe that Anheuser-Busch should implement the following:

Beer and beer-related operations. Anheuser-Busch's current goal of increasing market share to 40% by 1990 is appropriate. Since total beer consumption is projected to increase between .5% and 2% annually until the end of the decade, this will translate into total sales ranging between 77 and 85 million barrels through 1990. This will be accomplished by focusing on:

1. **The luxury-priced import market.** Forecasts for this segment indicate that luxury-priced imports will represent 8% of the total beer market by 1990 (as opposed to the current 3.1%). Anheuser-Busch should capitalize on this trend and investigate the potential for introducing new foreign beers to the U.S. and thus expand its product mix.

English and Japanese beers might constitute a good prospect because (1) they are not heavily marketed in the U.S. and (2) Anheuser-Busch has valuable contacts in the brewing industries of these countries. A reasonable goal for 1990 would be to reach total sales ranging between 3 and 3.5 million barrels (see Exhibit 4).

In summary, we recommend a two-pronged strategy that focuses on (1) reliable suppliers and (2) extensive promotion/advertising. Anheuser-Busch must give this endeavor full advertising support in order not to repeat its previous failure with Wurzburger Hofbrau. Initially the import should be test-marketed in the Northeast where there is a high concentration of high-income young professionals--this population segment comprises the highest proportion of luxury imports consumers. In a second phase, the import will be distributed and advertised nationwide.

2. **The light beer segment.** This segment is forecasted to represent 20% of the total beer market by 1990 (versus current 17.1%). Furthermore, it is an area where Anheuser-Busch's performance has fallen short of that of the competition.

Currently, the company segments the light beer market by price; this has not proved successful. We believe that a better approach would be to segment this market by sex and thus capitalize on the fact that the number of women who drink beer is increasing and that they tend to choose light beers more frequently than men. The Coca Cola Co. benefited greatly from a similar strategy applied to their diet sodas. Specifically, Natural Light should be repositioned to appeal to women. This approach would also take advantage of existing distribution channels for this product, e.g., supermarkets.

The current strategies for Bud Light and Michelob Light are appropriate and need not be revised at this point.

3. **Light alcohol beers (LA).** Anheuser-Busch currently plans to introduce a light alcohol beer next year; however, we do not foresee sufficient demand for this new product to justify this move. Our prediction is based upon the fact that there is an abundance of non-alcoholic beer substitutes already available in the market place. Furthermore, sales of LA would cannibalize our light beer sales since the product is likely to appeal to the same consumer groups.

4. **Other products.** Strategies for the super premium, premium, and popular-priced beers should remain unchanged. The goal here is to at least maintain the current level of sales.

5. **International expansion.** Since beer consumption in the U.S. is predicted to remain stable until the end of the decade, Anheuser-Busch is justified to seek out new markets abroad in order to increase its total sales. Current plans to enter Argentina, Chile, Peru, China, and Israel should be carried out. However, Anheuser-Busch will have to produce its beer abroad with the help of established local brewers and distributors. This approach was instrumental in their success in England, Japan and Canada.

Revenues from Anheuser-Busch International should account for 10% of total beer sales for the company by 1990.

A detailed implementation schedule is outlined in Exhibits 5 and 6.

Food related products. Although the baked goods industry is projected to experience minimal growth, we believe that Campbell-Taggart itself can grow within the industry. The company should be able to capitalize on the following three factors: (1) it is located in a super-growing region of the country where industry competition is minimal, (2) it benefited from a major capital expenditure program which modernized the facilities and (3) Anheuser-Busch's newly implemented marketing strategy.

Campbell-Taggart's objective should be to increase its total sales by 15% annually for the next five years and to develop nationwide. In order to meet this goal, the company should focus on (1) the development of a new white bread (heavier crust and texture) and (2) the production and sales of specialty crackers. However, the major part of Campbell-Taggart's growth is predicated on the internal development of the activities of the frozen food subsidiary. Specifically, we propose an expansion into additional ethic foods and low-calorie entrees (see Exhibit 7 for detailed implementation schedule).

The present goals and strategies for Anheuser-Busch's other food subsidiaries seem to mesh with the company's overall goals and need not be altered at this point. The same is true for the other non food-related subsidiaries.

Contingency plans. The range of the predictions which are displayed in Exhibit 2 reflect recognition of the fact that our forecast may prove inaccurate and/or unpredictable events may occur. Thus, we have developed the following contingency plans:

1. An increased interest in the products of microbreweries might endanger the success of Anheuser-Busch's luxury-priced import beers. The company could then consider producing these beers domestically in order to eliminate the microbreweries' competitive advantage (freshness).
2. Women may not respond to the positioning of Natural Light. If this occurs, Anheuser-Busch should consider discontinuing this brand.
3. Political problems abroad may compromise the company's international expansion. Anheuser-Busch must monitor the political environment in the countries it intends to enter and be ready to withdraw from those countries where unrest is prevalent.

Focusing on the growing segments of the beer market and expanding internationally, while capitalizing on the company's marketing expertise will ensure Anheuser-Busch's continued growth and success in the beer industry. Similarly, by stressing the cracker and variety/reformulated white breads segments of the baked goods industry, and marketing these products heavily, Campbell-Taggart will grow significantly. Campbell-Taggart's growth will be fueled also by the internal development of the frozen foods subsidiary.

The recommended strategy incorporates internal and environmental factors and ensures the overall continued success of Anheuser-Busch Companies.

Note: Various statistics quoted in the text were obtained from <u>Predicasts Forecasts</u> and <u>U.S. Industrial Outlook 1984</u>.

EXHIBIT 1

PRODUCT MIX

TYPE OF BEER	LIGHT	REGULAR	DARK
PRICE:			
POPULAR	NATURAL LIGHT (1977)	BUSCH (1955)	
PREMIUM	BUDWEISER LIGHT (1982)	BUDWEISER (1876)	
SUPER-PREMIUM	MICHELOB LIGHT (1978)	MICHELOB (1896)	MICHELOB CLASSIC DARK (1981)
LUXURY		WURZBURGER HOFBRAU (1979)	

EXHIBIT 2

PROJECTED INCOME STATEMENT
($ millions)

1984

	BEST	MOST LIKELY	WORST
OPERATING REVENUES			
BEER-RELATED	$5,974.9	$5, 496.9	$5,257.9
FOOD PRODUCTS	1,809.8	1,665.1	1,592.7
DIVERSIFIED OPERATIONS	187.4	172.4	164.9
TOTAL OPERATING REVENUE	7,972.9	7,335.0	7,016.1
FED AND STATE BEER TAXES	758.8	698.1	667.8
NET SALES	7,214.1	6,636.9	6,348.4
COST OF GOODS SOLD	4,920.0	4,526.4	4,329.6
GROSS PROFIT	2,294.1	2,110.5	2,018.8
MKT, ADMIN, R&D EXPENSES	1,522.8	1,401.0	1,340.1
OPERATING INCOME	771.3	709.6	678.7
OPERATING EXPENSE	93.3	85.9	82.1
EBT	677.9	623.7	596.6
TAXES	294.9	271.3	259.5
NET INCOME	383.0	352.4	337.1

EXHIBIT 2 (CONT.)

PROJECTED INCOME STATEMENT
($ millions)

1985

	BEST	MOST LIKELY	WORST
OPERATING REVENUES			
BEER-RELATED	$6,687.7	$6,152.7	$5,885.2
FOOD PRODUCTS	2,264.7	2,083.5	1,992.9
DIVERSIFIED OPERATIONS	215.5	198.2	189.6
TOTAL OPERATING REVENUE	9,168.8	8,435.3	8,068.5
FED AND STATE BEER TAXES	849.3	781.4	747.4
NET SALES	8,319.5	7,653.9	7,321.1
COST OF GOODS SOLD	5,673.9	5,220.0	4,993.0
GROSS PROFIT	2,645.6	2,433.9	2,328.1
MKT, ADMIN, R&D EXPENSES	1,751.2	1,611.1	1,541.1
OPERATING INCOME	894.3	822.8	787.0
OPERATING EXPENSE	108.2	99.6	95.2
EBT	786.1	723.2	691.8
TAXES	342.0	314.6	300.9
NET INCOME	444.2	408.6	390.9

EXHIBIT 2 (CONT.)

PROJECTED INCOME STATEMENT
($ millions)

1986

	BEST	MOST LIKELY	WORST
OPERATING REVENUES			
BEER-RELATED	$7,480.0	$6,881.6	$5,984.0
FOOD PRODUCTS	2,815.3	2,590.1	2,252.2
DIVERSIFIED OPERATIONS	247.8	228.0	198.2
TOTAL OPERATING REVENUE	10,544.1	9,700.6	8,453.3
FED AND STATE BEER TAXES	950.0	874.0	760.0
NET SALES	9,594.2	8,826.6	7,675.3
COST OF GOODS SOLD	6,543.2	6,019.8	5,234.6
GROSS PROFIT	3,050.9	2,806.9	2,440.8
MKT, ADMIN, R&D EXPENSE	2,013.9	1,852.8	1,611.1
OPERATING INCOME	1,037.0	954.1	829.6
OPERATING EXPENSE	125.5	115.4	100.4
EBT	911.5	838.6	729.2
TAXES	396.5	364.8	317.2
NET INCOME	515.0	473.8	412.0

EXHIBIT 2 (CONT.)

PROJECTED INCOME STATEMENT
($ millions)

1987

	BEST	MOST LIKELY	WORST
OPERATING REVENUES			
BEER-RELATED	$8,359.5	$7,690.7	$7,356.4
FOOD PRODUCTS	3,480.1	3,201.7	3,062.5
DIVERSIFIED OPERATIONS	285.0	262.2	250.8
TOTAL OPERATING REVENUE	12,125.7	11,155.7	10,670.7
FED AND STATE BEER TAXES	1,061.7	976.7	934.3
NET SALES	11,064.1	10,179.0	9,736.4
COST OF GOODS SOLD	7,545.7	6,942.1	6,640.2
GROSS PROFIT	3,518.4	3,236.9	3,096.2
MKT, ADMIN, R&D EXPENSE	2,316.0	2,140.7	2,038.1
OPERATING INCOME	1,202.4	1,106.2	1,058.1
OPERATING EXPENSE	145.5	133.8	128.0
EBT	1,056.9	972.3	930.1
TAXES	459.7	423.0	404.6
NET INCOME	597.1	549.4	525.5

EXHIBIT 2 (CONT.)

PROJECTED INCOME STATEMENT
($ millions)

1988

	BEST	MOST LIKELY	WORST
OPERATING REVENUES			
BEER-RELATED	$9,334.5	$8,587.8	$8,214.4
FOOD PRODUCTS	4,281.0	3,938.5	3,767.3
DIVERSIFIED OPERATIONS	327.7	301.5	288.4
TOTAL OPERATING REVENUE	13,944.6	12,829.0	12,271.3
FED AND STATE BEER TAXES	1,185.5	1,090.6	1,043.2
NET SALES	12,759.1	11,738.4	11,228.0
COST OF GOODS SOLD	8,701.7	8,005.6	7,657.5
GROSS PROFIT	4,057.4	3,732.8	3,570.5
MKT, ADMIN, R&D EXPENSES	2,663.4	2,450.3	2,343.8
OPERATING INCOME	1,394.0	1,282.5	1,226.7
OPERATING EXPENSE	168.7	155.2	148.4
EBT	1,225.3	1,127.3	1,078.3
TAXES	533.0	490.4	469.0
NET INCOME	692.3	636.9	609.2

EXHIBIT 2 (CONT.)

PROJECTED INCOME STATEMENT
($ millions)

1989

	BEST	MOST LIKELY	WORST
OPERATING REVENUES			
BEER-RELATED	$10,414.0	$9,580.9	$9,164.3
FOOD PRODUCTS	5,243.9	4,824.4	4,614.6
DIVERSIFIED OPERATIONS	376.9	346.7	331.6
TOTAL OPERATING REVENUE	16,036.3	14,753.4	14,111.9
FED AND STATE BEER TAXES	1,322.6	1,216.8	1,163.9
NET SALES	14,713.7	13,536.6	12,948.1
COST OF GOODS SOLD	10,034.8	9,232.0	8,830.6
GROSS PROFIT	4,679.0	4,304.6	4,117.5
MKT, ADMIN, R&D EXPENSES	3,062.9	2,817.9	2,695.4
OPERATING INCOME	1,616.0	1,486.7	1,422.1
OPERATING EXPENSE	195.5	179.9	172.1
EBT	1,420.5	1,306.9	1,250.0
TAXES	617.9	568.5	543.8
NET INCOME	802.6	738.4	706.3

EXHIBIT 2 (CONT.)

PROJECTED INCOME STATEMENT
($ millions)

1990

	BEST	MOST LIKELY	WORST
OPERATING REVENUES			
BEER-RELATED	$11,607.2	$10,678.7	$10,214.4
FOOD PRODUCTS	6,399.3	5,887.3	5,631.4
DIVERSIFIED OPERATIONS	433.4	398.7	381.4
TOTAL OPERATING REVENUE	18,441.7	16,966.4	16,228.7
FED AND STATE BEER TAXES	1,474.1	1,356.2	1,297.2
NET SALES	16,967.6	15,610.2	14,931.5
COST OF GOODS SOLD	11,571.9	10,646.2	10,183.3
GROSS PROFIT	5,395.7	4,964.0	4,748.2
MKT, ADMIN, R&D EXPENSES	3,522.4	3,240.6	3,099.7
OPERATING INCOME	1,873.3	1,723.5	1,449.1
OPERATING EXPENSE	226.7	208.5	199.5
EBT	1,646.7	1,514.9	1,449.1
TAXES	716.3	659.0	630.3
NET INCOME	930.4	855.9	818.7

EXHIBIT 3

PROJECTED REVENUES
($ millions)

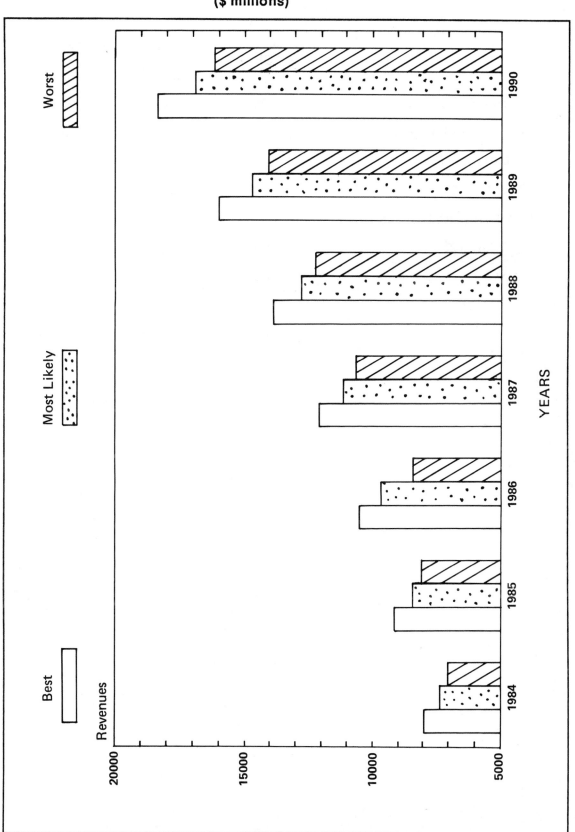

EXHIBIT 4

MARKET SHARE PROJECTIONS

	A B CURRENT 1983	A B CURRENT 1990	INDUSTRY PROJECTED 1990
LUXURY-PRICED IMPORTS	0%	4%	8%
SUPER-PREMIUM BEERS	13%	11%	11%
PREMIUM BEERS	69%	65%	45%
LIGHT BEERS	13%	17%	20%
POPULAR-PRICED BEERS	5%	3%	15%
MALT LIQUOR	NA	NA	1%
TOTAL	100%	100%	100%

EXHIBIT 5

BEER OPERATIONS
IMPLEMENTATION SCHEDULE
1985-1990

1985   Commence search for new luxury/import beer and product/distributor. Begin target marketing of Natural Light towards women, coupled with a $21.0M increase in advertising expenditures. The remaining $7.5M in advertising increases will be devoted to current product lines. Start construction of the Fort Collins, Colorado plant; begin expansion of Columbus and Jacksonville plants. Agressive international expansion in Australia, the Phillipines and Israel.

1986   Test market new luxury/import beer in Northeast region. Increase advertising expenditures for the luxury/import beer to $2.5M. Increase in capacity at Tampa plant (total capacity 5.4M barrels) will cover light beer expansion and increased demand in the South. This expansion will be supported by a $20.0M increase in advertising. Investigate market potential in Argentina, Chile and Peru; commence operations in China and Israel.

1987   Market luxury/import beer nationally, with heavy advertising ($19.0M) and promotional campaigns (national sales between 1.0M and 1.5M barrels). Complete constuction at Columbus and Jacksonville plants (capacities at 9.5M and 10.0M barrels respectively). An increase of $8.0M in advertising will support this expansion. Begin Budweiser production in South American country with best potential.

1988   Increase import sales to a range of 2.25M to 2.5M barrels nationwide. (increase import advertising by $5.0M). Complete construction of Fort Collins plant, which will be targeted to operate at 75% capacity, thereby producing 9.0M barrels this year. Advertising increases of $15.0M, primarily in the West, will also help to increase regional sales. Begin Budweiser production in either remaining South American market.

1989   Import sales levels to increase to number 4 position with 3.0M to 3.5M barrels, will advertising rising by $7.5M. Fort Collins plant to operate at full (12.0M barrels) capacity, with applicable advertising increasing by $10.0M. Begin expansion of Newark plant to increase capacity to 50%.

All necessary financing will be divided, with 55% being based on expansion of shareholder equity and stock issuance, and 45% from increases in their debt position. This should ensure a debt equity ratio that will remain between 55% and 65%. Both debt and equity should increase between 15% and 25% annually, as they have over the past decade.

EXHIBIT 6

PLANT CAPACITY

Plant:	1985	1986	1987	1988	1989	1990	% Change
ST. LOUIS	13.0	13.0	13.0	13.0	13.0	13.0	0.0
NEWARK	5.0	5.0	5.0	5.0	5.0	7.5	50.0
LOS ANGELES	10.5	10.5	10.5	10.5	10.5	10.5	0.0
TAMPA	1.8	5.4	5.4	5.4	5.4	5.4	300.0
HOUSTON	8.5	8.5	8.5	8.5	8.5	8.5	0.0
COLUMBUS	6.3	6.3	9.5	9.5	9.5	9.5	150.0
MERRIMACK	2.8	2.8	2.8	2.8	2.8	2.8	0.0
JACKSONVILLE	6.7	6.7	10.1	10.1	10.1	10.1	150.0
WILLIAMSBURG	8.3	8.3	8.3	8.3	8.3	8.3	0.0
FAIRFIELD	3.9	3.9	3.9	3.9	3.9	3.9	0.0
BALDWINSVILLE	7.2	7.2	7.2	7.2	7.2	7.2	0.0
FORT COLLINS	0.0	0.0	0.0	9.0	12.0	12.0	NA
TOTAL CAPACITY	74.0	77.6	84.2	93.2	96.2	98.7	133.0
PROJECTED SALES	66.7	70.0	73.5	77.2	81.1	85.1	127.6

EXHIBIT 7

FOOD OPERATIONS
IMPLEMENTATION SCHEDULE
1985-1989

1985   Hire a consultant to alleviate the management conflicts between Anheuser-Busch and Campbell-Taggart. Development and introduction of a new white bread with heavier crust and texture in the Midwest and Sunbelt. Replace 10% of cookie production with cracker production. Introduce refrigerated dough products in California and Pacific region. Begin development of new ethnic frozen food line.

1986   Expand distribution of white bread and variety breads to California and Pacific region. Continue the replacement of cookie production with cracker production by an additional 10%. Market new ethnic foods through current Mexican food distribution channels. Use heavy regional advertising to promote new product lines. Begin to develop high quality, low calorie frozen entrees. Begin building new refrigerated dough and cracker plants in California.

1987   Expand distribution of breads to Northeast region of the U.S. Begin expansion of cracker products to California and Pacific region. Expand refrigerated dough products to Central region of the U.S. Begin the introduction of frozen entrees in the Northeast and South with a big media blitz targeted at the middle income population between 25 and 50 years of age. Build new frozen food plant.

1988   Introduce cracker products in the Northeast and thus complete the national expansion program. Complete national expansion program for frozen dough products. Emphasize national expansion of frozen ethnic food and high quality, low calorie frozen entrees. Develop new product line in frozen foods, possibly vegetables and/or fruits.

1989   Introduce frozen vegetables and/or fruit products. Begin investigation of other frozen food products.

Financing of Campbell-Taggart, Inc.'s projected expansion will attempt to maintain a debt/equity ratio of 50%.

Levi Strauss & Co.[1]

Levi Strauss, a Bavarian immigrant who was lured to the West during the gold rush in search of prosperity, did not strike it rich in gold, but he found his fortune in jeans. His first pair of jeans was sold in 1853 to a San Francisco gold digger who wanted a sturdy pair of pants which would hold up in the mines. In time, his jeans became so popular that young Strauss set up a shop in San Francisco. Today, the headquarters of Levi Strauss & Co (LS & Co.) stands near the same location as young Strauss's shop.

It was not until the 1930's that Levi's jeans reached the eastern market. Although attempts were made to promote jeans for resort wear, the basic clientele continued to be limited. World War II, however, created a sharp increase in demand, and they were sold only to individuals engaged in defense work. It also marked a turning point for Levi Strauss. LS & Co. had been largely a wholesale operation prior to World War II, but after the war, they began concentrating on manufacturing and direct sales. Before the war, LS & Co.'s annual sales were around $8 million, but by 1961, sales reached $51 million mainly because of aggressive product diversification.

In 1981, LS & Co. was the largest manufacturer of jeans in the world, controlling about one third of the jeans market. Additionally, they were the largest firm in the apparel industry with products in virtually every product line and sales and profits by far the greatest in the apparel industry. According to LS & Co. chairman of the board, Peter E. Haas: "We'd like to outfit people from the cradle to the grave."

Levi's success has resulted in part from their skill in sensing an emerging new market and responding quickly and in part from their strong management and exceptional brand name acceptance. In addition, a focus on identifying market opportunities through segmentation in recent years has aided a diversification strategy. As a result, the company's growth and success has been strong despite the extreme competitiveness and cyclical nature of the apparel industry.

Top managers at LS & Co. are optimistic about the 1980s. Emphasis in the future will be on expanding women's wear and activewear and increasing the international market. A 1978 assessment by *The Wall Street Transcript* is valid today. It states, "There are few firms in any industry comparable to Levi Strauss from the standpoint of dynamic growth, above-average return on equity, competitive strength, and strong international consumer franchise" (*The Wall Street Transcript*, January 23, 1978).

KEY EXECUTIVES[2]

Walter A. Haas, Jr., joined the company in 1939 and served as its president from 1958 to 1970 and as its chief executive officer from 1970 to 1976. He was named chairman of the board in December 1970, and chairman of the executive committee in April 1976. He served in both of these positions until his retirement in 1981. He also served as a director since 1943. Haas controls 10.4 percent of the company's stock. This figure includes shares owned by his wife, children, estates, and trusts for which he votes. He is the great-grandnephew of Levi Strauss. He was 64 years old in November 1981.

Peter E. Haas joined the company in 1945 and became executive vice president in 1958. He became president of the company in December 1970, and chief executive officer in April 1976. In November 1981, he became chairman of the board. Haas controls 12 percent of the company's stock. This figure includes stock owned by his family and stock owned by trusts or estates for which he has the voting power. He graduated from the University of California in 1940 and from Harvard University's Graduate School of Business in 1943. He is the great-grandnephew of Levi Strauss and was 61 years of age in 1981.

---

[1]This case was prepared by Neil H. Snyder, Debie Alford, Karen Davis, Allison Gillum, Jim Tucker, and Jeff Walker of the MacIntire School of Commerce, University of Virginia. Reprinted with permission from L. L. Byars, *Strategic Management*, New York: Harper & Row, copyright 1984.

[2]The information included in this section was obtained from "Notice of Annual Meeting of Stockholders and Proxy Statement," Levi Strauss & Co., April 2, 1980, p. 1; Standard & Poor's *Register of Corporation's, Directors, and Executives*, 1980, vol. 2; and Standard & Poor's *Industry Surveys*, vol. 1, sec. 3, July 31, 1980, p. A95.

Robert T. Grohman joined the company in April 1974, as president of Levi Strauss International and was elected a vice president of the company in May 1974. In 1975 he was appointed international group president and senior vice president. He has been executive vice president since April 1976 and was president of the operating groups for fiscal years 1977-1980. He was named chief member of the office of the president in June 1978. In November 1981 he became president and chief executive officer. He has served as a director since 1974. He was 56 in 1981.

Francis J. Brann joined the company in 1965 and was elected vice president in November 1972. He assumed the position of Levi Strauss International division area manager central Europe in June 1974 and the position of president of the Canada and Latin American division in January 1976. He was named executive vice president of the U.S. sportswear group in June 1978 and was promoted to president of Levi Strauss USA in January 1980. He joined the board of directors in July 1979. Brann graduated from the University of San Francisco in 1961 and from City College of New York Graduate Business School in 1965. In 1981 he was 43.

Thomas W. Tusher joined the company in 1969. He was named president of Levi Strauss International in January 1980, having served as executive vice president of the International group since December 1976. During most of 1976 he held the position of president of the European division. During the previous five years, he functioned as general manager for various international divisions and areas. He was elected vice president of the company in April 1976, and senior vice president in December 1977. He joined the board of directors in July 1979. Tusher graduated from the University of California in 1963 and from Stanford University, Graduate Business School in 1965. In 1981 he was 39 years old.

Robert D. Haas joined the company in January 1973 as project analyst in inventory management and became Jeanswear product manager in August 1973. He then joined the Levi Strauss International group as marketing services manager in October 1975. He became director of marketing in May 1976, and assistant general manager-Far East division in December 1976. In November 1977, he was elected vice president of the company and was appointed director of corporate marketing development. He was elected senior vice president-corporate planning and policy in June 1978, and was appointed president of the New Business group in January 1980, when he joined the board of directors. In December 1980, he became president of the operating groups. In 1981, he was 38.

Exhibit 1 contains the names, positions, and ages of the key executives of Levi Strauss & Co.

THE APPAREL INDUSTRY

If one were forced to select one word which describes the nature of competition in the apparel industry, it would have to be <u>fierce</u>. In the United States alone, there are more than 15,000 manufacturers in the apparel industry. However, the industry is experienceing a trend toward consolidation (larger firms diversifying by buying smaller firms). This fact is evidenced by a 16 percent reduction in the number of domestic producers over the past five years. For the larger firms in the industry, consolidation via acquisition has led to rapid diversification of product lines and to an increased ability to cope with fluctuations in market demand. At the same time, it has resulted in market concentration. Currently, 5 percent of the firms in the apparel industry generate over 70 percent of industry sales.

Blue Bell, Inc. (manufacturer of Wrangler jeans), V.F. Corporation (producer of Lee jeans), and LS & Co. are the major competitors in the apparel industry in terms of sales. In 1979, Blue Bell had sales of $1.029 billion and V. F. Corporation had sales of $544 million. From 1974 to 1979, Blue Bell and V. F. experienced a 17.7 percent and 8.8 percent average annual sales growth, respectively. In comparison, LS & Co. had sales of $2.1 billion in 1979, and their sales have more than doubled since 1975.

Market saturation. According to Standard & Poor's, the U.S. apparel market has been saturated by both foreign and domestic producers. While imports of apparel had been growing gradually since the 1950s, in recent years imports have captured a considerable portion of the domestic market. Imports have continued to increase, albeit at a decreasing rate. Import volume doubled in the 1975 to 1978 period. Thus, domestic producers have found that it is becoming increasingly difficult to pass along to their customers the increased costs of raw materials, labor, energy, etc. In response to this trend, domestic manufacturers are turning toward mechanization, adoption of a global view of the business, diversification toward products that are more import-resistent, and a reliance on brand name marketing and product exclusivity to counteract pressure on price.

EXHIBIT 1

KEY EXECUTIVES

Name	Position and office	Age
J. P. Berghold	Vice president and treasurer	42
Thomas C. Borrelli	Vice president and president of the Jeanswear division	60
Francis J. Brann	Senior vice president and president of Levi Strauss USA, director	42
James W. Cameron	Vice president-human resources	40
Harry H. Cohn	Vice president and executive vice president of Group III - Levi Strauss USA, director	50
Robert T. Grohman	President, chief executive officer, director	56
Peter E. Haas	Chairman of the board, director	61
Robert D. Haas	Senior vice president and president of the operating groups, director	38
Walter H. Haas, Jr.	Retired November 1981, director	64
Thomas F. Harris	Vice president-Community affairs	
Roy C. Johns, Jr.	Vice president-corporate communications	51
Peter T. Jones	Senior vice president and general counsel director	50
David A. Kaled	Vice president-corporate planning and policy	37
Robert B. Kern	Vice president-corporate secretary, director	60
James A. McDermott	Vice president and executive vice president of Group II - Levi Strauss USA	44
Robert F. McRae	Vice president and president of the Canada division	48
Richard D. Murphy	Vice president-controller	37
Gerald E. O'Shea	Vice president and assistant to the chief operating officer	55
Alfred V. Sanguinetti	Senior vice president and president of Group I - Levi Strauss USA, director	52
Karl F. Slacik	Senior vice president-finance and chief financial officer	51
Peter T. Thigpen	Vice president and executive vice president of Group I-Levi Straus International	41
Thomas W. Tusher	Senior vice president and president of Levi Strauss International, director	39
William K. Warnock	Vice president, executive vice president of Diversified Apparel Enterprises and president of Koret of North America	59

Source: 10-K report for the fiscal year ended November 25, 1980. Standard & Poor's *Register of Corporation Directors and Executives* vol. 2 (1980), published by Standard & Poor's Corporation, New York.

Automation, particularly in the design and cutting area, is being used to increase productivity and thereby reduce cost pressures. In general, significant automation initiatives have been limited almost exclusively to the larger firms who can afford the increased investment in plant and equipment. This has resulted in even more competitive cost pressures for smaller firms which cannot afford the automated equipment. Larger firms with the resources to automate their manufacturing operations and reduce their average cost per unit will benefit through increased mechanization, but one consolation for smaller firms who choose to remain independent is that the largest cost component in production costs in the apparel industry is the cost of fabric. Thus, except for better frabric utilization, savings resulting from automation affect directly only a small proportion of total production costs. But modern equipment can reduce fabric usage. However, service centers are being set up to offer the use of automatic pattern markers to small companies on a pay-as-you-go basis. Also, by specializing in distinct niches, some small firms have avoided competition based purely on price.

Designer jeans. For a short time, designer jeans such as Gloria Vanderbilt, Calvin Klein, and Jordache were perceived as threats to the major producers of jeans. However, by 1981 the designer jean fad seemed to have peaked, and consumers began returning to the basic styles. Furthermore, designer jeans never accounted for more than an estimated 3 percent of the jeans market.

Counterfeiting of jeans. Jean counterfeiting is an emerging threat to the manufacturers of popular name brand jeans. Counterfeiting is a profitable undertaking since counterfeiters need not invest heavily to establish demand for their products (jean manufacturers have already done this), and they have no regard for product quality (jean manufacturers will bear the cost of dissatisfied customers).

For the most part, consumers who buy counterfeit jeans are unaware that they are not the real thing. These jeans are sold for a lower price than the "true brand," and they are often of inferior and/or inconsistent quality. Counterfeiters use lighter weight fabric; the seams in counterfeit jeans often come apart after one washing; and the zippers and rivets in counterfeit jeans are of low quality. Additionally, many counterfeiters purchase phony labels from labelmakers in New York and attach the labels to jean seconds and irregulars purchased from other jean manufacturers. Counterfeiting is a major concern for apparel manufacturers. They perceive counterfeits as a threat to the franchise as well as overall sales.

In 1980 alone, LS & Co. uncovered a U.S. counterfeiting operation that produced approximately 50,000 fake pairs of Levi's jeans per month. Moreover, LS & Co. recently won a $500,000 settlement in London from the operators of an international counterfeiting operation selling fake Levi's jeans in Europe. This underscores the tremendous value of Levi's trademark.

Outlook for the domestic apparel market. The future of the domestic apparel industry looks extremely good for various product lines such as activeware, sportswear, women's wear, jeans, and western styles. As the baby-boom population moves into a higher age bracket, emphasis on leisure remains high; the proportion of women in the work force is increasing; and the population is shifting to the Sunbelt. Thus, these segments should continue to grow.

Many firms who are surviving the effects of increased competition are doing so primarily because of diversification into various segments of the apparel market. By broadening their scope and focusing on different markets, firms find it easier to avoid the potentially serious negative effects resulting from rapid style changes which characterize the industry.

Activewear is becoming an important factor in the apparel industry, and it is expected to remain popular through the 1980s. The success of activewear is due largely to the popularity of sports and physical fitness in the United States. Additionally, activewear has both functional and fashionable qualities which make it versatile enough for use as everyday wear. Since "casual is the wave of the future" (*U.S. Industrial Outlook*, 1980; p. 367), and the refreshed, relaxed, and youthful appearance is also in vogue, the outlook for activewear is very good. Furthermore, the popularity of activewear is inducing strong growth in related sportswear apparel. LS & Co. is the only major apparel producer offering a full line of activewear.

Industry experts believe that women's wear has an exceptionally promising future since more women are entering the labor market. There is evidence of a strong trend toward dressier fashions, sportswear, activewear, and separates for women. This trend looks promising to the executives at LS & Co. since their recent acquisition of Koracorp Industries made them a leader in the production of women's sportswear.

The future of western styles looks bright also. Their popularity is expected to continue because of the trend in the United States and foreign countries toward wearing rugged American styles. From the perspective of the apparel producer, western styles are appealing for a number of reasons. First, most western-style clothes are made from cotton materials which are readily available and easy to work with. Second, they are durable, versatile, and comfortable. Thus, demand for these products is expected to remain strong for many years. Finally, corduroy products, which add color and variety to western styles, are experiencing increased demand. LS & Co. is encouraged by this trend since they are the leading producer of western styles in the world.

The outlook for the international market. As the U.S. apparel market has become more saturated, growth-oriented apparel producers in the United States have directed their attention toward the market potential overseas. Between 1974 and 1979, the value of U.S. apparel exports increased from $332.7 million to $819 million. Furthermore, industry analysts believe that by 1985, four percent of total U.S. apparel production will be exported. Large U.S. apparel firms have relied on their financial, marketing, and research and development capabilities to compete successfully with foreign producers. Additionally, the popularity of American styles overseas has resulted in increased demand for name brand U.S. products.

Countries in Western Europe, such as Italy, Belgium, Austria, Switzerland, and West Germany, offer the most promising possibilities for future export growth. According to *U.S. Industrial Outlook* (1980, p. 367), growth prospects in these countries look good for several reasons. First, they have high standards of living. Second, they are experiencing declining domestic production. Finally, apparel imports in these countries are increasing rapidly.

THE STRUCTURE AND PRODUCTS OF LEVI STRAUSS & CO.

Levi Strauss & Co. designs, manufacturers, and markets casual wear for just about every taste. Their product line includes everything from jeans, skirts, and suits to shoes. The majority of their products are manufactured and sold under the Levi's trademark. In 1980, Levi Strauss & Co. consolidated its three operating divisions into two units, Levi Strauss USA and Levi Strauss International. It also has miscellaneous other division and a corporate staff. Each unit contains several division which facilitate production and marketing in various segments of the casual wear market.

Levi Strauss USA. Levi Strauss USA consists of three groups which are divided into 10 operating divisions: Jeanswear, Youthwear, Resistol Hats, Womenswear, Koret of North America, Menswear, Activewear, Accessories, Employee Purchase Plan, and Retail Stores. Levi Strauss & Co.'s Jeanswear division is the largest jeans manufacturer in the United States, and the largest division in the company. Additionally, it is responsible for producing all styles of jeans (i.e. straight leg, bell bottom and prewashed). However, this group also produces various styles of shirts, jackets, vests, shorts, and western wear for men.

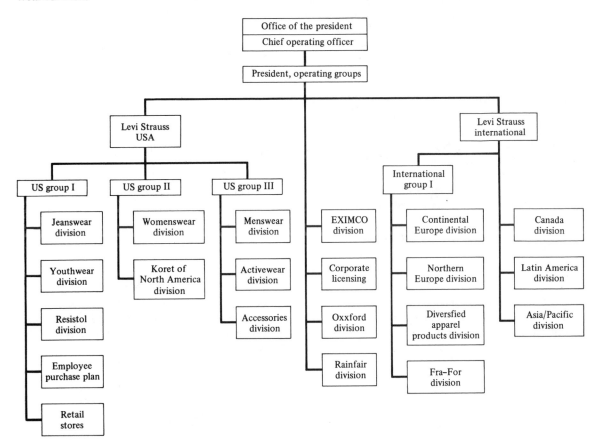

Exhibit 2 Operating structure of Levi Strauss & Company. (*Source:* 1980 Annual Report of Levi Strauss & Company.)

The Youthwear division is the second largest major product in the USA unit. It produces apparel for children from toddlers to teens, but it focuses primarily on the 7- to 14-year-old market. Like the Jenaswear division, its products range from jeans, jackets, shirts, and overalls to T-shirts. Sportswear for youngesters is a new product recently added to the Youthwear divisions.

Resistol Hats is the world's largest producer of brand name western and dress hats. This division was formally part of Koracap Industries which was a large and successful manufacturer in its own right.

Womenswear is another important product division in the USA unit. Products included in this division include pants, shirts, sweaters, and shorts. A recent introduction to the Womenswear line, Bend-Over pants which are made from a stretch material, is the hottest selling product in the group.

In the Levi Strauss & Co. 1979 annual report, the following statement was made concerning the Womenswear group: "Womenswear, the company's most rapidly growing division, nearly doubled its sales last year. . . . This sharp growth indicates the division's potential in the vast womenswear market, which exceeds the menswear in size."

Koret of North America division was formerly Koret of California. They produce high brand-loyalty apparel products.

The Menswear division manufactures stretch pants called Levi's Action Slacks which are becoming popular. Among the other products in the Menswear division are men's shirts, vests, sweaters, and jackets.

Activewear is the newest product division in the USA unit. This division manufactures such products as warm-up suits, shorts, ski-wear, and other sports apparel for both men and women. According to LS & Co.'s 1979 annual report, "The division's entry into the marketplace followed a three-year comprehensive study of the activewear market. . . . The activewear market was found to be large and highly fragmented, with no major American brands offering a full range of products." LS & Co.'s top managers indicate they will place substantial emphasis on activewear in the future as they attempt to carve out a niche for themselves in the market.

The Accessories division produces a wide range of products such as belts, hats, and wallets. The Accessories division produces the smallest sales volume of any product line in Levi Strauss & Co. Exhibit 3 shows sales figures for Levi Strauss USA from 1976 to 1980.

Levi Strauss International.   Levi Strauss International is the second component of the company's structure. The International unit is divided into four groups (International Group I and Canada, Latin America, and Asia/Pacific divisions) of which the International Group I is the largest. The International Group I is further divided into operating divisions. LS & Co.'s primary export product is jeans, but sportswear, youthwear, and womenswear have proven to be successful export items as well.

Exhibit 3 shows sales figures for the International Division from 1976 to 1980.

Other operating units. Four operating divisions have been separated from the two main operating units (Levi Strauss USA and Levi Strauss International) due to their unique nature.

The EXIMCO division was set up to develop special markets for LS & Co. and to manage sales in Eastern Europe, China, Switzerland, and Hong Kong. They provide Levi Strauss with the ability to take advantage of new opportunities in international markets.

The Oxford Division produces top-quality men's suits in the United States, and the Rainfair division producers industrial clothing and coated compounded products for industry. Both of these divisions produce products formerly produced by Koracorp Industries.

PRODUCTION FACILITIES

Levi Strauss & Co. has numerous plants and distribution centers located in North American and throughout Asia, Latin America, and Europe. Exhibit 4 presents a list of facilities LS & Co. owns or leases. According to *Fortune* magazine (November 19, 1979, p. 86), "During the next five years, the company plans to spend some $400 million to build no fewer than 40 new factories and enlarge several existing ones; more than $250 million will go into production facilities for sweaters, blazers, and a variety of other garments that were not in the company's product line a few years ago.

EXHIBIT 3

DIVISIONS' PERCENT OF TOTAL SALES ($ millions)

	1979 Sales	% Sales	1978 Sales	% Sales	1977 Sales	% Sales	1976 Sales	% Sales
Levi Strauss USA								
Division								
Jeanswear	743.1	57	658.7	61	695.5	65	569.1	66
Youthwear	217.8	17	184.2	17	171.6	16	126.8	15
Sportswear and Activewear	120.7	9	120.6	11	108.8	10	94.1	11
Womenswear	197.4	15	99.2	9	62.8	6	47.4	5
Accessories	15.6	1	14.3	1	33.6	3	26.5	3
Total	1294.6		1077		1072.3		863.9	
Levi Strauss International								
Europe	389.7	53	305.7	52	237.4	49	146.1	41
Canada	139.6	19	114.8	20	122.7	25	111.4	31
Latin America	134.7	18	103.5	18	79.3	16	51.7	15
Asia/Pacific	74.1	10	61.0	10	47.6	10	46.7	13
Total	738.1		585		487		355	

Source: 1979–1976 Annual Reports for Levi Strauss & Co.

EXHIBIT 4

FACILITIES OWNED AND LEASED

	Number of facilities	Square feet	Purpose
A. Facilities owned:			
Arkansas	1	295,000	Distribution center
	3	156,000	Manufacturing
California	3	282,000	Manufacturing
	2	323,400	Distribution center
Georgia	2	197,900	Manufacturing
Illinois	1	111,000	Manufacturing
Kentucky	1	324,200	Distribution center
Nevada	1	315,800	Distributioin center
New Jersey	1	50,000	Manufacturing
New Mexico	2	189,700	Manufacturing
North Carolina	2	262,400	Manufacturing
Pennsylvania	1	126,700	Manufacturing
South Carolina	1	54,600	Manufacturing
Tennessee	9	898,900	Manufacturing
Texas	16	1,559,000	Manufacturing
	1	123,000	Curing
	2	1,339,000	Distribution center
Virginia	2	99,700	Manufacturing
Wisconsin	2	283,000	Manufacturing
Argentina	1	72,700	Manufacturing
Australia	1	103,600	Manufacturing
	1	37,000	Distribution center
Belgium	4	213,500	Manufacturing
Brazil	1	38,300	Manufacturing
	1	250,000	Manufacturing and distribution center
Canada	4	236,200	Manufacturing
	1	96,000	Manufacturing and warehousing
	1	183,000	Distribution center
France	6	317,400	Manufacturing
	1	77,200	Manufacturing and warehousing
	1	116,600	Manufacturing and distribution center
Mexico	1	253,800	Manufacturing and distribution center
	1	104,000	Manufacturing
Puerto Rico	1	54,000	Manufacturing
	1	20,000	Distribution center
Sweden	1	18,800	Distribution center
United Kingdom	3	178,000	Manufacturing
	1	96,000	Distribution center
Total	85	9,518,300	

EXHIBIT 4 (continued)

FACILITIES OWNED AND LEASED

	Number of facilities	Square feet	Purpose	Term Expires
B. Facilities leased:				
Arkansas	5	238,400	Manufacturing	1981-1989
	2	45,000	Warehousing	1982-1989
California	1	18,000	Manufacturing	1985
	1	155,000	Distribution center	2013
	2	85,000	Warehousing	1986-2001
Georgia	2	145,900	Manufacturing	1984-1996
New Mexico	2	116,000	Manufacturing	1992-1994
	1	50,300	Manufacturing and warehousing	1989
North Carolina	1	25,000	Warehousing	1984
Ohio	1	105,000	Manufacturing	2006
South Carolina	1	92,000	Manufacturing	1991
Tennessee	3	142,900	Manufacturing	1983-1998
	3	75,500	Warehousing	1982-1986
Texas	9	377,700	Manufacturing	1981-1997
	1	200,000	Manufacturing and warehousing	2009
	1	15,900	Warehousing	1983
	1	310,000	Distribution center	1998
Utah	1	29,000	Manufacturing	1993
Argentina	1	51,000	Distribution center	1982
Australia	1	83,600	Manufacturing and warehousing	1983
Belgium	1	88,300	Distribution center	1986
	1	65,000	Warehousing	1981
Canada	1	105,900	Distribution center	2002
	8	429,300	Manufacturing	1981-2002
	2	31,200	Warehousing	1981-1986
France	1	32,300	Manufacturing and warehousing	1981
	1	37,000	Distribution center	1986
Germany	1	171,800	Distribution center	1987
Hong Kong	1	93,200	Manufacturing	1982
	1	50,700	Warehousing and distribution center	1981
Italy	1	43,100	Distribution center	1983
Japan	2	26,800	Distribution center	1985
Netherlands	1	17,900	Distribution center	1985
Norway	1	11,300	Distribution center	1981
Philippines	1	38,800	Manufacturing	1984
	1	32,500	Distribution center	1984
Switzerland	1	16,800	Distribution center	1981
United Kingdom	2	116,000	Manufacturing	1999-2000
	1	144,000	Distribution center and warehousing	2000
	1	20,000		
Total	70	3,933,100		

Source: 10-K report for fiscal year-end November 25, 1980.

MARKETING

The marketing orientation of Levi Strauss & Co. has undergone significant change since the company's inception in the 1850s. Originally, Levi's jeans were worn almost exclusively by gold miners who considered them to be essential equipment because they were both rugged and durable. However, in the 1950s jeans became a teenage fad, and later they became a trend. Thus, LS & Co. adjusted their marketing orientation to take advantage of this trend. Currently, Levi's products are oriented toward the more fashion conscious 20- to 39-year-old age group. There are 71.1 million people in this age group in the United States today, and there will be 77.6 million people in this age group by 1985.

Brand awareness. LS & Co. is the leading producer in the apparel industry. Much of their success can be attributed to the marketing strength they developed over many years of producing and selling jeans. The most important competitive advantage LS & Co. has, and their most important marketing strength as well, is wide consumer acceptance of the Levi's brand. LS & Co. sells high-quality products at reasonable prices, and this fact is recognized throughout the world.

Distribution. LS & Co. sells most of its products through department stores and speciality outlets. In addition, they promote many accessories (i.e. belts, hats, and totebags) inside retail esta-blishments by using attractive point-of-sale racks which complement the products on display. Pants specialty stores began to play a more dominant role in LS & Co's distribution system in the early 1970s. These stores and the more broadly oriented "Levi's Only" stores represent welcomed alternatives to distributing almost exclusively through department stores where sales have been sluggish recently. Approximately 90 percent of the products sold in Levi's Only stores are manufactured by Levi.

Advertising. LS & Co. employs both national and local advertising, and they utilize all advertising media (i.e. TV, radio, magazines, and newspapers). LS & Co.'s promotions emphasize quality and style as the two most important attributes of their products. The slogan "quality never goes out of style" appears whenever the Levi's brand name is advertised.

LS & Co. maintains flexibility in their advertising programs so they can shift their emphasis to high-volume markets quickly. They focus on anticipating consumer demand and gearing their advertising accordingly rather than attempting to dictate consumer preferences. Furthermore, they employ advertising programs which parallel and complement their special selling support.

Other marketing strengths. Include the following:

Diversification. Levi's extensive diversification is a major strength. They offer a wide variety of products to consumers throughout the United States and the world. This diversity makes LS & Co. less vulnerable to dramatic shifts in consumer preferences for any particular product or in any particular place.

Dependable delivery. LS & Co. employs an advanced computer system to define fashion trends and anticipate changes in consumer demand for apparel. This system enables LS & Co. to manufacture and inventory products which are selling well or are expected to sell well. Thus LS & Co. has achieved a reputation for dependable delivery.

Market research. When Levi Strauss develops a new product, they utilize test marketing to determine the most effective approach for advertising it. They concentrate on understanding the nature of demand for the product by identifying trends which might affect that demand and determining if that demand can be serviced. First, they segment the markets they serve according to consumer preferences and the types of retail outlets which serve them. Then, they identify locations where the Levi's brand has achieved acceptance. Thus, LS & Co. adjusts its advertising to meet the needs of specific products in specific markets.

Marketing weaknesses. Despite their numerous marketing strengths and their number one position in the apparel industry, LS & Co. has marketing weaknesses as well. First, their pricing policy is subject to Federal Trade Commission (FTC) regulations. Specifically, the FTC does not permit forced price maintenance by manufacturers at the retail level. In recent years, this has cost LS & Co. millions of dollars for out-of-court settlements of cases in which they were accused of price maintenance. As a result, LS & Co. is susceptible to price wars. Retailers will drastically cut the price of Levi's products to attract customers to their stores from their competitors. This may pose a possible threat to the quality image of a branded product.

PERSONNEL

The apparel industry employs approximately 1,134,000 production workers, and employment in the industry has been stable for five years. Heavy concentrations of jobs in the apparel industry are found in New York, Pennsylvania, California, North Carolina, and Texas, but most production is done in the South due to the low cost of labor.

Apparel production is highly labor intensive, and apparel industry wages are among the lowest of all manufacturing industries. This is because the production process used by apparel firms is suited to employing unskilled and semiskilled workers. Two major unions represent apparel workers (International Ladies Garment Union and Amalgamated Clothing and Textile Workers Union), and 81 percent of workers in the apparel industry are women.

LS & Co. employed over 44,700 individuals in 1979. Seventy-five percent (75 percent) of them were production workers, and over 60 percent of LS & Co. production workers were union members. Relations between LS & Co. and the production workers are satisfactory. As evidence of this fact, there has never been a major interruption in production due to labor disputes.

At LS & Co., in 1979, 11 percent of officials and managers were minority persons, 15 percent of officials and managers and 4 percent of sales personnel were women and the board of directors includes both minority persons and women. Further, LS & Co. supports minority economic development, and management's community concern is evidenced by its objective of allocating at least 3 percent of aftertax profits to social responsibility efforts. All LS & Co. plants have strong community relations programs, and LS & Co. encourages all employees to be socially concerned and socially active.

RESEARCH AND DEVELOPMENT

Research is considered one of LS & Co.'s most important competitive advantages. Their product research and development department is responsible for the company's progress in new fabrics and garments, and their goal is to improve functional performance. Additionally, an Equipment Research and Development Center is maintained by LS & Co. so that it can remain a leader in automated and semiautomated production equipment. Further, corporate marketing research has an online computerized data bank to monitor major fashion directions, general apparel pricing, retail point-of-sale trends, the company's image, and consumer attitudes toward products currently offered. Research also pretests the effectiveness of proposed advertisements and receptivity of the marketplace to new products.

FINANCIAL MATTERS AT LEVI STRAUSS & CO.

Exhibits 5, 6, 7, and 8 present LS & Co.'s 10-year financial summary, consolidated income statement, consolidated balance sheets, and consolidated statement of changes in financial position, respectively.

FUTURE

At LS & Co. the word *future* means diversification. In November of 1977, LS & Co. began a coordinated corporate strategy of diversification which it intends to continue into the future "at full speed." Four facts suggest this course of action:

1. "In all probability the jeans business in the United States is slowly maturing" (*Business Week*, May 19, 1979).

2. LS & Co. is generating more cash that it needs to finance its 20 percent annual growth in jeans.

3. Market research shows better returns could be made by putting the Levi's trademark or name on other products.

4. In all likelihood, antitrust laws would block an attempt by LS & Co. to acquire another jeans maker.

Peter Haas, chairman of the board, states "diversification has become the most prudent course we can follow."

Fortune Magazine (November 19, 1978) foresees two dangers in LS & Co.'s diversification plans. "One danger inherent in these ambitious plans is that keeping track of all the ever-changing fashions and maintaining the huge assortment of sizes and styles in all the new fields could tax the company's managerial capabilities beyond their limits." Also, LS & Co. is "vulnerable to the same profit-eroding markdowns the minute inventories get out of hand."

Robert T. Grohman, president and chief executive officer, says, "In order to maintain something close to the rate of growth we have experienced in the last five years, we are looking at much more rapid expansion in other segments." He adds, "We are not a fringe house and we are not high-fashion innovators, but we are looking at product lines that have a long-term appeal to the mainstream consumer." Furthermore Grohman says, "Our size and diversification give us tremendous flexibility."

Brenda Gall of Merrill Lynch, Pierce, Fenner & Smith says of LS & Co., "They have instant name recognition, strong ties with retailers, and the marketing talent to identify and go after basic, profitable product lines. They have many opportunities ahead of them, and their growth rate over the last five years is not unsustainable."

EXHIBIT 5

LEVI STRAUSS & CO. AND SUBSIDIARIES
TEN-YEAR FINANCIAL SUMMARY
For the Years Ended 1971-1980
($ millions except per share amounts)

	1980	1979	1978	1977	1976	1975	1974	1973	1972	1971
Net sales	$ 2,840.8	$ 2,103.1	$ 1,682.0	$ 1,559.3	$ 1,219.7	$ 1,015.2	$ 897.7	$ 653.0	$ 504.4	$ 432.0
Gross profit	$ 1,040.2	$ 793.8	$ 623.6	$ 562.6	$ 439.9	$ 347.4	$ 275.5	$ 184.4	$ 160.3	$ 129.6
Interest expense	25.0	12.4	11.2	20.0	12.2	13.1	13.7	10.1	4.3	4.4
Income before taxes	401.9	345.6	280.4	270.0	206.8	136.7	72.7	33.8	48.1	35.7
Provision for taxes on income	178.2	154.1	135.4	140.2	102.1	71.9	37.9	22.0	23.0	16.0
Net income	$ 223.7	$ 191.5	$ 145.0	$ 129.8	$ 104.7	$ 64.7	$ 34.9	$ 11.9	$ 25.0	$ 19.7
Earnings retained in the business	$ 170.2	$ 151.1	$ 110.0	$ 108.0	$ 94.8	$ 58.6	$ 29.6	$ 6.6	$ 20.9	$ 16.3
Cash flow retained in the business	213.3	176.9	125.5	128.7	110.6	71.7	45.7	17.7	28.6	22.5
Income before taxes as % of sales	14.1	16.4	16.7	17.3	17.0	13.5	8.1	5.2	9.5	8.3
Net income as % of sales	7.9	9.1	8.6	8.3	8.6	6.4	3.9	1.8	5.0	4.6
Net income as % of beginning stockholders' equity	32.8	33.3	31.3	35.8	39.5	31.4	19.8	7.0	16.8	23.2
Current assets	$ 1,122.5	$ 1,047.1	$ 824.2	$ 694.2	$ 570.1	$ 407.6	$ 383.5	$ 305.5	$ 252.4	$ 202.8
Current liabilities	452.4	489.7	302.4	263.5	226.6	155.4	188.1	155.7	98.2	67.9
Working capital	670.1	557.4	521.8	430.7	343.5	252.2	195.3	149.8	154.2	134.9
Ratio of current assets to current liabilities	2.5/1	2.1/1	2.7/1	2.6/1	2.5/1	2.6/1	2.0/1	2.0/1	2.6/1	3.0/1
Total assets	1,455.5	1,291.1	973.9	824.2	678.0	496.3	470.4	382.7	307.1	247.9
Long term debt—less current maturities	$ 138.8	$ 99.1	$ 83.3	$ 80.6	$ 79.2	$ 68.7	$ 72.8	$ 48.1	$ 37.6	$ 28.4
Stockholders'—equity	831.6	681.2	575.3	463.9	362.4	265.2	206.0	176.4	169.7	148.8
Capital expenditures	$ 119.8	$ 51.3	$ 42.9	$ 31.4	$ 19.5	$ 10.4	$ 24.3	$ 28.8	$ 17.6	$ 15.6
Depreciation	25.4	18.2	16.1	13.7	11.6	9.3	9.7	8.3	6.4	5.1
Property, plant & equipment—net	280.8	188.5	141.3	119.3	102.4	82.1	82.3	68.0	48.0	39.6
Number of employees	48,000	44,700	35,100	37,200	32,500	29,700	30,100	29,100	25,100	21,400
Per share data:										
Net income	$ 5.36	$ 4.58	$ 3.28	$ 2.93	$ 2.35	$ 1.47	$ .80	$ .27	$ .57	$ .47
Cash dividends declared	1.30	1.00	.80	.50	.23	.14	.12	.12	.10	.08
Book value (on shares outstanding at year end)	20.34	16.50	13.14	10.66	8.25	6.08	4.73	4.05	3.90	3.42
Market price range	44–30	$34\frac{1}{2}$/17	$19\frac{3}{8}$–$13\frac{5}{8}$	$15\frac{7}{8}$–$12\frac{1}{8}$	$13\frac{3}{8}$–9	$10\frac{3}{4}$–$3\frac{1}{8}$	$5\frac{5}{8}$–$3\frac{1}{8}$	$12\frac{1}{2}$–$4\frac{1}{4}$	15–$10\frac{1}{8}$	$16\frac{1}{8}$–$8\frac{3}{8}$
Average common and common equivalent shares outstanding	41,763,108	41,784,058	44,229,872	44,257,346	44,476,748	43,899,028	43,520,320	43,520,320	42,344,000	

Source: 1980 Annual Report for Levi Strauss & Company.

EXHIBIT 6

LEVI STRAUSS & CO. AND SUBSIDIARIES
CONSOLIDATED STATEMENT OF INCOME
For the Years 1978-1980
($000 except per share amounts)

	Year Ended		
	November 30, 1980 (53 weeks)	November 25, 1979 (52 weeks)	November 26, 1978 (52 weeks)
Net sales	$ 2,840,844	$ 2,103,109	$ 1,682,019
Cost of goods sold	1,800,665	1,309,263	1,058,439
Gross profit	1,040,179	793,846	623,580
Marketing, general and administrative expenses	635,870	464,086	344,536
Operating income	404,309	329,760	279,044
Interest expense	25,018	12,449	11,178
Interest and other income, net	(22,606)	(28,238)	(12,503)
Income before taxes	401,897	345,549	280,369
Provision for taxes on income	178,208	154,095	135,400
Net income	$ 223,689	$ 191,454	$ 144,969
Net income per share	$ 5.36	$ 4.58	$ 3.28
Average common and common equivalent shares outstanding	41,763,108	41,784,058	44,229,872

Source: 1980 Annual Report for Levi Strauss & Co.
[a]Dollars in thousands except per share amounts.

EXHIBIT 7

LEVI STRAUSS & CO. AND SUBSIDIARIES
CONSOLIDATED BALANCE SHEETS
For the Years 1979 and 1980
($000)

	November 30, 1980	November 25, 1979
Assets		
Current Assets		
Cash	$ 36,192	$ 27,454
Temporary investments of cash	51,693	195,297
Trade receivables (less allowance for doubtful accounts: 1980—$9,368; 1979—$8,340)	446,461	340,131
Inventories		
Raw materials and work-in-process	252,538	216,820
Finished goods	275,017	225,001
Other current assets	60,606	42,411
Total current assets	1,122,507	1,047,114
Property, plant and equipment (less accumulated depreciation: 1980—$113,301; 1979—$101,989)	280,783	188,495
Other assets	52,070	55,510
	$1,455,360	$1,291,119
Liabilities and stockholders' equity		
Current liabilities		
Current maturities of long-term debt	$ 14,963	$ 15,832
Short-term borrowings	48,642	53,535
Accounts payable	135,006	154,929
Accrued liabilities	93,875	83,802
Compensation and payroll taxes	55,313	57,636
Pension and profit sharing	20,982	27,545
Taxes based on income	68,309	85,069
Dividend payable	15,335	11,357
Total current liabilities	452,425	489,705
Long-term debt—less current maturities	138,754	99,126
Deferred liabilities	32,552	21,098
Stockholders' equity		
Common stock—$1.00 par value: authorized 100,000,000 shares: shares issued— 1980—43,998,808, 1979—21,999,404	43,999	21,999
Additional paid-in capital	59,837	82,424
Retained earnings	806,257	636,010
	910,093	740,433
Less treasury stock, at cost: 1980—3,105,482 shares: 1979—1,354,949 shares	78,464	59,243
Total stockholders' equity	831,629	681,190
	$1,455,360	$1,291,119

[a]Dollars in thousands.

EXHIBIT 8

LEVI STRAUSS & CO. AND SUBSIDIARIES
CONSOLIDATED STATEMENT OF CHANGES IN FINANCIAL POSITION
For the Years 1978-1980
($000)

	Year Ended		
	November 30, 1980 (53 weeks)	November 25, 1979 (52 weeks)	November 26, 1978 (52 weeks)
Working capital provided by:			
Operations:			
Net income	$ 223,689	$ 191,454	$ 144,969
Add items not currently involving working capital:			
Depreciation and amortization	30,004	20,430	17,606
Other, net	13,066	5,380	(2,140)
Working capital provided by operations	266,759	217,264	160,435
Common stock issued in acquisition of Koracorp Industries Inc.	—	37,261	—
Proceeds from long-term debt	54,586	8,400	14,411
Common stock issued to employees	6,322	4,999	5,077
Working capital provided	327,667	267,924	179,923
Working capital used for:			
Additions to property, plant and equipment	119,824	51,254	42,863
Cash dividends declared	53,442	40,391	34,972
Acquisition of Koracorp Industries Inc. (less working capital of $34,961):			
Property, plant and equipment	—	17,702	—
Other assets	—	4,885	—
Goodwill	—	39,341	—
Long-term liabilities assumed	—	(26,054)	—
Purchases of treasury stock	26,130	87,451	3,611
Reductions in long-term debt	14,958	15,505	11,766
Other, net	640	1,862	(4,379)
Working capital used	214,994	232,337	88,833
Increase in working capital	$ 112,673	$ 35,587	$ 91,090
Increase (decrease) in working capital, represented by change in:			
Cash and temporary investments of cash	$ (134,866)	$ (32,070)	$ 93,880
Trade receivables, net	106,330	99,006	37,886
Inventories	85,734	143,327	4,391
Other current assets	18,195	12,624	(6,188)
Current maturities of long-term debt and short-term borrowings	5,762	(48,003)	20,290
Accounts payable and accrued liabilities	9,850	(83,667)	(51,983)
Other current liabilities	21,668	(55,630)	(7,186)
Increase in working capital	$ 112,673	$ 35,587	$ 91,090

Source: 1980 Annual Report for Levi Strauss & Co.
[a]Dollars in thousands.

PART 3

New Cases

2 Cases

Apple Computer, Inc. - Fall 1985 [1]

Apple Computer, Inc., during Fall 1985 was reeling from the dramatic corporate events that some industry watchers compared to their favorite soap operas. Newspapers, popular journals and the trade press had almost daily reports of personality clashes and differences over management style that finally culminated in the September 17, 1985 resignation of the co-founder and chairman, Steven P. Jobs. The disputes did not end with his resignation, however. The former chairman's plan to start a new computer firm with five former Apple managers led Apple's top management and the board of directors to file a lawsuit charging Jobs with secretly scheming to use company research for his new venture and deceiving the company's board about his plans.

The events that led to the climactic closing of one chapter of Apple's history weave a tale of a company plagued by internal rivalries and bitter resentments. Perhaps the Fall 1985 episode began with the hiring of John Sculley in May of 1983 as the new president and chief executive officer. A former president of Pepsi-Cola, Inc. with no experience in the personal computer market, Sculley was hired to help Apple maintain market share in the personal computer market. Apple's market share had begun a downward slide in 1981. In a way, the hiring of Sculley marked the beginning of a transition for Apple from an entrepreneurial corporate culture to a professional corporate culture.

Although Jobs personally recruited Sculley and the two seemed to have a close working relationship, the alliance between the two men started to deteriorate in October 1984. A year earlier Sculley had consolidated the company's nine highly decentralized divisions organized along product lines into just three divisions. The new organization had one division for sales of all Apple products, another division for the production of the Apple II family of products and the third division for the development and production of the Macintosh (MAC). Jobs was named the general manager of the newly formed Macintosh Division.

As Jobs was both Chairman of the board and general manager, he and Sculley (the CEO) were faced with conflicting authority relationships: each was subordinate to the other yet they both had authority over one another. This structure created many conflicts in their management partnership. Although the MAC division was not performing up to par, Sculley felt reluctant to demand better performance from a general manager who was also the chairman of the board. Moreover, the people under Jobs' tutelage were often treated preferentially because Jobs believed that their mission was the most important aspect of the company. Jobs' behavior was met with particular resentment from Apple II personnel who felt slighted because their division brought in twice the revenues of the MAC division. This bitter resentment and rivalry between the two divisions was at least partly responsible for the resignation in February 1985, of Stephen Wozniak, Apple's other co-founder and designer of the original Apple.

The internal problems were exacerbated by the 1985 general slump in personal computer demand and by the failure of the Macintosh to successfully penetrate the business market. This turn of events prompted the board to insist that Sculley exercise his authority as CEO and hire a more seasoned general manager to turn the MAC division around.

Jobs initially agreed with Sculley that a change was needed. But when it came time to make the change, Jobs resisted. The ensuing power struggle ended in late May with the board supporting Sculley's decision to again reorganize the company, this time into functional divisions eliminating altogether the MAC division. Jobs was left with no operating authority whatsoever and no responsibility for any day to day activities. He retained his title of chairman of the board. In August, Jobs sold a fifth of his Apple

---

[1]This case was written by Theresa M. Brady under the supervision of Assistant Professor Daniel J. Power, University of Maryland at College Park. It was prepared as a basis for student analysis and discussion, and is not intended to illustrate either effective or ineffective handling of an administrative situation. Used with permission.

stock for an estimated $14 million, putting to rest any speculation that he might have been part of a plan to take Apple private in a leveraged buyout. For a few moments the turmoil of 1985 had begun to subside.

But no sooner had the dust finally settled from the upheaval of the drastic reorganization when the company was stunned by the resignation of Steve Jobs on September 17, 1985. Less than a week before, Jobs had informed Apple that he intended to start a new company and if the board felt that his plans would be in conflict with Apple, he would step down as chairman. For a short time the board considered investing in the new venture but when it discovered that Jobs had recruited five key Apple personnel including engineers who were privy to important research projects, rumors began to fly that Apple would ask Jobs to leave the company. Instead, Jobs, believing that the board was hostile, insisted on the board's immediate acceptance of his resignation. Jobs' new company would make a computer product for universities, one of Apple's fastest growing markets (Gray, September 18, 1985).

On September 23, 1985 Apple filed a suit in Santa Clara County Superior Court charging Jobs with planning to use proprietary information to create a company that would compete directly with Apple Computer.

REVISED DIRECTION - FALL 1985

Much of the conflict among Apple's key players centered on the direction the company should take. Steve Jobs believed that acquiescence to the **de facto** standard established by IBM was unnecessary. He reasoned that quality products, regardless of other factors in the marketplace, would be the motivating force behind purchases of computers. Products, not markets were to be emphasized. Jobs' drive to create new and different products gave the company a reputation for being innovative and earned Jobs the label of visionary.

John Sculley saw the personal computer business differently and in the end his views prevailed. The structure built by Sculley in the May, 1985, reorganization emphasized markets rather than individual products and was designed to bring a coordinated approach to bear on the business market. Third-party hardware and software manufacturers who had been largely rebuffed by Jobs in the past were welcomed by Sculley to work on attachments and programs for the Macintosh. The second quarter of 1985 letter to shareholders announced a new strategy "to coexist with IBM in the office." In a major speech in June, 1985, at the MacForum Conference in San Francisco, Mr. Sculley outlined Apple's direction. Excerpts from his speech appear in Exhibit 1.

HISTORICAL BACKGROUND

By 1985, the short history of Apple Computer had already taken on the trappings of folklore because it embodied the American dream: two young, self-made engineers had a vision of a computer product that would be understandable to and useable by the average person. They produced it, sold it, and soon turned their dream into a two billion dollar enterprise, the youngest company ever to enter the ranks of the Fortune 500.

The dream began in 1976 when Steven Jobs, 21, and Stephen Wozniak, 26, collaborated on a small computer board for personal use. In those days, the only computers available other than large expensive mainframes were those purchased through mail-order houses. The only purchasers were hobbyists and computer buffs. The Apple I, a bare bones assembled computer without keyboard or video monitor (which could be bought as extras and hooked on), took six months to design and forty hours to build. Since the machine was an improvement on the existing kits, and sold for under $700, the two soon had an order for fifty.

With that first order in hand, they raised about $1,350 by selling a used Volkswagon van and an HP programmable calculator. They set up shop in Jobs' garage and soon were doing well enough to form Apple Computer Company with Jobs as business manager and Wozniak as engineer.

From the beginning it was Wozniak who came up with the technical innovations. Jobs' contribution was envisioning and conceptualizing the product. Although he did not have the technical ability to create the machine, he knew what it should look like and what it should be able to do. His aggressive and energetic actions to get money from investors and credit from suppliers had positive results for the upstart company. Moreover, Jobs continually encouraged his friend Wozniak to keep trying. By his own admission, Wozniak would have been just as happy to only come up with a computer to show off at the local computer club (Gelman, Sept. 30, 1985).

EXHIBIT 1

**EXCERPTS FROM REMARKS BY JOHN SCULLEY
PRESIDENT AND CHIEF EXECUTIVE OFFICER
APPLE COMPUTER, INC.
MACFORUM CONFERENCE
JUNE 26, 1985**

• ...We remain a company that believes in the power of personal computers for individuals. And we believe our basic technologies are right for the market, both today and in the future.

• ...Apple Computer Company will be listening more to the needs of our customers in terms of what they want our products to be able to do. You will also see us rapidly building bridges with third party developers in order to broaden the product solutions available to the marketplace. This means we want to significantly improve our working relationship with those third party peripheral and software companies that can add the greatest value to our Apple II and Macintosh products...you'll see us take steps to make it easier for other companies to connect their products with ours. These steps will include a gradual transition to selective industry protocol standards as well as a new priority in the future for work station expandability.

• ...Apple Computer will be a market-driven company. This does not infer in any way that we will compromise in building great, innovative products, because innovation will still be a driving force for our company. But being market-driven means we will adopt innovation to the needs of our markets.

• ...you can expect to see Apple greatly increase its commitment to the success of the dealer base. Dealers will know -- without a doubt -- that Apple expects to reach its markets primarily through the dealer channel...we will be making a transition in our university and college sales from a direct-only selling approach...

• ...The marketing message for Macintosh that has largely focused on ease-of-use will now begin to shift its emphasis to the **power** of the Macintosh system with the hardware peripherals and power software now on the market...we are establishing a high engineering priority internally to simplify the development tools for those who want to write Macintosh software...we will try to do a better job on a non-disclosure basis in keeping third party developers informed on where we are going with future products.

• ...We are a company that builds personal computers for individuals. This is because we firmly believe that the information revolution is one that will touch the lives of individuals even more than it will affect institutions. A personal computer can be far more than a smaller version of its large mini and mainframe cousins. Macintosh was created to be a "power tool for the mind" just as the automobile and airplane have been "power tools for the body...By making Macintosh easy to use, we not only have created a landmark user interface that can bring personal computing to many who otherwise would have been intimidated by the complexity of computers, but we are now making it intuitive for even the power users.

• ...we are One Apple. We have put our individual egos aside and we are putting teamwork in its place...it is clear that we are going to have to do incredible things right now in order to continue to succeed. And that starts with clearing up ambiguities in Apple's directions, clearing up channel conflicts and getting the message out to all who are interested that Apple intends to be a constructive player in this industry.

It was not long before demand outstripped the capacity of Jobs' garage and overtaxed their capital. Believing they had a product with great commercial and social value, Jobs and Wozniak set out to find professional managers. Their first recruit was A.C. "Mike" Markkula, Jr., whom they met through a mutual friend. Markkula had successfully managed marketing in two semiconductor companies that had experienced dynamic growth--Intel Corporation and Fairchild Semiconductor.

After researching the personal computer market and assessing Apple Computer's chances, the three men developed plans for acquiring the necessary capital, management expertise, technical innovation, software development, and marketing. Initial financing came from Markkula and a group of venture capitalists that included Venrock Associates and Arthur Rock and Associates. Apple Computer, Inc. was incorporated on January 3, 1977.

Apple remained a private corporation until December, 1980, when it made an initial public offering of 4.6 million shares of common stock. In May, 1981, there was a secondary offering of 2.6 million shares of common stock by approximately 100 selling stockholders, all of whom acquired their shares through employee stock plans or private placement.

Apple's stock reached its peak in 1983, the year John Sculley was hired as the CEO, when it traded for $62 a share. By August 1985, the price had fallen considerably to $16.

In 1985 Apple Computer ranked 234 on the Fortune 500, had over 4,000 employees, served an international market and had annual sales approaching two billion dollars.

MICRO-COMPUTER INDUSTRY

The microcomputer industry was characterized by the manufacture and sale of very small computers with microprocessors as central processing units. These machines usually sold for less than $15,000 (McCrossen, June 6, 1985). The boundaries separating superminis and mainframes and between minis and micros, however, had become blurred as performance gaps between product categories were filled in and new technologies overtook the old.

The driving force behind the expansion of the computer market in general and the microcomputer market in particular was the continued improvement in the price/performance ratio for available equipment. In other words, as the performance improved the prices were remaining the same; or the prices for a given level of performance were falling. According to Standard & Poor's *Industry Surveys*, the overall computer industry had improved price/performance by approximately 20%-25% per year in 1985 and was expected to continue to do so for the next decade. Perhaps more interesting was that the development of the microprocessor had contributed to a reversal of the traditional price/performance relationship. Previously, the rule of thumb was that for twice the price one could buy twice the performance. In 1985, a dollar would buy more processing power at the low end of the performance range than at the high end. This cost advantage for smaller systems was the impetus for the trend towards decentralized data processing. Microcomputers could provide systems dedicated to one user at a fraction of the cost of a large scale system.

Demand forecast. In 1985 the entire computer industry suffered its worst slump in over a decade. Even IBM, far and away the staunchest competitor in all segments of the market, had to scale back on two separate occasions what were conservative earnings forecasts. Experts disagreed on the cause and duration of the declining demand. To a large extent the causes were as different in the separate market categories as the categories themselves. Since Apple competed only in the small-scale microcomputer market, the analysis of the 1985 collapse in demand is limited to that market.

In a letter to shareholders written at the end of Apple's 1985 third quarter, Sculley and Jobs listed their reasons for the pause in the computer industry:

> We believe the pause is mainly the result of two things. First, a large number of computer products from several manufacturers have been announced or rumored -- but have not yet begun to ship. This causes some customers to hesitate, awaiting the opportunity to see and evaluate the new products before buying. Second, the economy appears to have slowed in recent months.

Industry experts delved a little deeper into the industry sluggishness reflected in both the home and business markets. The home market was believed to be saturated because by 1985 hobbyists already had their machines and the number of professionals who needed PCs to work at home was limited. The next layer of home users was difficult to penetrate because many consumers, try as they might, failed to see a need to have a computer in their homes. William Rupp, a manager for an east coast computer dealer, noted in a Fall 1985 interview:

> You've got a different customer now. I think everyone has recognized that. You had your frontier ones that had to be the first ones on the block with something new. We've sold out all those folks. Now we have to get to the people who are thinking about buying a PC but haven't found a good reason yet. This is clearly a harder sale.

A perceived lack of need was combined with a frustration with computers because they were more difficult to use than customers were led to believe. Moreover, the day the computer would run the washing machine and arrange schedules never came. While some experts believed that it was up to the computer hardware and software manufacturers to find useful applications for the home market, others believed that the demand would be stimulated by other industries.

Dennis Gilbert, an expert on purchasing computer systems, claimed in a Fall 1985 interview that:

> ...the need for the computer won't be established by hardware or software manufacturers but by the ways in which businesses are going to be doing their business... But unlike earlier projections, this change will not occur suddenly... It is no longer the case that one piece of software, like VisiCalc, is so compelling that people rush out to buy hardware to use it. It will be a collection of services that will be appealing to different segments of the marketplace whose resistance has worn thin. Instead of computer companies establishing a need for computers, it may very well be large retailers like Sears, J.C. Penney or Montgomery Ward which will provide the impetus. It's not clear to me that the market will necessarily be technologically-driven.

The commercial or business market for PCs was also nearing saturation, although planned purchases for 1985 and the use of PCs in offices in 1985 were up over the previous year (see Exhibits 2 & 3). Nonetheless, for the first time in years funds allocated for the purchase of microcomputers declined as a percentage of average data processing budgets in 1985 (Brandt, July 15, 1985). The business market was stalled partly because the industry had yet to come up with an effective means to tie computers into cohesive information systems. Not to be ignored, however, was the influence of the sluggish economy and the strong U.S. dollar. Customers, entertaining thoughts of a possible impending recession, curtailed or deferred all capital equipment purchases which included computer systems.

Another factor contributing to the slack demand was that customers were pausing to "digest" the systems they had purchased in recent years to figure out whether the manchines were worth the money. Beyond basic writing, filing and figuring, the machines were not used for much else. Indeed most users exploited only 5% of the machine's full capability (Kneale, Sept. 16, 1985). Exhibit 4 reflects the attitude of office personnel in 1985 regarding computer applications.

Just how soon demand would turn around was uncertain. One thing that was clear, however, was that the phenomenal pace of the growth rate of the PC market experienced up until and including 1984 would probably not be seen again. The revolution had become an evolution, so that although growth would indeed occur, it would not be at the same rate.

Market segments. In 1985 the microcomputer market could be roughly divided into five major segments: home, business, government, education and international sales. Exhibit 5 shows both 1984 and projected 1990 computer shipments by application market.

The home market included applications such as games, educational programs for children, accounting and other programs for professionals who worked or had their businesses in their homes and hobbyists who enjoyed tinkering with electronic toys. This segment was temporarily saturated in 1985 and was expected to remain sluggish through 1986 and possibly 1987.

The business segment was only slightly better as a market for microcomputers in 1985 for reasons decribed earlier. There was, however, a growing demand from business for computers to tie together isolated personal computers so that employees could share information. The demand was coming largely from departments or work groups within large corporations. It was estimated that the demand was growing 30% a year, which was more than twice the rate of the overall industry. In 1985 mid-range computer systems, which cost anywhere from $10,000 to $350,000, were being used to solve the problem. Yet these systems were not the only effective means for workers to share information. Local area networks (LANs) allowed personal computers to zap information back and forth between each other, share files and printers and gain access to computers outside the department. Apple Computer had just introduced its own LAN to attract corporate customers who had been reluctant to buy the stand-alone Macintosh. Clearly a standard was yet to be set for the future automation of the office; connectivity was the key but there were many ways to play in the market. An estimated 4 million departments and work groups existed in companies in 1985. They were expected to buy $5.3 billion worth of departmental computer gear in 1986 (Brandt, July 15, 1985).

An important but often overlooked segment was the federal government. In 1985 it was the nation's single largest purchaser of personal computers. While sales to companies and individuals slumped, federal agencies were buying personal computers by the tens of thousands. Government purchases represented an attractive market segment because nearly 1.4 million white-collar federal employees relied on information to do their jobs. Moreover, the government had flexible procurement procedures for PC purchases and they were often made in large volumes. Cutbacks in staffs coupled with increasing demands for productivity were other reasons that stimulated demand.

The government segment was especially appealing because awards to suppliers were not usually based on price alone. Government agencies also considered such variables as the expansion capabilities of the system, service support and other factors. Thus profit margins tended to be higher. Furthermore, unlike other segments experiencing declining demand, the federal government was just beginning to make major purchases of PCs. When personal computer sales were booming during the years prior to 1985, the government was only starting to put in place its procurement policies for computer purchases.

A third category, the education market, was smaller than either the business or home markets but unlike either of those segments, this market was growing in 1985. Apple was the dominant player in this segment.

Another growing market for PCs was in Europe. Just when the U.S. market was in a pause, Europe's was coming on strong. In 1985 Europeans were expected to buy 50% more machines than they did in 1984. Although the number of office workers in Europe (60 million) was equal to that in the United States, the number of installed personal computers was only one-third of America's six million. So the potential market was great and American companies held 70% of what already existed in 1985. Apple Computer had the second largest market share in all of Europe; it was number one in France (Calonius, August 19, 1985).

Competition. The early to mid-1980's saw hundreds of computer firms begin operations. Some failed quickly; others struggled with the intense competition and survived. As evidenced by Apple's humble beginnings in a garage and initial financing through the sale of a Volkswagen van and an HP calculator, barriers to entry into this industry were not enormously high. But entrance did not insure survival. In 1985 even some previously strong computer firms faced bankruptcy; others scaled back production and laid off employees.

Among Apple's major competitors were IBM, Commodore, Atari, and AT&T. Exhibit 6 lists a number of competitors along with information on their products. Each of these firms followed separate business strategies attempting to penetrate the microcomputer industry:

IBM. The staunchest competition came from the giant IBM which demonstrated its prowess with its phenomenally rapid dominance of the PC market. IBM introduced its PC in 1981; by 1984 its share of the PC office market was 60% and was expected to rise to 75% in 1985. Its ability to penetrate this segment so quickly stemmed from its already dominating presence in the data processing departments of corporate America. IBM was the only company that actively participated in almost every computer industry segment so its salespeople could tap customers throughout a company. The major strengths of the colossal firm were its strong brand image, customer awareness, reputation, heavy R&D effort and a large, well-trained sales force acknowledged by general consensus to be the best in the country.

In addition, IBM was able to sustain competitive advantage. By virtue of its enormous size the company enjoyed economies of scale, making it the low-cost producer in many cases. This allowed the firm to slash prices in any segment where it was weak. Ultimately strength was gained by IBM through eliminating competitors who could not compete with the lower prices for a sustained period of time. With gross margins of about 40% in 1984, IBM had plenty of room for price cuts if it needed them (McCrossen, June 6, 1985).

Even if companies attempted to avoid head-to-head competition with IBM by finding market niches not yet approached by the corporation, they were likely to be "blown out of the water" if the niche proved profitable. IBM was able to exploit any new opportunity because its manufacturing facilities were modern and effficient. In short, competitors survived only by offering products with significant advantages over IBM, usually a lower price or higher performance for comparable equipment.

IBM's penetration into the office market had set **a de facto** standard prior to 1985. With the exception of Apple, most PC makers made machines that were compatible with IBM. Apple's goal was to provide a machine "for the rest of us". The problem was, by 1985, there were few of "us" left. IBM became the safe purchase as the slogan "no one every got fired for buying IBM" became popular. Indeed, customers said they assumed they would continue to buy most of their equipment from IBM over the next five years, not only for the safety of buying from the market leader, but also because of IBM's superior record for service and support (McCrossen, June 6, 1985).

For 1985 and 1986 IBM had its priorities set on penetrating two of the fastest growing markets in the industry -- office and factory automation. Automation implies the facilitation of the flow of information between data processing mainframes, word processors, workstations, robots, printers, copiers, storage devices, and any other electronic machine that manipulates text or data. In 1985 IBM had yet to develop the connections necessary for compatibility across its product lines. At that time its systems, developed separately for different purposes, had different hardware and operating systems that could not communicate with each other. It was expected that IBM would develop a local area network to tie all its systems together by 1986 or 1987.

Commodore. Commodore was one of the first major U.S. competitors for Apple with its Commodore PET (Personal Electronic Transactor). As the years passed, however, it became less and less of a threat as it tried to fend off criticism of its delivery and service. The company had lost considerable market share by 1985 and like many other companies in the unstable and volatile microcomputer industry, Commodore posted a loss for fiscal year 1985. Its shaky financial condition forced its auditors to qualify their report on the computer maker's earnings after the company had to obtain waivers from its banks on certain conditions of its loan agreements. Moreover, the company's long term debt was reclassified as current (Smith, Sept. 27, 1985).

In the fall of 1985, Commodore attempted to turn its financial woes into prosperity with the introduction of two new product offerings, the C-128 and the Amiga. The C-128 was an enhanced version of the firm's venerable C-64. It was aimed at the low end home market and sold for $300 through the mass market retail channel.

Most of the company's energy, however, was focused on the promotion of the new, full-fledged personal computer aimed at the business segment -- the Amiga. This new product represented significant competition to Apple's Macintosh since it used similar but enhanced technology and sold for much less. According to descriptions in technical journals at the time, the Amiga promised lightning-fast desktop-metaphor graphics in color and twice as much memory and disk storage as the Macintosh. It also had software to exploit the multitasking, graphics, sound and animation capabilities of the hardware. A crucial feature, not available with the Macintosh, was an option for a disk that enabled the computer to run most business-oriented programs written by the IBM PC.

Although technically appealing, the Amiga faced an uphill sell since the introduction to the market of many software programs was delayed until late 1985. The disk option which would make the machine IBM-compatible was also delayed until the end of the year. Nonetheless, Commodore launched a $40 million marketing plan in September 1985 to promote the Amiga which sold for $1,295 plus $195 for a display screen.

Atari. For many years Atari was not a direct threat to Apple since its products were aimed at an entirely different market -- the game business. When it turned out that computers which only ran games were a passing fad, the company started to lose money and began to be viewed as an Achilles' heel by its parent company, Warner Communications. Then in July, 1984, the founder and head of Commodore, Jack Tramiel, left his company and bought Atari from Warner. Tramiel promised to make Atari financially solvent by the end of 1985.

Although the company had yet to turn around completely by the fall of 1985, it had announced a number of new products designed to have more mass appeal than its previous offerings. Prominent among the new machines was a computer line with Macintosh-like capabilities, the 130ST and the 520ST. To demonstrate the likeness to the Macintosh, the computer was dubbed the "Jacintosh". The major difference between the two machines was price. The 130ST sold for $400 as opposed to $1,600 for the comparable 128K Macintosh; the 520ST went for $799 compared with $2,500 for the 512K Macintosh. The new machine could use neither Apple software nor Atari software and it was not IBM-compatible. It did have a color screen; the MAC machine was black and white.

Jacintosh's introduction to the marketplace in the summer of 1985 was less than spectacular. It arrived three months late, with no publicity and no software to run on it. Some of the first machines to hit the market failed to work because microchips on the inside had become loose. To make matters worse, Atari applied stringent conditions to dealers who agreed to sell the product, such as small margins and the assumption of all responsibility for service.

AT&T. AT&T was not free to enter the PC market until January 1, 1984, when it divested its local telephone operating companies as part of an antitrust settlement. AT&T had always had vast expertise in computers but had been prevented from entering the market because of a 1956 consent decree with the Justice Department that had limited its business oeprations to "regulated" telecommunications services and equipment. But by the time the giant telecommunications firm shook itself of the strings attached to its operations, it faced two major hurdles: first, the PC market was already dominated by IBM and Apple; second, the public had pegged AT&T only as a phone company and was reluctant to view it any other way. Consequently, AT&T's foray into the PC market left it with less than a four percent share in 1985.

Nonetheless, AT&T was not yet ready to throw in the towel in 1985. Recently freed from a Federal Communication Commission (FCC) regulation requiring separate subsidiaries for manufacturing and marketing, the company had revamped its computer strategy to take better advantage of its strength as a communications company. It introduced an array of new products that combined communications and computer technologies. In March, 1985, the company introduced a new AT&T UNIX PC which was based on a more powerful version of the microprocessor that powered the Macintosh. It had a price tag of $5,000 and could be expanded to handle ten users. Capitalizing on AT&T's expertise, the new computer had a built-in modem and communications software. A score of popular software was introduced with the model but Lotus Development Corp. had not yet decided to adapt Lotus 1-2-3 to UNIX.

Early on, AT&T had decided to bypass the home markets and concentrate solely on the business market. To sell its UNIX PC it used its direct sales force which had access to virtually every corporation in America. It should be noted, however, that as a regulated monopoly with a guaranteed rate of return for so many years, AT&T was not known for its marketing ability. Nonetheless by mid-1985 shipments were ahead of expectations.

In some quarters, however, AT&T's progress in the computer world was not viewed optimistically. In September of 1985, the *Wall Street Journal* reported that Moody's Investors Service Inc. was considering downgrading its double A-1 rating of AT&T's debt and preferred shares. According to Moody's the review was prompted by AT&T "disappointing performance in its attempt to enter more competitive, high technology markets." The investors service firm was "seeking to determine whether AT&T (could) compete successfully in the office automation industry" (Guyon, Sept. 11, 1985).

Other competitors. Literally hundreds of firms competed in the PC market in 1985. Even companies that had filed for Chapter 11 bankruptcy protection were taking on new managements and taking second stabs at the potentially lucrative but somewhat elusive PC market.

Specifically, Victor Technologies, Osborne Computer and Franklin Computer -- in Chapter 11 bankruptcy proceedings -- sought to carve out niches in the microcomputer market. Their new plans involved selling through dealers who tailor computers for specific tasks such as accounting or machine-shop management.

Another potential competitor was Tandy Corporation. Although the firm had lost market share between 1980 and 1985, its strength was its extensive distribution system, unmatched by any competitor. Tandy Corporation operated Radio Shack stores in the U.S., Canada, and Europe. As of June 30, 1984, there were 9,018 Radio Shack stores including 5,928 owned by the company, and 3,090 owned by dealers or franchised.

A different strategy was followed by another successful computer maker, Compaq Computer Corporation. Rather than rely on distribution channels, this firm instead concentrated on producing computers that were as close to being clones of the IBM PC as the law allowed. The Company's distribution strategy involved pricing its products to dealers so that they could gross 36% on sales made at the suggested retail price compared with 33% on sales made of IBM computers. The company had been profitable since the third quarter of 1983. In 1984 it earned an estimated $11.4 million which represented an 11.6% return on $98.3 million of shareholders' equity.

Other firms with IBM-compatible desk top machines in 1985 were Wang Laboratories, Inc., Data General Corp., Datapoint Corp. and Sperry Corp.

Competitive forces. Sales of microcomputers were dependent on other forces in the marketplace. Software availability, industry standards, retail shelf space and market strategies were as important to the sale of personal computers as the products themselves.

The decision to buy a particular brand of computer was usually based on the number or type of software applications that could run on the computer. Indeed, the publication of VisiCalc, a spread sheet software package, was the catalyst for the phenomenal success of the Apple II because it provided the first practical application for personal computers. Later, it was the development of the Lotus 1-2-3 spreadsheet that stimulated sales of the IBM PC and led to the dominance of IBM in the business market.

The IBM presence was so strongly felt that any company with an operating system other than the PC-DOS used on IBM's machines had to convince software firms to write programs for their computers. It represented a chicken and egg situation as software developers had no incentive to produce programs unless they could be sure of high-volume sales of the computers. Yet volume sales would not occur without ample software availability.

Perhaps equally important to the success of a personal computer were the distribution channels maintained by the computer firms. Independent retail stores accounted for nearly half of all personal computer distribution in 1985 (McCrossen, June 6, 1985). The competition to convince dealers to carry a computer manufacturer's products was intense due to the limited shelf space in stores as well as the unwillingness or inability of salespeople to learn the ropes of more than just a few machines. In 1985 the dominant products on retail shelves were IBM, Apple and Compaq. The retail nature of the personal computer industry led to the high advertising expenditures required to make inroads into the market.

A fast emerging strategy for microcomputer makers in 1985 was to shift from an emphasis on horizontal markets to vertical markets. Vertical marketing involved selling computer systems tailored to the unique needs of particular industries. For many small and new companies, this was the only way to survive in an industry with hundreds of competitors, some with enormous resources enabling them to fight vigorously to maintain market share. So rather than go head-to-head with the giants, companies chose an industry and designed a computer system with special software and/or hardware that solved critical problems faced only by that particular industry. In addition, they trained their salesmen to be knowledgeable in the business they were targeting, advertised in trade publications and provided customers with cradle-to-grave service. For these computer companies, the beauty of the strategy was that the vast majority of vertical markets were too small for IBM to find worthwhile.

PRODUCTION

Due to the slowness in the microcomputer industry, Apple had phased out three of its manufacturing facilities by September of 1985. This left the company with three plants: a highly automated plant in Fremont, California which built the Macintosh and the LaserWriter printer and had just begun to build the Apple IIc; a plant in Singapore which produced the Apple IIe; and a plant in Ireland which built the European model of the Apple IIe.

The assembly plant in Fremont was the result of two years of research and development carried out in Japan. Built at a cost of nearly twenty million dollars, the plant was one of the most modern and automated plants in the world. The high efficiency and advanced technology of the process meant that rejects numbered less than one percent and that the plant was able to produce more than 2,000 units a day at a cost considerably lower than that of the non-automated plants. Each step of the manufacturing process took a maximum of 27 seconds but the average time for most steps was only 13 seconds. Apple was one of the few companies to build computers with computers. In mid-1985 the factory was producing MACs at a rate of less than half its monthly capacity of 80,000 (Sevy, June/July, 1985).

MARKETING

Products. In 1985 Apple had just two product lines: the Apple II and the Macintosh. The Apple III was discontinued in 1984 and the Lisa (Macintosh XL) was discontinued in the summer of 1985. Apple also sold peripheral devices, operating systems and applications software packages.

The Apple IIe was the second successor to the original Apple II and was popular in the education and home markets. It also had a following in the small business market. The computer had almost limitless expandibility plus a large software base, making it a versatile and appealing personal computer. The second product in the Apple II family, the Apple IIc, was introduced in 1984 to attract customers who were not interested in putting boxes, cards, cables and components together. It was a compact, complete machine that was transportable and could be set up easily and quickly. This product was not intended to be a replacement of the IIe but an expansion of the Apple II product line. The Apple II family was the company's cash cow but in 1985 it was not bringing in the record revenue it had in the past.

The Macintosh line, which was not compatible with the Apple II products, was introduced in January, 1984, with a splashy ad aired during the Super Bowl that depicted IBM as Big Brother and offered the Macintosh as an alternative business computer. Originally hailed as technologically advanced, easy to use and having outstanding graphics capability, the Macintosh failed to impress the business market at which it was aimed. Exactly one year after the introduction of the Macintosh, Apple announced the "Macintosh Office" which was to have consisted (initially) of the computer, the LaserWriter printer, a local area network called Appletalk, and a file server. The introduction of the file server, a device that would provide a multiuser data base and accounting functions, never materialized. In the fall of 1985, Apple all but scrapped plans to produce the file server and left it to third-party vendors to develop their own versions of the software.

Unlike the Apple IIe which allowed specialized add-on hardware and software, the Macintosh was a closed machine. Jobs, who directed the development of the Macintosh, believed that this personal computer should be as simple to use as a telephone; that it should be one complete package like any other applicance in the home. Consequently the Macintosh was loaded with special software, making it difficult for programmers to make new software. In addition, the machine had no slots into which outside manufacturers could slide circuit boards for such functions as expanding the computer's memory or adding a superfast mathematical processor. In the fall of 1985, it was estimated that between 600 and 700 software programs had been written for the Macintosh. By comparison, there were over 3,000 programs that could run on IBM PCs and their clones. Based on the commitment Sculley made in his June, 1985 speech with respect to opening up the Macintosh to third-part hardware and software companies, the situation was expected to change in 1986.

Apple introduced a number of new products in September, 1985, but they received very little media attention because their announcements came the same week that Jobs resigned. The long awaited hard disk drive for the Macintosh was among the new products. Also included was a $399 color monitor and a $499 hard disk drive for the Apple II, and a $595 enhanced Image writer printer and $399 modem for the MAC.

The company was working on two projects that were expected in 1986 or 1987. One was Project Phoenix, a code name for a new Apple II computer; the other was Project Jonathan, the next-generation Macintosh which would be capable of color grpahics and equipped with a modem allowing the computer to transmit data over telephone lines (Bellew, Aug. 2, 1985).

Promotion/Distribution. In April, 1985, Fortune Magazine quoted John Sculley as saying: "We've got the products, but the big question is, have we got the ability to sell them? Is Apple a credible enough name for large corporations? Or are people going to say, 'Hey we love Apple in schools, we love you in the home -- but in business?" (Kessler, April 15, 1985).

Between 250,000 and 275,000 Macintosh PCs were sold in the first year the product was marketed which was more than the IBM PC sold in its first year. But sales began to erode in 1985. Market analysts attributed the decline in sales to a number of factors including lack of business software, the inability of the machine to hook into IBM's computer environment, and the perception that the Macintosh was not a business computer.

Apple had hoped that the introduction of Jazz, a piece of software developed by Lotus Development Corporation for the Macintosh which combined writing, financial analysis, filing, communications and chart-making functions, would provide the means to finally propel the computer into the business environment. Apple's hopes were dashed when Lotus delayed bringing the spreadsheet package to the market until May 1985, 17 months after Macintosh was first introduced. When Jazz was finally offered, it did not go over well in the marketplace. Computer magazines had both favorable and unfavorable reviews of the Jazz program but sales of the software quickly declined after a fast start (Davis, Aug. 16, 1985). One computer retailer sold just 32 programs in two months compared to 500 a month of the popular spreadsheet, Lotus 1-2-3. Some retailers blamed the slow sales on the limitations of the Macintosh, which they claimed had internal software that made Jazz run very slowly.

Lack of software was only one obstacle that kept Apple out of the business world. Many believed the company's refusal to acknowledge the IBM **de facto** standard contributed to its reduced credibility as a computer maker for business. In 1985, Apple changed tactics and began to make statements implying that IBM would always be the major player and that Apple products would have the ability to link up with IBM mainframes. The company moderated its predictions that the Macintosh would become an alternative to the IBM PC. One computer watcher, Dennis Gilbert, saw the change this way:

> Within the last year and a half, statements by both Jobs and Sculley were not implying 'we don't need IBM'; they were saying very compatible words. But the implication was that their linking to the IBM world would be through networking; that the network they were developing would be able to plug to IBM equipment. But you wouldn't be able to take a program that ran on an IBM, for example, and slip it into the Macintosh.

Beyond the product related reasons for Apple's limited pentration into corporate America, the company also suffered because it had no sales force with direct access to corporations. During the early '80s, the company tried to fill the void by establishing a 60-person direct-sales staff. The staff was meager compared to IBM's army of 6,000 to 7,000 direct-sales personnel. Even so, the company decided in 1985 that the small national sales force was doing more harm than good and all but abolished it in the May reorganization. (Salespeople were kept on already established accounts.) It turned out that the direct-sales force had alienated the independent dealers who provided most of Apple's revenues. Dealers accused Apple salespeople of elbowing them out of markets by offering low-cost Macintoshes to potential corporate customers at prices the dealers couldn't match.

As the company approached FY 1986, its efforts were refocused on the company's vital link to the market: the 2,200 independent dealers that sold Apple products. In August 1985, the company introduced a series of incentives aimed at encouraging dealers to push its machines more aggressively. The incentives included discounts of about 4% on bulk orders of certain Apple products and contributions of $1,500 to marketing programs for dealers who order six or more Macintosh computers. In addition, the company ran training seminars which provided dealers with technical information so that they could design computer systems for the customers using Apple equipment. Apple encouraged the dealers to try to penetrate such industries as advertising and publishing which relied on graphics to sell their products.

Besides its distribution channels, Apple attempted to sell its products through a unique advertising technique called "event advertising." Rather than have TV commercials, say, every night during prime time or during the news hour, the company chose a major event like the Super Bowl to introduce a new product or launch a new marketing direction. The company once bought all the advertising space in a special election edition of *Newsweek*. Another time it bought nearly all the commercial time for a CBS showing of "Death of a Salesman."

For the 1985 Christmas season, Apple originally had planned a low advertising and promotional budget in order to keep costs down. In September, however, the company reversed its earlier plans and said it would mount a big advertising campaign during the Christmas selling season. The campaign, the company said, would rival but probably not top, the $17 million blitz the company had the previous year.

FINANCIAL POSITION

After experiencing phenomenal growth in its first eight years in business, Apple reported its first quarterly loss in the third quarter of fiscal year 1985. The loss of $17.2 million was the result of a costly reorganization combined with a precipitous decline in sales. Revenues for the third quarter slumped to $374.9 million compared with $435.3 million in the second quarter and $698.3 million in the first quarter. It cost the company $40.3 million to reorganize; this one-time charge was expensed in the third quarter of 1985. Despite the loss, Apple ended the period with cash and temporary investments of $254.6 million. In addition the company had no long term debt.

Apple was expected to recover in the final quarter of 1985 with higher than expected sales of personal computers to schools.[2] It was estimated that the firm would post a net income of between $12.1 million and $15.2 million for the fourth quarter ending September 30, 1985. Revenues were expected to be between $390 million and $405 million. With revenues only increasing slightly, Apple officials attributed the improvement in the bottom line figure to stringent cost-cutting measures imposed during the reorganization. Apple's chief financial officer, David J. Barram, commenting on the improvement in the

---

[2]As this case was completed, Apple announced its actual year-end financial results. A press release regarding FY 1985 financial performance is included as Exhibit 7.

financial position for the fourth quarter of 1985, said "... our manufacturing costs are lower, we have less excess capacity and our gross profit margins are higher. We are also controlling our inventory better" (Gray, Sept. 23, 1985).

Exhibits 8 and 9 reflect Apple's financial picture over the last several years.

ORGANIZATIONAL STRUCTURE

The $40.3 million reorganization that sent Jobs off to a small office he called Siberia, also sent 1,200 workers into the job market. Sculley viewed the layoff as a necessary cost cutting measure in the face of declining demand in the personal computer market. The new streamlined organization reflected a departure from a "walk-around management" style to a professional organization more characteristic of Fortune 500 companies. The two product divisions were organized into one in an effort to end internal rivalry and overlapping functions.

Critics believed that the loss of Jobs and the changes in organizational structure would hurt the company known for its innovation, vision and creativity. Others felt that the company got too big for Jobs' entrepreneurial nature; that his emphasis and zeal for new technology and new projects often meant that both the needs of the marketplace and other Apple products were ignored.

Jobs took more with him than just his vision and skills. He also took some key middle managers whose absence was sure to be felt by Apple. Those individuals included Don Lewis, marketing manager for Apple's educational sales and a key figure in the company's successful sales campaign in the university market; Bud Tribble, manager of software; Richard Page, senior engineer and an Apple Fellow who was involved in several prototyped Apple computers; George Crow, a hardware engineering manager; and Susan Barnes, U.S. sales and marketing controller.

As the company entered FY 1986, it had a major gap in engineering (Pollach, Sept. 23, 1985). Mr. Sculley was looking for a high level engineering manager to guide product development and design, functions Steve Jobs had skillfully performed in the past. The new manager would be required to play a role in developing new versions of the Apple II and the Macintosh, as well as devices and strategies to link machines together into complete office systems.

The senior management team reflected a transformed Apple from a company of young independent free thinkers to one heavily weighted toward the pragmatic East Coast establishment with almost all of them over 40. Biographies of the top managers appear in Exhibit 10.

PERCEPTIONS OF APPLE

The following comments were made by people outside of Apple who had reason to formulate an opinion:

> Will somebody tell me what kind of company Apple is? Is it a business-personal-computer company? A consumer-computer company? An education-computer company? Is the Macintosh a business machine? An artist's tool? A document processor?
>
> Michael Schrage
> Business Reporter
> *The Washington Post*
> September 23, 1985

> My personal research into the extreme devotion Macintosh owners feel for their machine has uncovered the fact that what they love most is their ability to produce good-looking documents. Their documents look good because they combine effective fonts and pictures or diagrams or highlighting. Most IBM PC users still send their documents to grahics designers when they want them to look as good as documents coming from the MAC.
>
> Alan Paller
> Computer Reporter
> *Government Computer News*
> August 30, 1985

Apple is more dealer-oriented than IBM; they've been in the dealer business a little bit longer. IBM is pretty big and pretty bureaucratic. Apple is more 'Loosey Goosey'. We could call Apple today and place an order; we could call them 3 times today and place 3 orders and they would all eventually arrive here. With IBM, you have to forecast a year in advance and forecast again by quarters and place a monthly order. Anything beyond that is a special order and special orders are only filled after the people who have done their homework and their forecasting have received their orders. And IBM offers no promises which often results in our getting a system unit but no monitors or a keyboard without a system unit. . .

> William A. Rupp
> Clinton Computers
> Alexandria, VA
> September 20, 1985

Apple doesn't really have a market strategy. Their strategy has been dictated by the market instead of the other way around. Apple is in any market in which its products happen to sell. Their success in the home and education markets is more by default than by any preplanned strategy. . .

The best place for Apple to be in is the single-user market. Their best attempt to get into the business market totally backfired for two reasons. First, Apple doesn't belong in the large business market because it has virtually no access to that market segment. It therefore lacks an essential marketing ingredient -- distribution channels. The only distribution channel Apple has is the dealer base which is retail so its interested in pushing x number of boxes per month. This is not the mentality required for success in the Fortune 500 market. The second reason Apple's strategy for the large business market failed is because they totally missed the point in positioning the Macintosh. They tried to transform the way people think and attempted to convince the user to go against everything they believed in -- and that included trying to make them believe they didn't need IBM.

> Evan Moltz
> International Data Corp.
> Framingham, MA
> September 26, 1985

Apple was enticed into believing that it needed to penetrate the business market in order to be successful. But there's a lot more room for computers out there than just the business sector. I think Apple's attempt to appeal to business was a big mistake; the emphasis on the large business market was particularly ill-conceived. Even before the company introduced the Macintosh, it was not concerning itself with what the large buyers really needed.

The absence of hard disk availability for the Macintosh exemplified Apple's ignorance of how to enhance its products for the business market. And it wasn't for lack of technology; Apple simply didn't believe the hard disk was important so they didn't provide them until they realized how strong the demand for them was...

> Tim Caffrey
> International Data Corp.
> Framingham, MA
> September 24, 1985

Apple is caught in a squeeze caused by poor product positioning in the office market, and weakening demand in the consumer/home market. Apple's products are overpriced, in our opinion, with the price/value relationship becoming more out of balance in the II family.

> Robert T. Cornell
> Paine Webber
> August 8, 1985

REFERENCES

1. Annual Report, 1984 Apple Computer Inc., Cupertino, Calif.

2. "Apple Computer to Mount Big Holiday Ad Campaign," *Wall Street Journal*, September 18, 1985, p. 2.

3. Bellew, Patricia, "Apple Has Loss of $17.2 Million In Its 3rd Period," *Wall Street Journal*, July 19, 1985, p. 4.

4. Bellew, Patricia, "Apple Computer Intensifies Marketing," *Wall Street Journal*, August 2, 1985, p. 4.

5. Brandt, Richard and Lewis Geoffrey, "The New Computer Wars," *Business Week*, July 15, 1985, pp. 96-104.

6. Burton, Kathleen, "Vertical Marts Hold Promise for Micro, Mini Vendors," *Computer World*, July 22, 1985, p. 78.

7. Calonius, Erik, "As a Market for PCs, Europe Seems As Hot As the U.S. is Not," *Wall Street Journal*, August 19, 1985, p. 1.

8. Cornell, Robert T., "Apple Computer," *Paine Webber Update*, August 8, 1985.

9. Davis, Bob, "Sales of Lotus's Jazz Computer Program Slump After a Fast Start, Dealers Say," *Wall Street Journal*, August 16, 1985, p. 4.

10. Gelman, Eric, "Showdown in Silicon Valley," *Newsweek*, September 30, 1985, pp. 46-50.

11. Gray, Patricia, "Apple Says Net for Fiscal 4th Quarter Will Be Higher Than Earlier Forecast," *Wall Street Journal*, September 23, 1985, p. 7.

12. Gray, Patricia Bellew, "Apple Sues Jobs, Charging Misuse of Firm's Research," *Wall Street Journal*, September 24, 1985, p. 4.

13. Gray, Patricia Bellew and Miller, Michael W., "Apple Chairman Jobs Resigns, Citing Firm's 'Hostile' Response to New Venture," *Wall Street Journal*, September 18, 1985, p. 2.

14. Guyon, Janet, "AT&T Debt, Preferred Ratings Studied by Moody's for Possible Downgrading," *Wall Street Journal*, September 11, 1985, p. 2.

15. Kessler, Felix, "Apple's Pitch to the Fortune 500," *Fortune*, April 15, 1985, pp. 53-56.

16. Kneale, Dennis, "The Unfinished Revolution," *Wall Street Journal*, September 16, 1985, (Section 3) p. 1.

17. Levy, Gerard, "Levy's Corner," *MacMag*, June/July 1985.

18. Lewis, Geoffrey and Maremont, Mark, "AT&T Makes A Second Stab at the Computer Market," *Business Week*, April 1, 1985, pp. 89-92.

19. Lewis, Geoffrey, "AT&T UNIX Takes a Stand Against Big Blue," *Business Week*, April 22, 1985, pp. 74-76.

20. Leyenberger, Arthur, "The New Atari Computers: Power Without the Price," *Analog Computing*, Issue 28, p. 4.

21. Markels, Alex, "Apple Accepts Jobs' Kiss-Off," *MIS Week*, September 23, 1985, p. 6.

22. McCrossen, Melanie, "Computers and Office Equipment," *Industry Surveys*, Standard & Poor's, June 6, 1985, pp. C73-C95.

23. Miller, Michael W., "Atari Turnaround Depends on $799 Machine," *Wall Street Journal*, September 30, 1985, p. 6.

24. Miller, Michael W., "Apple's Jobs to Sell 850,000 Shares Valued at More Than $13.5 Million," *Wall Street Journal*, August 2, 1985.

25. O'Reilly, Brian, "Compaq's Grip on IBM's Slippery Tail," *Fortune*, February 18, 1985, pp. 74-83.

26. Paller, Alan, "Mouse Essential for New Trend: 'Macmemos'," *Government Computer News*, August 30, 1985, p. 1.

27. Pollack, Andrew, "Now, Sculley Goes It Alone at Apple," *New York Times*, September 22, 1985, Section 3, p. 1.

28. Schrage, Michael, "U.S. Is Now Biggest Buyer of Computers," *The Washington Post*, September 11, 1985, p. D1.

29. Second Quarter Report 1985, Apple Computer Inc., Cupertino, Calif.

30. Small, David, "Outpost Atari," *Creative Computing*, April 1985.

31. Smith, Randall, "Commodore International Will Spend $40 Million Marketing Amiga Computer," *Wall Street Journal*, September 27, 1985.

32. Third Quarter Report 1985, Apple Computer, Inc., Cupertino, Calif.

33. Uttal, Bro, "Behind the Fall," *Fortune*, August 5, 1985, pp. 20-24.

34. Williams, Greg, Edwards, Jon, and Robinson, Phillip, "The Amiga Personal Computer," *Byte*, August, 1985, pp. 83-100.

35. Wise, Deborah, "Three Computer Makers and Chapter 11: Trying to Write a Happy Ending," *Business Week*, March 4, 1985, pp. 112-113.

PERSONAL INTERVIEWS

1. Caffrey, Tim, Director of Strategies for Microcomputers and Office Systems, International
    Data Corporation, Framingham, MA, Personal Interview, September 24, 1985.

2. Gilbert, Dennis, Program Analyst, National Bureau of Standards, Gaithersburg, MD, Personal
    Interview, September 23, 1985.

3. Moltz, Evan, PC Market Analyst, International Data Corporation, Framingham, MA, Personal
    Interview, September 26, 1985.

4. Rupp, William A., Director, Corporate and Government Sales, Clinton Computers, Alexandria,
    VA, Personal Interview, September 20, 1985.

EXHIBIT 2

PLANNED PC PURCHASES

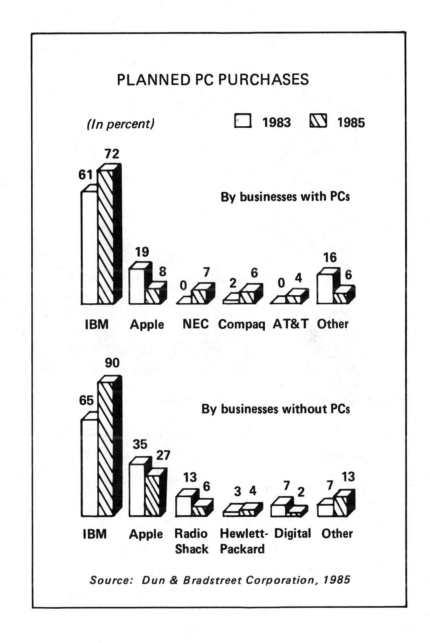

EXHIBIT 3

PC USE IN OFFICES

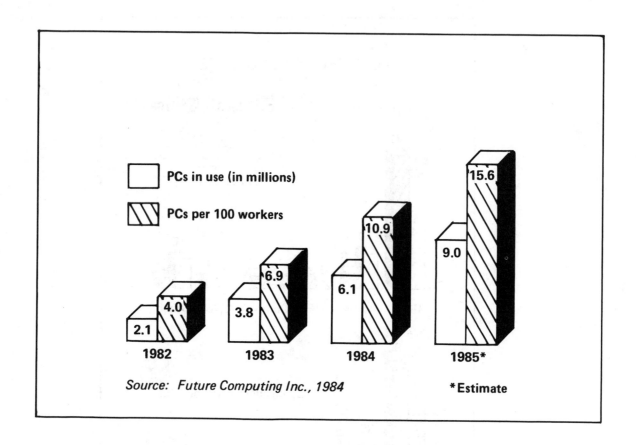

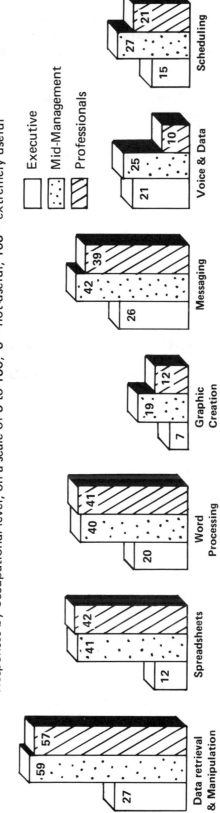

EXHIBIT 4

ATTITUDES TOWARD COMPUTER APPLICATIONS

Responses by occupational level, on a scale of 0 to 100; 0 = not useful, 100 = extremely useful

Executive

Mid-Management

Professionals

Source: American Telesystems Corporation, 1985

Scheduling: 15, 27, 21

Voice & Data: 21, 25, 10

Messaging: 26, 42, 39

Graphic Creation: 7, 19, 12

Word Processing: 20, 40, 41

Spreadsheets: 12, 41, 42

Data retrieval & Manipulation: 27, 59, 57

EXHIBIT 5

**1984 WORLDWIDE PERSONAL COMPUTER SHIPMENTS BY
APPLICATION MARKET,
UNITS (Left) & DOLLAR VALUE (Right)**

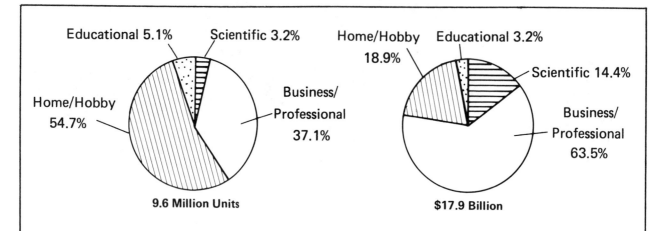

**1990 WORLDWIDE PERSONAL COMPUTER SHIPMENTS
BY APPLICATION MARKET,
UNITS (Left) & DOLLAR VALUE (Right)**

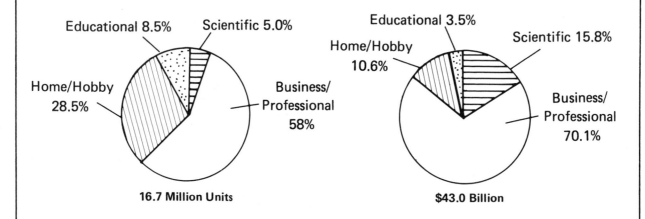

Source: International Data Corporation, EDP Industry Report, August 30, 1985. Copyright 1985 by
International Data Corporation. Used with permission.

EXHIBIT 6

PERSONAL COMPUTER CENSUS
DOLLAR VALUE OF 1984 WORLDWIDE SHIPMENTS,
AS OF JANUARY 1, 1985

NAME OF MANUFACTURER	COMPUTER MODEL	AVERAGE PURCHASE PRICE	DATE FIRST INSTALLED	NUMBER INSTALLED IN U.S.	NUMBER INSTALLED OUTSIDE U.S.	TOTAL NUMBER INSTALLED
IBM	PC	$3,000	10/81	1,645,000	310,000	1,955,000
	PC Jr*	1,200	6/84	250,000	0	250,000
	PC-AT	5,795	6/84	22,000	3,000	25,000
	Portable	2,200	6/84	98,000	2,000	100,000
	XT	4,000	5/83	340,000	95,000	435,000
Apple	Apple II, IIe	1,425	5/77	1,535,000	435,000	1,970,000
	Apple III*	3,500	11/80	44,000	16,000	60,000
	Apple IIc	1,195	4/84	300,000	50,000	350,000
	Lisa*	10,000	6/83	15,600	4,500	20,100
	Lisa II*	4,500	6/84	96,000	4,000	100,000
	Macintosh	2,195	6/84	235,000	40,000	275,000
Commodore	64	250	8/82	2,150,000	1,800,000	3,950,000
	Executive 64	1,000	2/83	30,000	30,000	60,000
	PET/CBM	1,000	10/77	225,000	310,000	535,000
	Super Pet	1,995	7/81	54,400	68,600	123,000
	VIC/20	150	6/81	1,390,000	1,300,000	2,690,000
Hewlett-Packard	110	2,295	6/84	14,500	500	15,000
	150	3,995	10/83	55,000	55,000	110,000
Tandy/Radio Shack	TRS 80-100	650	6/83	168,000	27,000	195,000
	TRS-80/1	1,000	9/77	247,500	27,300	274,800
	TRS-80/16	9,000	6/82	69,200	7,800	77,000
	TRS-80/2000 Series	2,800	12/83	60,000	5,000	65,000
	TRS-80 Color	399	9/80	445,000	55,000	500,000
	TRS-80/II,IV	1,200	9/81	275,000	55,000	330,000
	TRS-80/III	6,000	7/79	102,000	14,000	116,000
Compaq	Compaq, Compaq Plus, Deskpro	3,000	2/83	210,000	2,000	212,000
Zenith	Z89, Z90, Z110, Z120, Z150, Z160	5,400	6/82	160,000	40,000	200,000

*Discontinued

Source: Abstracted from International Data Corporation report. Copyright 1985 by International Data Corporation. Used with permission.

EXHIBIT 7

APPLE PRESS RELEASE

Press Information

FOR RELEASE AFTER 8:30 AM (E.D.T.)
THURSDAY, OCTOBER 17, 1985

Contact: **Dan Eilers**
Assistant Treasurer
(408) 973-3314

or

Barbara Krause
Manager, Public Relations
(408) 973-3719

APPLE ANNOUNCES INCREASE IN SALES FOR FISCAL 1985, SAYS REORGANIZATION IS WORKING

CUPERTINO, California--October 17, l985--Apple Computer, Inc. today announced that net sales for fiscal year 1985 increased 27 percent over the previous year.

Apple posted sales of $1.918 billion and profits of $61.2 million or $.99 per share for the fiscal year which ended September 27, 1985. Sales in the previous fiscal year were $1.516 billion with profits of $64.1 million or $1.05 per share.

Apple posted a gross profit margin of 46 percent in the fourth quarter, the highest achieved in nine quarters. The company's net sales for the fourth quarter were $409.7 million, with earnings of $22.4 million or $.36 per share. In addition, Apple's cash balance increased by $82.4 million during the fourth quarter. The company finished the year with $337.0 million in cash on hand, the highest in the company's history.

"It's working," said Apple's president and chief executive officer John Sculley. "These financial results offer the most compelling evidence possible that the steps we've taken to streamline the company are producing results faster than anyone thought possible last summer. We managed down inventories, built up cash to our strongest position ever and still have no debt. Sales to education remain solid, retail sales have been increasing since July, and orders from dealers for the holiday selling season are brisk.

Apple Computer, Inc.
20525 Mariani Avenue
Cupertino, California 95014
(408) 996-1010
TLX 171576 TWX 9103382054

EXHIBIT 7 (continued)

APPLE PRESS RELEASE

APPLE COMPUTER, INC.
CONSOLIDATED STATEMENTS OF INCOME

(In thousands, except per share amounts)	Three Months Ended (Unaudited)		Year Ended	
	Sept 27, 1985	Sept 28, 1984	Sept 27, 1985	Sept 28, 1984
Net sales	$409,709	$477,400	$1,918,280	$1,515,876
Costs and expenses:				
Cost of sales	221,670	270,337	1,117,864	878,586
Research and development	19,059	15,495	72,526	71,136
Marketing and distribution	104,805	121,573	470,588	392,866
General and administrative	28,365	25,123	110,077	81,840
	373,899	432,528	1,771,055	1,424,428
Operating income before unusual item	35,810	44,872	147,225	91,448
Unusual item'- provision for consolidation of operations *	3,373	-	(36,966)	-
Interest and other income, net	4,654	3,861	9,786	17,737
Income before income taxes	43,837	48,733	120,045	109,185
Provision for income taxes	21,480	17,927	58,822	45,130
Net income	$ 22,357	$ 30,806	$ 61,223	$ 64,055
Earnings per common and common equivalent share	$ .36	$ .50	$ .99	$ 1.05
Common and common equivalent shares used in the calculation of earnings per share	61,897	61,402	61,895	60,887

* Includes plant and equipment write-downs, facility lease cancellations, employee compensation and other charges related to the consolidation of operations.

EXHIBIT 7 (continued)

APPLE PRESS RELEASE

APPLE COMPUTER, INC.

CONSOLIDATED BALANCE SHEETS

(In thousands)	Sept 27, 1985	Sept 28, 1984
Assets		
Current Assets:		
Cash and temporary cash investments	$337,013	$114,888
Accounts receivable	220,157	258,238
Inventories	166,951	264,619
Prepaid income taxes	70,375	26,751
Other current assets	27,569	23,055
Total current assets	822,065	687,551
Net property, plant and equipment	90,446	75,868
Other assets	23,666	25,367
	$936,177	$788,786
Liabilities and Shareholders' Equity		
Current liabilities	$295,425	$255,184
Deferred income taxes	90,265	69,037
Shareholders' equity	550,487	464,565
	$936,177	$788,786

EXHIBIT 8

APPLE COMPUTER - CONSOLIDATED STATEMENTS OF INCOME

Three years ended September 1984 *(Dollars and shares in thousands, except per share amounts)*	1984	1983	1982
Net sales	$ 1,515,876	$ 982,769	$ 583,061
Costs and expenses:			
Cost of sales	878,586	505,765	288,001
Research and development	71,136	60,040	37,979
Marketing and distribution	392,866	229,961	119,945
General and administrative	81,840	57,364	34,927
Total costs and expenses	1,424,428	853,130	480,852
Operating income	91,448	129,639	102,209
Interest and other income, net	17,737	16,483	14,563
Income before taxes on income	109,185	146,122	116,772
Provision for taxes on income	45,130	69,408	55,466
Net income	$ 64,055	$ 76,714	$ 61,306
Earnings per common and common equivalent share	$ 1.05	$ 1.28	$ 1.06
Common and common equivalent shares used in the calculations of earnings per share	60,887	59,867	57,798

Source: Apple Computer Annual Report, 1984, p. 36

EXHIBIT 9

APPLE COMPUTER - CONSOLIDATED BALANCE SHEETS

September 28, 1984 and September 30, 1983

(Dollars in thousands)	1984	1983
Assets		
Current assets:		
Cash and temporary cash investments	$114,888	$143,284
Accounts receivable, net of allowance for doubtful account of $10,831 ($5,124 in 1983)	258,238	136,420
Inventories	264,619	142,457
Prepaid income taxes	26,751	27,949
Other current assets	23,055	18,883
Total current assets	687,551	468,993
Property, plant and equipment:		
Land and buildings	24,892	19,993
Machinery and equipment	68,099	51,445
Office furniture and equipment	30,575	22,628
Leasehold improvements	26,008	15,894
Total property, plant, and equipment	149,574	109,960
Accumulated depreciation	(73,706)	(42,910)
Net property, plant, and equipment	75,868	67,050
Other assets	25,367	20,536
Total assets	$ 788,786	$ 556,579
Liabilities and Shareholders' Equity		
Current liabilities:		
Accounts payable	$ 109,038	$ 52,701
Accrued compensation and employee benefits	20,456	15,770
Income taxes payable	11,268	-----
Accrued marketing and distribution	50,638	21,551
Other current liablities	63,784	38,764
Total current liabilities	255,184	128,786
Non-current obligations under capital leases	-----	1,308
Deferred income taxes	69,037	48,584
Commitments and contingencies	-----	-----
Shareholders' equity:		
Common stock, no par value, 160,000,000 shares authorized 60,535,146 shares issued and outstanding in 1984, and 59,198,397 shares issued and outstanding in 1983	208,948	183,715
Retained earnings	259,101	195,046
Accumulated translation adjustment	(633)	-----
	467,416	378,761
Notes receivable from shareholders	(2,851)	(860)
Total shareholders' equity	464,565	377,901
Total Liabilities and Shareholders' Equity	$ 788,786	$ 556,579

Source: Apple Computer Annual Report, 1984, p. 37.

EXHIBIT 10

BIOGRAPHICAL SKETCHES - APPLE TOP MANAGERS

JOHN SCULLEY: In 1985 John Sculley was president, chief executive officer, and a director of Apple Computer, Inc. Mr. Sculley became president in April, 1983. Before joining Apple, Mr. Sculley was president and chief executive officer of Pepsi-Cola Company for five years. Mr. Sculley graduated in 1961 from Brown University with a B.A. degree in architecture. He also had a Masters in Business Administration from the Wharton Business School.

DAVID J. BARRAM: David J. Barram joined Apple Computer, Inc. in April 1985 as vice president and chief financial officer. In this position, he was responsible for Apple's planning, internal financial controls, the Management Information Systems (MIS) group and treasury functions. A graduate of Wheaton College, Barram earned a bachelor's degree in economics and political science. In addition, he held a master's in business administration from Santa Clara University.

ALBERT A. EISENSTAT: Albert A. Eisenstat joined Apple Computer Inc. in 1980 as vice president, secretary and general counsel. In 1985 he had maintained this seat on the executive staff for five years. In this role, Eisenstat oversaw the legal, tax and community affairs departments; and served as secretary on the board of trustees. Prior to his position at Apple, Eisenstat was senior vice president and general counsel for Bradford National Corporation, a large national financial transaction processing company based in New York City. His academic background included a B.S. in Economics from the Wharton School of Finance at the Unviersity of Pennsylvania and a Bachelor of Laws degree from the New York University School of Law.

DELBERT W. YOCAM: In 1985 Delbert W. Yocam was executive vice president and group executive of product operations for Apple Computer, Inc. He oversaw development and engineering, product management, manufacturing, quality, distribution and service for all Apple products. In addition, Yocam was responsible for all OEM product operations. Previously, Yocam held the position of executive vice president and general manager of the Apple II group which developed, engineered, manufactured and marketed all Apple II products. He joined Apple in 1979 as director of materials. Yocam held a bachelor's degree in business administration from California State University at Fullerton. He also had completed the master's program in business administration at California State University at Long Beach with an industrial management major and a marketing minor.

WILLIAM V. CAMPBELL: In 1985 William V. Campbell was executive vice president of sales, marketing and distribution at Apple Computer, Inc. He was responsible for developing and implementing sales strategies for all Apple products. Before joining Apple in July of 1983, Mr. Campbell was director of marketing communications for the film division of Eastman Kodak Company, and prior to that, a vice president of J. Walter Thompson. Before entering the advertising industry, Mr. Campbell was head football coach at Columbia University for five years. In 1985 he was a director of the National Football Foundation and Hall of Fame. Mr. Campbell held both bachelors and masters degrees in economics from Columbia University.

JAY ELLIOT: Jay Elliot was vice president of human resources for Apple Computer, Inc. in 1985. His worldwide responsibilities included staffing, employee development, compensation, benefits and employee relations. Elliot joined Apple in May of 1982 as director of human resources. Prior to his employment at Apple, Elliot was a personnel manager for Intel. He joined Intel after 14 years with IBM Corporation. Elliot graduated from San Jose State University with bachelor of science degrees in management and mathematics.

Federal Express - 1985[1]

"It's never been done before. Isn't that what Federal Express is all about?" is how Daniel Copp, vice president for communications, responded to guest host Joan Lunden's query about the world's first corporate teleconference spanning the globe. A complex array of satellite links brought employee audiences in London, Toronto, Los Angeles, Dallas, and several other American cities into the Memphis Coliseum to share in the company's 1984 Family Briefing. Showcasing to its employees the latest in satellite communications technology was just an added attraction of the gala event. The real reason for the meeting was to point Federal Express employees in a brand new direction.

In June 1984, via worldwide teleconferencing, Federal Express' senior executives announced a new company mission called "Mission II." Federal Express had expanded its mission from "an integrated air-ground network for moving time sensitive documents and packages." "Mission II" meant that Federal Express would offer competitively superior, broad-based networks for rapid movement of documents. On July 2, 1984, Federal formally introduced ZapMail, an electronic, high quality facsimile transmission system. In so doing, Federal entered the electronic/telecommunications industry. Moreover, ZapMail was to be an extension of the reliable ground network that would allow 2 hour coast-to-coast, guaranteed delivery. A separate strategy was developed to launch ZapMail in the new uncharted waters of the electronic mail market.

Mission II

The goal of Mission II was simply stated as "winning the all out war against competition while changing forever how the game is played." To achieve Mission II, management outlined five long term strategies:

1. Increase customer service reliabilty levels (in meeting guaranteed delivery commitment times) from 99.5% to 100%. If 350,000 shipments are processed each day, then 1,750 customers during the day could become dissatisfied with late arrival of their time sensitive goods or correspondence. This would gradually erode Federal's reputation for reliability and is unacceptable.

2. Give the customer better value for money spent. For example, this was done by moving next day delivery back from noon to 10:30 am (after which volume soared 30%). Also, by providing Saturday services, "hundredweight" pricing for multiple shipments, and state-of-the-art electronic parcel tracking, Federal Express intends to maintain its dominant market leadership postion.

3. Expand service to more areas (95% of population is currently served). This would be done by installing more remote drop boxes, opening more business service centers (at least 300 total), and expanding international service to Europe via the 1984 Gelco acquisition and service to the Far East.

4. Push technology to the limit. COSMOS is an industry-unique, high-tech package and fax transmission tracking system. DADS (digitally assisted dispatch system) allows efficient, timely courier route dispatch information update through hand-held and truck mounted microprocessors. ZODIAC offers more efficient sorting by zip code using the latest in optical character scanning techniques. More efficient material handling and sort systems technologies will be developed and implemented.

5. Achieve superior financial performance so the company can borrow more money to invest in future growth opportunities, such as ZapMail. By adopting a "Q = P, or quality equals productivity"

---

[1]Prepared by Robert S. Berlin under the supervision of Assistant Professor David M. Schweiger, University of Houston-University Park. Used with permission.

program, each employee is tasked to work smarter and innovate more productive ways to perform job duties. As Mr. Barksdale, chief operating officer, stated, Federal Express must lower its unit operating costs to improve its competitive position. This would allow Federal to offer lower prices as an inducement for its customers to use more of its services.

Not mentioned was the use of lower price offerings as a means of combating price-cutting tactics and share-grabbing strategies of competitors like Purolator and the US Postal Service. Also looming in the background was a hot new air express market entrant respectfully called the "Brown Giant," United Parcel Service.

The strategy to launch ZapMail electronic facsimile mail service was broken into three phases:

1. ZapMail fax machines installed and operational in business service centers and remote "closet" locations by July 2, 1984. The goal was to achieve 10,000 messages/day by the end of December 1984. By March 1985, messages were hovering around 3000/day.
2. ZapMail "Imagers," enhanced office versions of the original, will be leased to customers and located on their premises. The goal to install 3000 by May 31, 1985 was met; and, orders had been placed with NEC for over 10,000 machines.
3. At some future date, modified office ZapMailers will be placed in public access areas for general public use.

Mr. Oliver, senior vice-president for marketing, stated that each phase was dependent upon suc-cessful implementation of the preceding phase. Mass media advertising and promotional activities would be scaled to build demand based on one key factor: the abilty of the operating system to assimilate existing demand while meeting the crucial 2 hour delivery commitment.

To achieve all five major long term strategies and the successful launching of ZapMail, Mr. Smith, CEO, re-emphasized Federal's commitment to the company philosophy "People, Service, Profits." Actions and leadership demonstrated in fulfilling this motto form a cohesive corporate strategy giving direction, pride, and a sense of purpose to employees. This is evidenced by action-oriented programs such as: Guaranteed Fair Treatment, Open Door policy, No Lay Off policy, profit sharing , annual attitude surveys with corrective feedback, annual wage reviews, employee suggestion incentive/award programs, frequent informal "brown bag" lunch meetings with the CEO, and an up-front, open approach to keeping employees informed within the company. Mr. Smith stated his philosophy that by taking care of his employees, they will in turn give the extra effort needed to perform the demanding customer service commitments which set Federal Express apart from its competitors. Only satisfied, repeat customers pay salaries and benefits. Hence, "Profits" will accrue from Federal's competitively superior services.

THE FORMATIVE YEARS

From new venture start-up in 1972 to present day Wall Street darling and leader of the growth industry it created, Federal Express Corporation embodied the American business dream. Founded on the philosophy of "People, Service, Profits," Federal Express earned over $2 billion in 1985 in what is considered a $5 billion overnight air express market. In 1972, Federal Express was conceived with the mission of providing reliable overnight delivery of high priority small package business shipments. What set Federal apart from air cargo freight forwarders, such as Emery and Airborne, was the fact that it owned and operated its own airline. This provided an integrated air-ground delivery network in which Federal Express controlled all aspects of package movement from origin to destination. Initial studies commissioned by Federal indicated that only 10% of the airline fleet flew after 10:00 pm and that over 60% of all airline movement occurred between 25 major markets. In contrast, over 80% of all urgent shipments originated or terminated outside the same 25 key markets.

Freight forwarders, on the other hand, were at the mercy of the scheduled airlines. Giants in the freight forwarding business, such as Emery, were earning comfortable returns and did not see a need for "guaranteed, reliable" overnight small package delivery. John Emery scoffed at the idea of purchasing aircraft. Such a move by Emery earning 15% return on equity in the early 70's, would have been considered foolish given the acceptable profits enjoyed by majors in the staid, regulated air cargo industry.

Total control of package movement under the "hub and spokes" concept gave Federal Express the unique performance advantage it needed to guarantee next day delivery by 12:00 noon in its primary service areas. Freight forwarders were no longer in the same league when it came to air movement of business packages. Federal Express had changed the rules of how the game was played. A new air express industry was born.

EARLY STRATEGIES

From 1971, when the first business plan was developed, until the company became profitable in 1976, Federal's early strategies were:

1. Finding new financial sources and keeping current investors committed so that the company could continue operating.
2. Establishing air-ground logistics and key market service areas (which included aircraft acquisition, sort system and network development).
3. Building immediate demand by increasing consumer awareness with attention-grabbing, multi-media advertising targeted to key market areas.
4. Becoming profitable as quickly as possible.
5. Attaining a dominant leadership position in the market that it created.

When the company became profitable in 1976, it faced a serious threat to market expansion and revenue enhancement. Package volume on major routes had outgrown the lift capacity of its fleet of limited-load Falcon jets. Reportedly, as many as 7 Falcons were needed on peak nights to lift cargo from New York to Memphis. Lift problems created excessive fuel and operting costs, even though nightly volumes were increasing steadily and the company's profit outlook was strengthening. Holding Federal back from using larger, more fuel efficient aircraft was Part 298 of the Civil Aeronautics Board regulations. This regulation limited payload per aircraft to 5000 lbs. Larger loads were subject to route and rate regulation by the CAB under the auspices of protecting the certified air cargo carriers, which included major scheduled airlines.

It had become painfully clear to senior management that relief from this obscure CAB regulation was absolutely necessary for Federal to lower unit costs and grow. From early 1975 until late 1977, Mr. Smith, CEO, worked in Washington, mustering political support and fighting objections from formidable opponents like the scheduled airline lobbyists of the Air Transport Association and the Air Freight Forwarders Association.

Federal sought legislative relief rather than CAB certification for several reasons. Legislative relief would provide an immediate cure. Certification, on the other hand, was a lengthy, bureaucratic process that could have taken 2 to 10 years for completion. Opponents would have pressured the bureaucratic machinery through countless hearings to the point of stalling Federal's certification. The company could ill afford to spend $500,000 to $1 million needed to fund the certification process while being deprived the opportunity of expanding its business. Through persuasive and skillful lobbying efforts, Mr. Smith achieved a major strategic success for Federal Express when President Carter de-regulated the air cargo industry by signing Bill PL 95-163. The company became free to choose its own routes, its own aircraft, and to set its own freight rates as long as they were not predatory. Had it not been for air cargo de-regulation, Federal's growth would have flattened out and the company would have been only moderately profitable. More importantly, investors and lenders would have lost interest in Federal. Limited lift capacity of the Falcon fleet meant limited revenue-generating ability.

De-regulation shifted growth strategy into high gear. Larger aircraft, improved sort systems and an expanded ground fleet were acquired in a concerted effort to increase service levels in key markets. In 1975, Federal Express handled 19,000 packages per day. Ten years later, they exceeded 450,000 documents and parcels each day. Much of this growth was made possible through a unique advertising strategy never before used by members of the air cargo industry. In stages, Federal employed innovative, humorous mass media advertising which poignantly touched the human side of business situations common to its targeted audience: everyday business people, clerks, secretaries, and professionals. With broadcast media and a touch of humor, Federal Express effectively communicated its service message for "when it absolutely, positively has to be there overnight." This aggressive promotional and advertising strategy helped create the market and stimulate demand for overnight delivery of high priority goods.

Federal Express made several other strategic moves to secure its dominant market leadership position. By introducing the "Courier Pak", Federal impressed its customers with appealing, standardized shipping boxes and pouches. Customers were left with the impression that they could depend on Federal Express from origin to destination. Moreover, the shipper believed that the bright purple, orange and white package would be delivered to the addressee and not the shipping dock. Package design became the silent salesman. An off-shoot of the Courier Pak was the Overnight Letter. In 1981, Federal took advantage of Postal Service regulation changes that allowed private delivery of "extremely urgent" mail. The Overnight Letter product was desinged for letters up to 2 ounces. A special attention-getting envelope was introduced. With a planned effort to lower unit costs, Federal achieved a tremendous product breakthrough and revenue enhancement. In 1985, the Overnight Letter accounted for nearly 33% of total volume shipped. Additionally, the use of technology was pushed by management to lower unit costs and improve service levels. The company developed innovations such as OCR, DADS, and COSMOS. Adapting technology to improve operations had been a key strategy from the beginning.

COMPETITIVE ADVANTAGES AND COMPANY RESOURCES

During an interview with Mr. Smith, six competitive advantages were highlighted that distinguish Federal Express from its competitors:

1. **Image and reputation for services:** Over the years, Federal has achieved a rock solid reputation among its customers for meeting its delivery commitments. This unique market identity is based on the repeated satisfaction of customers who are reliability sensitive. In 1985, it became the only air express company to offer a "money back" guarantee against late delivery.

2. **Different and expert approach to aviation:** "Super Mod," a major corporate project, has showcased hundreds of aircraft technical modifications and improvements intended to increase lift efficiency. As a result of aircraft nose dock innovations, a DC-10 can be unloaded in a record 7 minutes. In contrast, UPS must add 20 to 30 minutes to each end of its sort because of its use of loaders and unloaders between aircraft and the hub. Also, Federal Express has its own DC-10 flight simulator and has eliminated dependency on other airline flight training facilities.

3. **Electronic telecommunications advantages:** COSMOS provides customers with immediate knowledge of shipment whereabouts. A modified COSMOS tracks electronic mail messages to make sure they aren't lost as a result of quirks in the phone lines. POLARIS gives rapid, accurate billing information. Project SUN involves launching 2 satellites by early 1989 so that Federal will no longer be dependent on AT&T leased phone lines for ZapMail transmissions. To centralize customer support, Federal organized 4 regional service centers to direct inquiries and pick-up requests. Within minutes, a Houston pick-up request phoned to the Memphis service center is relayed back via computer and phone lines to the Houston dispatch office computer. Through digital communications, new dispatch information is radioed without problem of channel congestion to the on-board computer of the nearest van and updated on its CRT screen (DADS). The major focus of this technology is to lower unit costs and improve customer service.

4. **Employee commitment is high:** According to Mr. Smith, employee commitment is higher than industry standards. Observations made by interviewers of the hub operation, Zap Central, general offices, local business service centers, and couriers confirm a high level of employee job commitment. Leadership, genuine concern for employees, and an attitude toward open communication emanate from senior executive offices. Action-oriented employee suport programs have helped to develop employee commitment. The 1984 Family Briefing on Mission II and frequent "brown bag" lunch question and answer periods conducted by Mr. Smith are examples of how senior management has kept employees informed and in tune with company goals. Video tapes of employee meetings with the CEO are circulated throughout the company for viewing. Also, employees are brought in from around the country to participate in special "informal" meetings with the CEO. Commented Charles Hartness, Director of Human Resources Analyses, "We believe employees come to us motivated. Our job is to make sure they don't become de-motivated." He also indicated that despite their technological lead, it will be employees who guarantee Federal's future competitive advantage.

5. **Size and coverage:** Federal Express enjoyed a 42% market share by 1984 year end and is expected to surpass a 45% share by the end of 1985 (see Exhibits 1, 3 and 4). It serves over 40,200 communities or 95% of the total U.S. population. Only UPS has greater total coverage, 98.5% because of its extensive ground network. Federal operates 61 aircraft which serve 145 airports. Over 11,000 vans support the ground transportation system. With nearly 31,000 worldwide employees and over 600 flight crew members, Federal Express is the biggest in the business and it is still growing. Aggressive placement of over 1500 drop boxes and 300 business service centers has increased depth of coverage in key markets. Mention should be made of Federal's strategy of gradual expansion into international markets as a result of the 1984 acquisition of Gelco International. Its large domestic customer base will be offered greater coverage

to Europe and the Far East. (The International Civil Aviation Organization projected an 11% annual growth rate for trans-Pacific air cargo shipments through 1992.)

6. **Flexibility:** The ability to implement sweeping changes quickly throughout such a large organization has resulted in strong management, high employee commitment, and superior internal communciations. Project Earlybird was such an example. In the fall of 1982, UPS entered the air express industry with its Next Day and 2nd Day air package services. UPS guaranteed delivery only on the day scheduled. Emery, Airborne, and Purolator had matched Federal's guaranteed 12:00 noon next day delivery time. However, it was the entry of the "Brown Giant," UPS, into the market that eliminated Federal's freedom to set prices (even though the reliability claims of the other 3 competitors were questionable at best). Market research showed UPS's Next Day service was intended to take away 28% of Federal's customers.

In an effort to counter UPS and distance themselves from competition, Federal announced it was moving the clock back from 12:00 noon to 10:30 a.m. guaranteed delivery in its primary service areas. "We can't let UPS have customers think their service is comparable to ours, " said Fred Smith during one of his frequent meetings with employees. Moving quickly, 10:30 a.m. delivery was started within 6 weeks of its announcement. Research indicated this made a great psychological difference in the minds of Federal's customers and would stimulate increased volume. The introduction of Saturday services in October 1983 and "heavyweights" (upping limits from 70 to 150 lbs.) also show how Federal responded to differentiate itself, expand the market and counter-attack competition.

Some additional factors in the air-ground courier network have created internal company strengths. "Bypass" operations, which sort like-destined items at origin into separate containers, have reduced sort loads at the Memphis SuperHub. "Bleed-off" operations have been initiated in high density areas, such as at the new Newark regional hub. Parcels from Boston going to New York don't make the trip to Memphis. Instead, they travel by specially routed Federal Express trucks. About 15,000 packages/day were being "bled-off" in 1984 as this project was implemented. Other regional hubs were planned for Boston, Philadelphia, Harristown, Albany, and Tampa. One study showed that truck delivery saves 75% of air package delivery costs. "NOVAK" high density sort systems continue being expanded at the SuperHub to handle high volume flows to major areas such as Los Angeles and Chicago. Many of these programs are geared not just to increase efficiency, but to reduce the need for future aircraft purchases.

Though not readily apparent, Federal Express has assembled some of the country's leading telecommunications and data processing talent. Research and development facilities were built in Colorado Springs. To market office model ZapMailers, Federal recruited its own telecommunications sales force from companeis such as IBM, Xerox, and Rolm. In the areas of sort systems development and aviation, Federal's engineering talent is second to none. Through 1985, Federal lead the industry with the brightest and sharpest people.

Perhaps one of Federal's greatest strengths is the fact that it is not unionized. It is management's firm belief that they do not need a union to represent employee interests to management. Employees have resisted union organizing efforts in the past. The unique way in which sorters and couriers perform their duties to meet demanding customer commitments requires the highest degree of flexibility. Approximately 2,800 part-time employees (of whom over 90% are college students) man the hub. Not unionized, they enjoy the benefit of having tuition paid by the company. Despite this benefit, average unit labor costs at the Memphis hub are lower than Emery's Dayton hub which is controlled by Teamsters.

From "no-brainers" to "Bravo Zulus," a pervasive corporate culture has strengthened the framework of shared values and common goals. Employees are value-driven. They understand clearly the need to work together to meet the rigorous customer commitments that set Federal's high reliability above all others. "No-brainers" need no comment. "Bravo Zulus" are awards for excellence above and beyond normal requirements. Managers may affix Bravo Zulu naval flag stickers to written work or the flags may hang openly, such as at the SuperHub. Company doctrine is covered in 40 hours of leadership training given to each manager. It was remarked that the Gelco acquisition involved no problems in acclimating Federal's managers to foreign customs. Instead, acculturation of new overseas employees into Federal Express posed the greatest challenge.

From a hardware perspective, Federal has state-of-the-art facsimile machines developed under license by NEC. Federal's push into satellites, Project SUN, should give it total control of vital telecommunicaitons links used for its ZapMail network and parcel tracking systems.

A marketing strength unusual to the air cargo industry is Federal's high recognition and its total dominance of consumer awareness. "Federal Express" has become part of every day business vernacular. Advertising has emphasized convenince and reliability. All that is needed to use overnight service or

ZapMail is a telephone. Federal's long term relationship with the advertising firm of Ally & Gargano has served it well. Federal ranked 4th in 1983 and 14th in 1984 in terms of overall advertising cost efficiency ratings.

From 1980 through 1984, Federal Express enjoyed an ideal pricing situation. Because of their low cost position, Federal's price charged per package was substantially lower than the average (per package) operating expense incurred by competition. Its profit margin was the highest in the industry. However, 1984 saw competitors lowering their operating costs closer to Federal's (see Exhibits 1, 2, and 3).

AIR EXPRESS INDUSTRY ANALYSIS

By year end 1984, Federal Express commanded nearly a 42% share in its traditional stronghold, the overnight delivery of documents and parcels. Standard & Poor's *Aerospace & Air Transport Industry Survey* reported a banner year for air freight movement in 1984. Yet, the fastest growing segment was the express shipping of small packages, letters and documents -- most of which weighed under 5 lbs. Standard & Poor's reported that this sector had grown more than 20% annually from 1979 through 1984. It is expected to continue for several more years. From data compiled during the first 9 months of 1984, the Air Transport Association reported that the number of small package/express shipments increased 39% among the scheduled carriers, the Postal Service, and small shipment carriers. Predicasts, a Cleveland research firm, reported that overnight delivery revenues were growing at a rate of 50% a year. In 1977 they reported that overnight shipments represented only 9% of the total small package delivery market. By 1985, overnight small package express commanded a 33% share and was still climbing. Competition for the growing air express market intensified as companies scrambled to complete new sorting hubs, purchase or lease aircraft, and expand their ground coverage (see Exhibits 4, 5 and 6).

United Parcel Service. "Our customers wanted it, and we saw that they wanted it" is how John Alden, VP-customer service, described UPS' entry into the high pressure air express industry. As the number 2 competitor, they captured an estimated 16% of the market since their September 1982 market entry. Building from its existing customer base, UPS achieved a 74% revenue growth over 1983. It built an airline over its vast ground network, capitalized on its reputation for reliable service, and brought "integrity to overnight pricing" by offering rates as much as 50% below its competitors. By 1984, UPS owned 64 aircraft with 88 more under contract. Their Louisville sorting hub could handle 200,000 packages/day with a planned expansion under way to increase overnight capacity to 500,000. It will be able to handle 100 aircraft, which is twice the current schedule.

Though it serves only 88% of the US population with overnight delivery, UPS has refrained from adding "on call" package pick-up, sophisticated shipment tracking, early morning delivery, and many other customer conveniences. Air shipments are delivered by the same ground network handling surface shipments. Vehicles cover a route system and lack radio dispatching. However, in June 1985, UPS introduced its Next Day Air Letter and Air Pak in direct competition with Federal Express, Emery, Burlington Northern, Purolator, Airborne and DHL.

Even though UPS is still learning to operate its own airline and air hub, it is dedicated to improving its present capabilities and introducing new customer services. To UPS' detriment, the Teamsters thwarted a plan to add part-time drivers assigned to delivering air express shipments. Union negotiations have always been a delicate issue for UPS because of their influence over wages and operating flexibility. Even so, UPS could be a formidable competitor to Federal Express if they decide to match product and services one-for-one. Fred Smith of Federal Express once remarked that "UPS could put the hurt on us." With 1984 revenues of $7 billion and current assets of $900 million, the privately held UPS has shown the financial strength needed to be in the business "...for the long haul and to make a reasonable profit."

Purolator Courier. In 1984, Purolator held 14% of the air express market. With an air hub in Indianapolis, Purolator layered an airline over its extensive ground delivery network. Overnight deliveries within 400 miles of origin are sent by truck. Traditionally, Purolator targeted the industrial market and has built on its base business to compete against Federal Express. In 1985, Purolator stepped up its mass marketing program designed to increase name recognition and to promote its full range of services and low prices.

In anticipation of increased demand for express services, they committed heavily to capital investments in aircraft and facility improvements. To increase their sorting hub capacity four-fold, $70 million was required in 1984 and in 1985. Purolator also became a contract carrier for MCI Mail. By end of the third quarter 1985, Purolator's courier operations were no longer profitable.

U.S. Postal Service. With a 1984 market share of 13% and revenues of nearly $500 million from overnight products, the Postal Service has stirred great controversy. Private couriers have charged that the federal government is in direct competition with them with no threat of ever going broke. Surface mail rate increases paid by the public could subsidize inefficient express operations. Gordon Morison, assistant postmaster general-customer service, dismissed these criticisms by pointing out that the USPS was chartered to provide optimal service to its customers, the U.S. public. Besides, "It's a real growth marketplace. There's a lot of room out there."

Despite its poor service image, the Postal Service enjoys a large customer base, nationwide office network and subsidized rate structure. It has used patriotic advertising to promote its reliability and low cost to capture market share. Future developments include increasing drop boxes in major cities and expanding international service.

Airborne Express. Though fifth ranked in 1984 with an 8% market share, Airborne's 1984 operating results showed impressive gains over 1983 in all areas except profit margins which held constant at 3%. For 1984, Airborne reported a 63% shipment volume increase, a 32% corporate account revenue increase, and a 35% increase above targeted drop box installations.

Planned for 1985 are continued heavy investments in aircraft acquisitions, hub sorting systems and airport development. The air fleet should total 31 by the end of 1985, with 30 additional lease aircraft. Sorting hub capacity is planned to reach 240,000 by year end 1986. Operating from an old Air Force base in Wilmington, Ohio, Airborne is the only air courier with its own airport.

Airborne's strategy is to become a high service, price-competitive air express and air freight organization. Marketing programs and advertising have imitated Federal Express. During 1985, Airborne planned to add 1500 more drop boxes, build 10 more service centers, and integrate a computer tracking and billing service called FOCUS. Airborne is committed to providing service coverage to all Standard Metropolitan Statistical Areas within the U.S. and to expanding international service. Mass media advertising has been targeted to the infrequent user. A $1 million "Lotto" sweepstakes was promoted to increase recognition and spur sales.

Emery Air Freight. Emery's annual report said 1984 was a turn-around year. Emery started recovering from massive investments it had made in its new Dayton sorting facility and aircraft acquisitions (now totaling 65). Sixth ranked with only a 4% market share, Emery increased revenues 11% domestically and 37% internationally. In the U.S., shipments of documents and envelopes were up 38%, packages under 70 lbs. were up 10%, and packages over 70 lbs. were up 6%. Most significantly, international door-to-door service increased 250%. John Emery predicted the company's 1984 overseas freight revenue of $250 million would grow to $1 billion by 1990.

Employing an aggressive marketing strategy, Emery offered a broad range of overnight products without weight or size limitations. "We need to be a service innovator, not just a 'me-too' competitor," said Emery. "We want Emery to be kind of the Burger King of air freight, 'Have it your way' is the main theme." Building from its strong international customer base, Emery intends to boost its domestic air express business. A mass media advertising campaign was launched to deliver the message to secretaries and businessmen that Emery is the overnight full-service courier to use for deliveries worldwide and door-to-door. As stated by John Emery in the 1984 annual report, their corporate mission is "To provide excellence and service superiority--striving to become Number One in our Strategic Business Units."

DHL Worldwide Express. DHL entered the domestic overnight market in late 1983. However, they have operated as an international overnight courier for 13 years. One market study attributed DHL with moving 70% of all overseas-bound small packages under 70 lbs. Though estimates indicate that DHL earned only a 2% domestic market share in 1984, it entered the market with a full service offering similar to Federal Express. Its strategy is to use its strong international reputation and wide customer base to fuel domestic expansion and to prevent erosion of their international overnight business. DHL has also become the contract courier for Western Union's Easylink electronic mail service.

Burlington Northern Air Express. Burlington Northern is a member of Burlington Air Freight Inc., a Pittston Company. In 1984, Burlington earned a 1% market share and revenues of about $50 million. Table 3 shows that the Pittston Company has experienced financial troubles. Until the company returns to profitability, Burlington's growth potential is limited.

Burlington Air Express followed an incremental strategy by offering overnight service to its existing heavy weight freight customers. Packages are shipped on scheduled airlines with limited customer services. However, they do provide computerized tracking and an attractive rate structure.

ELECTRONIC MAIL MARKET ANALYSIS

Incorporating the latest advances in telecommunications technology, the same-day, electronic transmission of correspondence is a market in its infancy. Two major types of electronic mail have forged their beginnings: personal computer-based mail, and high resolution facsimile document transmission. Both systems rely on the use of land-based telephone lines.

PC based electronic mail is considered the fastest growing segment of the computer industry. Though still in its fledgling stage, analysts have estimated electronic mail use to be growing at an annual rate of 60% with estimated 1984 revenues of $200 million. International Resource Development, Inc., a market research firm, estimated that 250 million electronic mail messages were sent in 1984 and that usage numbers would grow to 25 billion messages annually by 1994. The Electronic Mail Association has projected that in the next 10 years, electronic messages will be a part of standard business routine. Before then, several obstacles must be overcome. Users must have access to computers and know how to use telecommunications software. Because of technical compatibility problems, the subscriber to one electronic mail system can not send messages to subscribers of competing services. There is evidence that system incompatibility problems may be resolved. In October 1984, a committee of the International Telecommunications Commission agreed on a set of international tecnhical standards that would permit interconnection between all electronic communication systems regardless of country or company of origin.

Two types of PC based mail products dominate market offerings. First is the multiple subject information services, such as CompuServe, The Source, GE InfoNet, ITT Dialcom, GTE Telenet, and others promoting use of computer accessed electronic mailboxes. These services are sold to businesses and computer hobbyists. However, they have several drawbacks. Only same service subscribers can communicate with each other. If electronic mailboxes are not checked within a prescribed period, messages will be deleted from memory; and, some services can not create hard copy from local printers.

The second type of PC based same-day documents transmission is an enhanced version of the electronic mailbox/information services. These systems allow the user to generate a text message on a personal computer and to access system-dedicated communications networks. Once linked to the communications network, the sender selects one of several methods of transmission to the addressee. Offered by MCI Communications' MCI Mail and Western Union's Easylink, both companies have established strong footholds in the electronic mail market.

MCI Communications Corporation. Touted as "the nation's new postal system," MCI Mail was introduced in September 1983. Five delivery methods, each with different rate structures, were offered:

1. Electronic Mailbox; $18 per year and $2.45 for the first page, $1 for each additional page.
2. Mail Service; $2 to print up to 3 pages and mail the message first class in a distinctive orange envelope.
3. Overnight Courier Delivery; $8 for up to 6 pages delivered by Purolator by noon the next day.
4. 4 Hour Courier Delivery; $30 delivered by Purolator within 4 hours.
5. International Telex; access and time charges are based on destination.

Considered to be a strong, well managed company, MCI achieved a 9% profit margin on 1984 revenues of $1.7 billion. It invested $40 million in the development and introduction of MCI Mail and has continued an aggressive advertising campaign. Despite MCI's financial strength, it was estimated in early 1985 that MCI Mail was loosing $35 million annually and would not break even before 1986.

Western Union. To replace its commerically obsolete telex service, Western Union introduced Easylink in 1983. With an initial investment of $115 million, Easylink tied into Western Union's vast communications network. Like MCI Mail, Easylink offers several service options:

1. Electronic Mailbox; from $.31 to $.57, messages are limited to 200,000 characters. Messages left for 10 days will be sent as a Mailgram with a $.50 collect charge.
2. Mailgram; overnight delivery rates vary based on length of text.
3. Mail Service; three day delivery, rates vary based on length of text.
4. Telegram; rates vary based on length of text.
5. 2 Hour Delivery; rates by DHL courier.
6. Overnight Delivery; rates by DHL courier.
7. Telex Network; charges vary based on the destination and length of message.

During the first three months, customers pay only for messages sent. Afterwords, a $25 monthly minimum fee is charged.

In 1983, Western Union experienced an operating loss of $66.9 million on revenues of $1.04 billion. Easylink service lost $24 million in 1984. On the positive side, monthly Easylink communications had reached 2.5 million by year end 1984, up 31% from a year earlier. Even so, Western Union has banked its hopes on Easylink and related product improvements to pull the company from the brink of financial disaster.

The FAX machine option. "We are selling the secret of ZapMail," claims Panafax, a worldwide manufacturer and distributor of high resolution fax transmitters. "Canon has all the FAX you need to keep in touch with business around the world," says another major manufacturer. Ricoh and AT&T have entered into an arrangement to market high quality fax transmission systems. The intentions of IBM and Xerox are not yet known. Both AT&T and IBM have satellite based communications networks and market personal computers. All of these companies possess highly developed, well established office products divisions with strong direct sales or distributor networks.

Same-day facsimile document transmission allows the sender to transmit both text and graphics in hard copy format. Most prevalent today are fax machines in technology groups II and III. Group II machines can send a one page copy in 2 to 3 minutes. Not only is it the most expensive in terms of phone transmission time, but its copy quality on coated paper is poor. Group III machines can transmit one page in less than one minute. They give good copy quality, but still require coated paper. Only machines of the same technology level can link together. Machines are generally leased or purchased at a cost of $3,000 to $10,000 per unit. Major fax manufactures are committed to improving transmission quality, speed, and product acceptance.

ZAPMAIL BENEFITS

"Convenience" underscores ZapMail's advertising and personal selling strategy. All the user needs is a telephone - no personal computer and no special software skills. Federal Express sweats the details, not the customer.

When a customer phones in a request for pick-up, a courier is dispatched to take the document to the nearest ZapMail transmitter and send it over land phone lines to the machine nearest its intended destination. The document is routed by courier and delivered to the addressee, all inside a 2 hour window. Though an expensive service option, other alternatives are available to the high volume user.

By leasing its own Federal Express ZapMailer, the customer can send messages to other customers who have ZapMailers at attractive rates without accessing company couriers. No bigger than the standard office copier, the ZapMailer, complete with LED display screen, is easy to use. It can even make photo copies. In event of machine failure, Federal offers back-up courier service at no charge until it repairs the machine. ZapMail claims a lower per page cost of $.70 to $.90 versus a $1.50 per page cost charged under competitive lease-buy arrangements.

The ZapMailer is the only fax machine on the market that employs new Group IV technology. It gives high resolution copy on plain bond paper and fast transmission. Copies may be broadcast simultaneously to 50 different stations. All messages are tracked by COSMOS as a safeguard against loss in transmission. The ZapMailer offers one company interface, with no telephone company involvement or reliance on an outside courier service, such as with MCI Mail-Purolator. Messages may be sent by

ZapMail for 10:30 am next day delivery by courier for $.25 per page and a $5 delivery charge. Two hour courier delivery costs $10 from the ZapMailer.

NEW CHALLENGES

An International Resources Development study has forecast electronic mail volume to increase ten-fold over the next ten years. However, it projects a fall by half of all telegram and facsimile transmissions while predicting a slower rate of growth for the courier services.

Debate continues to rage over what form the electronic mail market will take. Backed by the results of $3 million of market research, Federal Express claims that 30% of the entire overnight document market is actually frustrated same-day demand. Potentially 150,000 customers per day need same-day service. The size of the market is estimated at $1.5 billion per year.

Over the next 10 years, Federal Express has earmarked $1.2 billion for ZapMail investment. By the end of 1984, the company had invested over $100 million. In the quarter that ended November 1984, Federal Express incurred a $60 million pre-tax operating loss.

Unfortunately, analysts believe that Federal Express needs 27,000 ZapMail messages a day just to break even. In February 1985, ZapMail messages reached a record 3,950/day. By October 1985, messages were expected to be nearly 10,000/day. As of June 1985, the total number of office ZapMailers installed was 4500, well above the original goal of 3000. Even though orders had been placed for 10,000 machines, Federal hopes to have 7500 installed by January 1986.

While ZapMail appears to have gotten off to a slow start, Federal's overnight delivery business has grown at breakneck speed. In March 1985, the number of documents and packages sorted each night had exceeded 380,000. By October 1985, the number was expected to break 500,000. Improved levels of international service had contributed substantially to the growth in overnight delivery.

As Mr. Barksdale remarked during the 1984 Family Briefing on Mission II, the corporate goal and mission will change with changes in electronic technology. But the corporate philosophy of "People, Service, Profits" will never change. It has been the cornerstone of past success. Creating a "future of our own making" is what Federal Express is all about. After all, the meeting theme song intoned, "Where were you 10 years ago? They said it couldn't be done."

EXHIBIT 1

FINANCIAL DATA - MAJOR COMPETITORS

	FEDERAL 1984	AIRBORNE 1984	EMERY 1984	PUROLATOR 1984
ACCOUNTS RECEIVABLE	$207,256	$44,619	$97,345	$102,385
INVENTORY	$39,725	$3,909	$2,520	$36,279
OTHER CURRENT ASSETS	$81,155	$6,363	$32,782	$84,062
TOTAL CURRENT ASSETS	$328,136	$54,891	$132,647	$222,726
PROPERTY & EQUIPMENT	$1,427,281	$135,936	$186,743	$230,211
DEPRECIATION	$314,642	$41,523	$48,268	$91,882
OTHER LONG TERM ASSETS	$85,030	$16,428	$51,682	$17,636
TOTAL ASSETS	$1,525,805	$165,732	$322,804	$378,691
CURRENT LIABILITIES	$255,910	$41,160	$98,968	$106,003
LONG TERM DEBT	$435,158	$28,865	$30,000	$38,379
OTHER LIABILITIES	$117,016	$18,287	$17,496	$26,523
RETAINED EARNINGS	$391,314	$42,082	$117,530	$162,332
OTHER EQUITY	$326,407	$35,338	$58,810	$45,454
TOTAL LIABILIITIES	$1,525,805	$165,732	$322,804	$378,691
REVENUES	$1,436,305	$417,854	$683,556	$716,431
OPERATING EXPENSES	$1,271,097	$395,011	$607,806	$640,722
INTEREST	$36,350	$1,621	$12,619	$5,410
OTHER	($23,402)	$1,486	$23,511	$23,316
EBIT	$152,260	$19,736	$39,620	$46,983
TAXES	$36,830	$8,907	$14,634	$15,198
EBAT	$115,430	$10,829	$24,986	$31,785
CURRENT RATIO	1.282	1.334	1.340	2.101
QUICK RATIO	1.127	1.239	1.315	1.759
DEBT TO TOTAL ASSETS	0.285	0.174	0.093	0.101
TIMES INTEREST EARNED	5.189	13.175	4.140	9.684
INVENTORY TURNOVER	36.156	106.895	271.252	19.748
AVERAGE COLLECTION PERIOD	51.947	38.441	51.267	51.448
FIXED ASSET TURNOVER	1.291	4.426	4.936	5.179
TOTAL ASSET TURNOVER	0.941	2.521	2.118	1.892
PROFIT MARGIN	0.080	0.026	0.037	0.044
RETURN ON TOTAL ASSETS	0.076	0.065	0.077	0.084

EXHIBIT 2

MARKET AND FINANCIAL DATA

	1980	1981	1982	1983	1984
PACKAGES (000)					
FEDERAL	17,272	22,149	32,000	43,000	67,000
MARKET	40,485	48,537	65,757	82,845	115,996
REVENUE PER PACKAGE					
FEDERAL	$24.05	$26.61	$25.12	$23.44	$21.44
MARKET	$37.39	$38.06	$33.52	$30.73	$26.62
OPERATING EXPENSES PER PACKAGE					
FEDERAL	$18.78	$20.24	$19.63	$18.14	$17.30
MARKET	$32.65	$32.84	$28.97	$25.79	$22.04
OTHER EXPENSES PER PACKAGE					
FEDERAL	$3.02	$3.69	$3.04	$3.24	$2.41
MARKET	$2.48	$2.85	$2.58	$3.05	$2.95

1985 PROJECTED PERCENTAGES OVER 1984
No change in Revenue per Package

MARKET GROWTH	25% INCREASE
REVENUE PER PACKAGE	NO CHANGE
OPERATING EXPENSES PER PACKAGE	NO CHANGE
OTHER EXPENSES PER PACKAGE	NO CHANGE
FEDERAL'S MARKET SHARE	57.76%

EXPECTED RESULTS AT	100% OF CURRENT MARKET SHARE	90% OF CURRENT MARKET SHARE	80% OF CURRENT MARKET SHARE	70% OF CURRENT MARKET SHARE	60% OF CURRENT MARKET SHARE
PACKAGES	83,750	75,375	67,000	58,625	50,250
REVENUE (000)	$1,795,381	$1,615,843	$1,436,305	$1,256,767	$1,077,229
OPERATING EXPENSES (000)	$1,448,926	$1,304,034	$1,159,141	$1,014,248	$869,356
OTHER EXPENSES (000)	$202,168	$181,951	$161,734	$141,517	$121,301
NET (000)	$144,288	$129,859	$115,430	$101,001	$86,573

5% Decrease in Revenue per Package

MARKET GROWTH	25% INCREASE
REVENUE PER PACKAGE	5% DECREASE
OPERATING EXPENSES PER PACKAGE	NO CHANGE
OTHER EXPENSES PER PACKAGE	NO CHANGE
FEDERAL'S MARKET SHARE	57.76%

EXPECTED RESULTS AT	100% OF CURRENT MARKET SHARE	90% OF CURRENT MARKET SHARE	80% OF CURRENT MARKET SHARE	70% OF CURRENT MARKET SHARE	60% OF CURRENT MARKET SHARE
PACKAGES	83,750	75,375	67,000	58,625	50,250
REVENUE (000)	$1,705,612	$1,535,051	$1,364,490	$1,193,929	$1,823,367
OPERATING EXPENSES (000)	$1,448,926	$1,304,034	$1,159,141	$1,014,248	$869,356
OTHER EXPENSES (000)	$202,168	$181,951	$161,734	$141,517	$121,301
NET (000)	$54,518	$49,067	$43,615	$38,163	$32,711

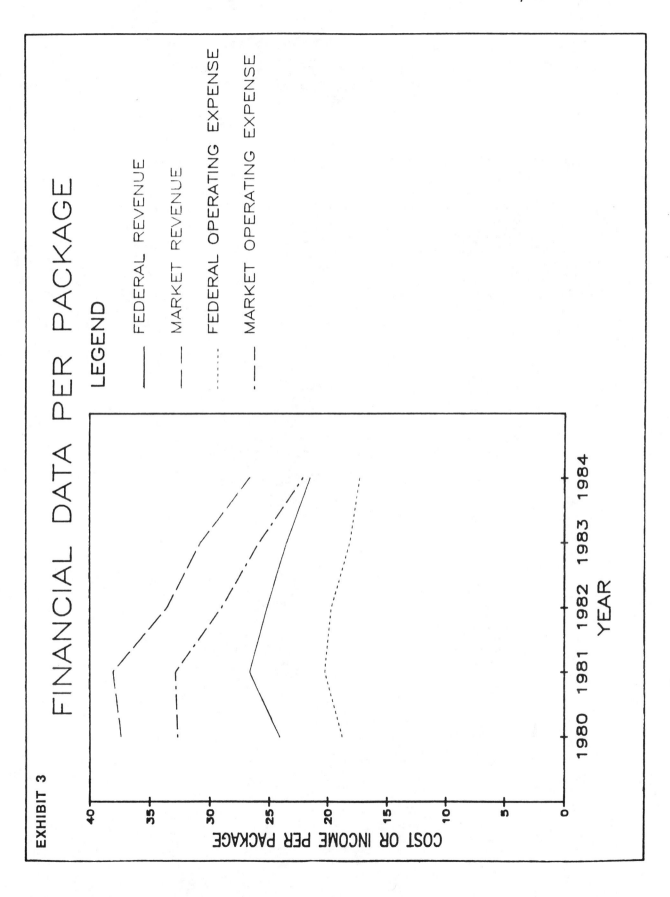

EXHIBIT 3

FINANCIAL DATA PER PACKAGE

LEGEND

—————— FEDERAL REVENUE

— — — MARKET REVENUE

.... FEDERAL OPERATING EXPENSE

—·—·— MARKET OPERATING EXPENSE

COST OR INCOME PER PACKAGE

40 35 30 25 20 15 10 5 0

1980 1981 1982 1983 1984

YEAR

EXHIBIT 4

OVERNIGHT MARKET COMPETITORS
1984 ESTIMATED REVENUES

Competitor	Share %	$ Millions
1. Federal Express	42	$ 1,720
2. United Parcel Service	16	675
3. Purolator Courier	14	590
4. U.S. Postal Service	13	500
5. Airborne Express	8	305
6. Emery Air Freight	4	175
7. DHL Worldwide	2	100
8. Burlington Air Express	1	50
Totals	100	$ 4,115

Information taken from the following sources:

1-6   Business Week, December 17, 1984, pg. 111.
7   Estimated from San Francisco Business Journal, September 17, 1984, "Firms Vie to offer same-day delivery".
8   Estimated from 1983 Pittston Company Annual Report (parent company).

EXHIBIT 5

SAME-DAY MARKET COMPETITORS

I.   PERSONAL COMPUTER BASED SERVICES

    1.   MCI-MAIL; MCI Communications, Inc., Delivered by Purolator Courier.
    2.   EasyLink; Western Union Corporation, Delivered by DHL Corporation.
    3.   CompuServe
    4.   The Source
    5.   GE InfoNet
    6.   ITT Dialcom
    7.   GTE TeleNet

II.   FACSIMLE MACHINE MANUFACTURERS

    1.   Canon
    2.   Panafax
    3.   Ricoh
    4.   Others

III. FACSIMILE / COURIER INTEGRATED NETWORKS

    1. ZapMail; Federal Express Corporation

Information taken from multiple sources.

EXHIBIT 6

COMPARATIVE FINANCIAL DATA
($ 000,000 except EPS)

	Federal Express[1]	United Parcel Service[2]	Purolator Courier[3]	U.S. Postal Service[4]	Airborne Express[5]	Emery Air Freight[6]	DHL Worldwide Express[7]	Burlington Northern Air Express[8]
Revenues								
Domestic					333	544		
Int'l					85	257		
Total	1,436	7,000	713	500	418	818	600	1,230
Net Income	115	600	32	N/A	11	32	N/A	-79
EPS	2.52	N/A	4.56	N/A	1.85	1.70	N/A	-2.08
Current Assets	328	900	223	N/A	55	176	N/A	301
Inventories	40	N/A	36	N/A	4	N/A	N/A	41
Total Assets	1,526	N/A	379	N/A	166	380	N/A	1,060
Current Liab.	256	850	106	N/A	41	106	N/A	216
Total Debt	691	N/A	171	N/A	89	212	N/A	530
Net Worth	772	N/A	208	N/A	76	168	N/A	531
RATIO ANALYSIS								
Current	1.28	1.06	2.10	N/A	1.33	1.66	N/A	1.40
Quick	1.13	N/A	1.76	N/A	1.24	N/A	N/A	1.21
Debt	0.45	N/A	0.45	N/A	0.54	0.56	N/A	0.50
T.I.E.	4.54	N/A	14.31	N/A	14.09	7.50	N/A	-1.51
Avg. Coll. Period	52	N/A	52	N/A	38	49	N/A	59
Fixed Asset TO.	1.29	N/A	5.15	N/A	4.43	4.94	N/A	2.61
Total Asset TO.	0.94	N/A	1.88	N/A	2.52	2.15	N/A	1.16
Profit Margin	0.08	0.09	0.04	N/A	0.03	0.04	N/A	-0.06
ROI	0.08	N/A	0.08	N/A	0.07	0.08	N/A	-0.07
RONW	0.15	N/A	0.15	N/A	0.14	0.19	N/A	-0.15

Notes:
1. Information based on 1984 Annual Report (Year Ending May 31, 1984).
2. Information based on company released information - privately held - As of Year Ending 1984.
3. Information based on 1983 Annual Report (Year Ending December 31, 1983).
4. Government Agency; estimated 1984 Revenues in overnight business.
5. Information based on 1984 Annual Report (Year Ending December 31, 1984).
6. Information based on 1984 Annual Report (Year Ending December 31, 1984).
7. Estimated - privately held- As of 1983.
8. Information based on 1983 Pittston Company Annual Report.

N/A = Information not available

Strategic Management Skills Glossary

Acceptability test examines the attitudes that major stakeholders will have toward the proposed strategic business plan.

Analyzing means separating a situation into parts and examining the parts in an attempt to understand what is occurring.

Assessing involves estimating the value or worth of elements of a situation.

An **assumption** is a condition, relationship or state of affairs that is regarded as true without actual knowledge that it is or without direct supporting facts.

Barometric techniques examine the relationships between causal or coincident events to predict future events.

Brainstorming is a technique that encourages individual team members to free themselves from any inhibitions and constraints and to generate as many creative ideas as possible. It is quite useful for generating ideas.

A **company profile** summarizes an analyst's perspective on how a company is performing and why. The following three types of comparisons are usually used to develop a company profile: historical comparisons, competitive comparisons, and normative comparisons.

Contingencies are important low probability events that have been anticipated by a planner. If these events occur, plans may be adversely affected.

Contingency plans are statements of actions that will be taken if a specific contingency occurs.

Corporate culture includes the assumptions, values, traditions, and behaviors that prescribe the actions of individuals within a firm.

Corporate strategy is the pattern of company purposes and goals, and the major policies and actions for achieving them, that defines the business or businesses the company will be involved with and the kind of company it will be.

Devil's advocate approach develops a solid argument for a reasonable recommend-ation, then subjects that recommendation to an in-depth, formal critique completed by a formally-appointed devil's advocate. Through repeated criticism and revision, the ap-proach leads to mutual acceptance of recommendations.

Diagnosing is the process of determining the cause and nature of problems. Usually you will need to draw inferences and make judgments to reach a diagnosis.

Differentiation is a generic strategic thrust that emphasizes providing customized and specialized products and services for all segments in an entire market.

A **diversification strategic thrust** involves acquiring related or unrelated businesses, and in some cases major new product line development programs.

Economic feasibility test focuses on returns and costs in both the short and long-term.

Environmental scanning is a process of examining and forecasting competitor actions, industry forces and industry and company-specific threats and opportunities.

Environmental turbulence refers to the amount of change and complexity in the environment of a company. The greater the amount of change in environmental factors, such as technology and governmental regulations, and/or the greater the number of environmental factors that must be considered, the higher the level of environmental turbulence.

Focus is a generic strategic thrust that emphasizes segmenting an entire market and focusing on only one or few segments. Companies following a focus thrust emphasize providing either a differentiated product or service to the segment or providing a low cost product or service for the chosen segment.

General managers are those managers who are responsible for the performance of an entire organization or a significant part of an organization which is often called a strategic business unit (SBU).

An **industry** is a group of companies or organizations providing similar products and/or services to an identifiable set of customers or clients.

Inferring means reaching conclusions using reasoning based upon what is known and as-sumed about a situation.

Interpreting means providing your own conception and explanation of a situation.

Judging is the process of forming opinions and estimates relevant to a situation or problem.

Marketing mix is the combination of product, price, promotion, and place decisions made by managers to position products and services.

Mechanical extrapolations involve the use of statistical techniques, such as a moving average, to evaluate past data for the purpose of projecting relationships into the future.

A **mission statement** is a broad statement of a firm's direction and purpose.

Monopolistic competition occurs in an industry with a few large and medium-sized competitors and many small competitors. The larger competitors are severely restrained in their ability to set prices.

Monopoly means that a single company dominates and controls prices in an industry.

A **multinational expansion thrust** may involve joint ventures with partners in other countries, wholly-owned subsidiaries, or expanded distribution channels.

Nominal group technique is a structured approach to problem solving and decision making that clearly divides idea generation and idea evaluation into two stages. It is useful for eliciting ideas and information from team members. The technique uses a 10-15 minute period of silent brainstorming and then ideas are recorded using a round-robin method. Ideas are then discussed and rated. In some groups as many as 10-12 people participate.

Oligopoly involves four or five large competitors that control most of the output of an industry; such firms can implicitly collude to set prices.

Operational risk refers to the possibility that new strategies and plans will fail.

Opinion polling involves surveying knowledgeable individuals (such as executives, industry analysts, sales representatives, or purchasing agents) to develop a consensus regarding future events.

Opportunity, company-specific, is a benefit or potential benefit that may result from the interaction between present or future positive environmental variables and industry-wide opportunities, and company strengths.

Opportunity, industry-wide is a benefit or potential benefit that all or most companies in an industry may realize.

Organizational dependence refers to the ability of managers to influence the actions of customers and suppliers. The lower the influence of managers on customer and supplier actions, the greater the organizational dependence on customers and suppliers. For example, a company with a single major customer is often very dependent on that customer for future sales.

Organizational design refers to both a process of fitting the organizational hierarchy, authority relationships, information and communication systems, and reward systems to a corporate strategy and strategic plan and the current state of the organizational hierarchy, authority relationships, etc.

Organization hierarchy refers to how people and tasks are grouped. For example, an organization may be structured in functional units such as accounting and marketing, with only one type of specialist working in each of these units. Or, an organization can be structured in product units. In this instance, specialists of all types are grouped together within one unit.

Overall cost leadership is a generic strategic thrust that emphasizes providing products and services at the lowest per unit cost within an entire market.

Perfect competition refers to an industry with many small firms none of which can influence or set prices.

Planning is the process of designing a consistent integrated program of actions that when carried out will accomplish specific goals.

Planning horizon is the time frame for planning strategic activities and for accomplishing strategic goals. This time frame is often 5 years, but the appropriate horizon depends on the industry. For example, 2 years in the fashion industry and 10 or 15 years in the forest products industry.

Policies are formal statements of a company's practices, procedures, or intentions. Policies guide managerial decision making and actions to ensure compliance with the corporate strategy.

A **portfolio reorganization thrust** involves actions to change the SBUs of a corporation.

Search, breadth first, is one of the strategic management information search strategies. The goal is to examine many sources and topics, then search for detailed information as needed.

Search, depth first, is one of the strategic management information search strategies. The goal is to research in detail only a few major topics first and then broaden the search to other areas as that becomes necessary.

Stakeholders are all groups that have a vested interest in a firm's performance and actions. These groups may be external to the firm, e.g., members of the local community, stockholders, customers, suppliers, and creditors; or internal to the firm, e.g., top managers, line managers, staff, and hourly employees.

Standard Industrial Classification (SIC) is a U.S. government classification system that divides economic activities into broad divisions (manufacturing, mining, retail trade, etc.). Each division is further broken down into major industry groups (two-digit SIC code), then into industry sub-groups (three-digit SIC code) and, finally, into industries (four-digit SIC codes). For example, the SIC code for home refrigerators is 3632 while the SIC code for home laundry (washing) machine is 3633. Thus, a firm that manufactures both refrigerators and home laundry machines would compete in two industries identified by SIC codes 3632 and 3633.

A **strategic business analysis** critically evaluates a company's current position, internal strengths and weaknesses, and external threats and opportunities.

A **strategic business plan** is an action-oriented document that describes the mission, strategic thrust, and major actions for an entire organization or an SBU. The plan also usually includes resource allocations, major implementation steps and pro forma financial statements.

Strategic business units are planning units within a large, diversified company. A strategic business unit (SBU) must serve an external, rather than internal, market; must have control over its own destiny; should have a clear set of external competitors; and should be a true profit center.

Strategic fit indicates how well the firm's mission and strategies fit its internal capabilities and its external environment.

Strategic goal-setting is a process of generating and setting a mission and long-run corporate performance goals.

Strategic group mapping categorizes industry competitors into meaningful groups based on at least two strategic variables.

Strategic industry analysis involves an overview of strategic forces affecting a target industry, an analysis of strategies of companies in the industry, and forecasts and recommendations.

Strategic management is an ongoing planning and analysis process that attempts to keep a firm co-aligned with its environments while capitalizing on internal strengths and external opportunites and minimizing or avoiding internal weaknesses and external threats. Strategic management is also a future-oriented, proactive management system.

A **strategic management team** is a group of individuals working cooperatively to deal with strategic management tasks and problems. A group of top managers is often considered a team; also boards of directors or task forces may be called strategic management teams.

A **strategic thrust** is a broad statement of strategic actions that are intended to occur during the planning horizon.

Strategy control involves monitoring current plans and the strategic planning process to improve both future company performance and the strategic planning process.

Strategy evaluation and choice is a process that reconciles strategic actions, market opportunities, corporate strengths and resources, values of general managers, and legal requirements and social responsibilities to select a "best" mission, strategic thrust, and set of strategic actions.

Strategy implementation is the action step in the strategic management process. Strategy implementation involves providing leadership, communicating with managers, making adjustments in the strategic business plan, and many tactical plans and day-to-day decisions.

Strengths are internal characteristics of an organization that make it uniquely adapted to carrying out its tasks, or characteristics of the organization that competitors do not have, which create a competitive advantage.

Threat, company-specific, is a problem or potential problem that may result from the interaction between company weaknesses and present and future negative environmental variables and industry-wide threats.

Threat, industry-wide, is a problem or potential problem for all or most companies in an industry.

Time traps are activities and decisions that are an unproductive use of time.

Trade associations are voluntary groups formed by companies or professionals to promote their collective interests.

Weaknesses are internal characteristics of an organization that inhibit its ability to carry out tasks, or characteristics that the organization does not have that competitors do, which create a competitive disadvantage.

Workability test determines if what is proposed can really be accomplished as planned and whether it is likely that the intended results will be realized.

Student Teams
On Videotape

STUDENT TEAM #1 won the 1984 Rutgers University at Camden/Harrah's Invitational MBA Case Competition, Atlantic City, New Jersey, May, 1984. The other MBA teams in this competition were: Rutgers University at Camden; Temple University; The Pennsylvania State University; and Rice University. Student team #1 analyzed two cases on the videotape: American Safety Razor and Levi Strauss. Its members received their MBA degrees from the University of Maryland in May of 1984.

ROBERT C. LESLIE received his undergraduate degree from Susquehanna University; his MBA major was Finance. He is currently an Investment Advisor, United Mine Workers of America Health and Retirement Funds, Washington, D.C.

MARTA QUINN received a B.A. from Michigan State University; her MBA major was Public Policy. Ms. Quinn recently moved to California and is organizing and managing the West Coast regional office for Greenfield, Belser, Inc., a consulting firm.

BRIAN K. TRACEY received his undergraduate degree from Frostburg State College; his MBA major was Finance. He is currently working as a Corporate Banking Representative for Equitable Bank of Baltimore, Maryland.

FRANCISCO D. VALERIANO received his undergraduate degree from The American University; his MBA major was Finance. He is currently Manager, Credit Cycle Consulting, Citicorp Credit Services, Inc., New York, New York.

STUDENT TEAM #2 placed second in the 1985 Rutgers University at Camden/Harrah's Invitational MBA Case Competition, Atlantic City, New Jersey, May, 1985. The other teams in this competition were: Boston University, which placed first; the Pennsylvania State University; the University of Pittsburgh; and Rutgers University at Camden. Student team #2 analyzed one case on the videotape: Anheuser-Busch. Its members received their MBA degrees from the University of Maryland at College Park in May, 1985.

RITA C. HUMMEL received her undergraduate degree from the University of Maryland at College Park; her two majors in the MBA program were Finance and Accounting. She is currently Staff Supervisor, Financial Management, AT&T Communications, Washington, D.C.

GREGORY J. KURGANSKY received his undergraduate degree from the University of Maryland at College Park; his MBA major was Finance. He is currently Data Processing Manager of Business Operations and User Education in the Engineering & Information Systems Centers and Assistant to the Director at the Maryland Institute for Emergency Medical Services Systems.

LEO W. LATONICK received his undergraduate degree from the United States Naval Academy; his two majors in his MBA program were Accounting and Finance. He is currently Senior Associate Analyst, Strategic Planning Department, Federal Systems Division of the IBM Corporation, Washington, D.C.

PEGGY H. LANDINI received her undergraduate degree from the University of Maryland at College Park; her MBA majors were Management Information Systems and Marketing. She is currently a Marketing Representative with the IBM Corporation, Baltimore, Maryland.

STUDENT TEAM #3 was one of the four final teams in the MBA Case Competition at the University of Maryland at College Park, April, 1985. On videotape this team analyzed the Anheuser-Busch case. This team also completed the written student report on Anheuser-Busch that is included in this book. All of the team members received their MBA degrees from the University of Maryland at College Park in May, 1985.

KAREN J. FREETO received her undergraduate degree from Wheaton College (Norton, Massachusetts); her MBA major was Management Science. She is currently a Staff Consultant with the Price-Waterhouse Accounting Firm, Washington, D.C.

SHERRY L. GREENWALD received her undergraduate degree from the State University of New York at Stony Brook; her MBA major was Marketing. She is currently an Office Systems Consultant with Copy Products Unlimited.

CHRISTINE LEMYZE received her undergraduate degree from the University of Paris; her MBA major was Finance. She is currently a Marketing Representative, IBM Corporation, Washington, D.C.

ROBERT E. WALTON received his undergraduate degree from Washington & Lee University his MBA major was Finance. He is currently an Area Merchandise Manager with Woodward & Lothrop, Washington, D.C.

Index